MEMOIRS OF THE LIFE,
RELIGIOUS EXPERIENCE, MINISTERIAL TRAVELS,
AND LABOURS OF MRS. ELAW

*Re*GENERATIONS
AFRICAN AMERICAN LITERATURE AND CULTURE

Also in this series:

Appointed: An American Novel
Edited by Eric Gardner and Bryan Sinche

The Hindered Hand
Edited by John Cullen Gruesser and Hanna Wallinger

Sketches of Slave Life and *From Slave Cabin to Pulpit*
Edited by Katherine Clay Bassard

Memoirs of Elleanor Eldridge
Edited by Joycelyn K. Moody

The Colonel's Dream
Edited by R. J. Ellis

Freedom's Witness: The Civil War Correspondence of Henry McNeal Turner
Edited by Jean Lee Cole

A Nickel and a Prayer: The Autobiography of Jane Edna Hunter
Edited by Rhondda Robinson Thomas

Hearts of Gold
Edited by John Ernest and Eric Gardner

SERIES EDITORS

John Ernest, Professor and Chair of English, University of Delaware

Joycelyn K. Moody, Sue E. Denman Distinguished Chair in American
Literature, University of Texas at San Antonio

MEMOIRS

of the Life, Religious
Experience, Ministerial Travels,
and Labours of Mrs. Elaw

by Zilpha Elaw

Edited by

Kimberly D. Blockett

WEST VIRGINIA UNIVERSITY PRESS / MORGANTOWN

ISBN 978-1-952271-26-7 (cloth) / 978-1-952271-27-4 (paperback) /
978-1-952271-28-1 (ebook)

Library of Congress Control Number: 2021037012

Cover Design by Than Saffel
Cover image: Frontispiece of *Memoirs of the Life, Religious Experience, Ministerial Travels, and Labours of Mrs. Elaw.* Courtesy of Marietta College Legacy Library.

For Nellie Y. McKay (1930–2006)—who still speaks to me about the urgency and purpose of studying Black lives.

CONTENTS

Acknowledgments

It is impossible to study Zilpha Elaw without being keenly aware of her seemingly solitary life as an itinerant alongside her roles as a daughter, sibling, wife, and mother. Acknowledging the hidden struggles and necessary support systems for women to work, I extend my gratitude first and foremost to my family. My parents, Margie Cromer and Charles Blockett, have supported my own comings and goings, even when they had no idea why or where I was journeying. My children, Alyxe, Leo, CJ, and Niara, bemusedly cheered when "that book that she's been working on forever" finally had a publication date. Kevin Brooks—who, unlike his wife, never had any doubts about the book getting published—prepared my favorite meal, opened a great bottle of wine, and boasted to anyone listening. This is the family that has lovingly and unfailingly grounded my life as an academic, and I'm always pleasantly surprised by their interest in my work.

My own interest in Elaw was a complete surprise to me, since it was never my intention to be a literary historian. Studying, much less searching for, Zilpha would never have occurred to me had Nellie McKay not forced me to read William Andrews's *Sisters of the Spirit*, an anthology of spiritual autobiographies that I thought would hold little interest for me. I have never been so utterly wrong and hope that I have learned my lesson. In the project's infancy, the Ford Foundation and the Smithsonian Institution (Anacostia Museum) fellowships enabled the time I needed to learn how to be a historian and, indeed, how to sleuth. During the early stages of my research, I needed extensive time in the London City Archives, the British Library, and the John Rylands Library's Methodist Archives and Research Centre. Due to the rental costs in Greater London, I'd given up on being able to stay in England long enough to exhaust the resources of all three archives. Unbelievably, with only an email introduction, the sister of a friend of a friend, Angela Phillips, and her husband, Mike Flood Page, offered me their third-floor suite for a month and fed me exquisite, healthy meals. They refused any payment, and I am eternally indebted to them for their kindness and friendship.

The last stages of research and writing I completed with generous funding from the Massachusetts Historical Society National Endowment for the Humanities fellowship and Harvard Divinity School's Women's Studies in Religion Program. Director Ann Braude's writing colloquiums were critical interventions for moving our projects forward. The unexpected bonuses of that year were the research librarians at Andover Library, and the graduate students in my Black Women's Movement and Spirituality course were an absolute joy. The introduction for this edition is much improved from the insightful and timely feedback of my Penn State Brandywine colleagues: James Berkey, Chris Brown, Annie Jansen, and Angela Putman. Susan Ware, Brandywine's librarian (now retired), provided invaluable support and assistance throughout the project. I'm also grateful for the thorough reports from anonymous readers and the loving, multiple reads by ma belle-sœur, Lyvette Brooks Jones. My hardworking and super reliable research assistants, Kelli Coles, Satomi Minowa, and Nicole Prucha, relieved lots of stress during this project and always produced excellent work. Nicole was a lifesaver: I'm not sure how I would have crossed the finish line without her. The series editors, John Ernest and Joycelyn Moody, have offered ongoing support and encouragement. And finally, none of my scholarship would be possible without my sister scholars—a network of friends, writing communities, and accountability partners. My life and work have been greatly enriched by too many to list, but I must give print hugs to Shanna Greene Benjamin, Rebecca L. Davis, P. Gabrielle Foreman, Cora Fox, DoVeanna Fulton, Lynn Jennings, Shirley Moody-Turner, Elizabeth Todd-Breland, Keisha Watson, Yolonda Wilson, and Rafia Zafar. Thank you all for your unwavering support and solidarity.

INTRODUCTION

On Monday evening, according to announcement, Mrs. Elaw, a lady of colour, from America, preached to the [Primitive Methodist Chapel in Keighley]. As soon as the doors were opened the rush and pressure of the crowd became so tremendous that several were taken out severely crushed, and it was with considerable difficulty the service could be commenced.

   —*Leeds Mercury*, April 17, 1841

Primitive Methodist Chapel.—A coloured lady, dignified with the euphonious name Mrs. Zilpha [Elaw] Shum, preached twice at the above place of worship on Sunday last, to large audiences. It is very strange that the Methodists, with their much vaunted notions of propriety, should encourage such unseemly and Barnum-like exhibitions.

   —*Lincolnshire Chronicle*, March 6, 1857

Zilpha Panco Elaw Shum (c. 1793–1873) spent the majority of her adult life doing things she was not supposed to do and going places she was not supposed to go. As a teenage orphan, she angered her Quaker indenturers by joining the new and controversial Methodists.[1] As a young wife and mother, she ignored her husband's denial of her call to preach. As a widowed mother, she left her only child to heed that call. Once Elaw decided to dedicate her life to evangelism, she was unstoppable. Elaw preached throughout New England in the 1830s when racists mobs were burning churches and kidnappers sold free Blacks into slavery. In the antebellum South, Elaw told enslavers that they were on a road to Hell. At midcentury, when the narrow pathways for women preachers began to close, Elaw sailed to England, pronounced the nation's white male ministers deficient, rose to celebrity preacher status, and wrote a book about the many thousands of souls she moved.[2] *As far as we know, there is not another Black woman who did what she did when she did it.* But in the voluminous histories of early British Methodism, Elaw's work is not mentioned. Zilpha Elaw was audacious, and her punishment was historical erasure. In the official records of Methodism, the largest Protestant denomination of the nineteenth century, it is as if Zilpha Elaw Shum never existed.

The epic erasure of Black women in history is not new, nor are the valiant efforts to recover buried and hidden records. But how do we find those who were denied acknowledgment, let alone recognition? When nation-builders and history-makers omit names in their minutes, overlook the women who organized their events, and make invisible the women who made visible the largest Protestant movement of the 1800s, how do we bring those hidden figures out of the shadowy corners of archives? Recovering "recalcitrant" Black women requires radical methodology. It's an arduous, unruly process of reading between the lines for traces and whispers of what lies beneath and around the written story, reading the minutiae of the "unimportant" lives, and reading hundreds of tidbits to cross-reference against the historical events described in the readily available records of "important" lives. Working backward from the journals and letters of white men to find evidence of a Black woman's life was the essential methodology to reconstruct Zilpha Elaw's life, critical to understanding the histories of women, evangelism, and transatlantic racism. This scholarly edition of Elaw's narrative forges a path to right a wrong.

Ignoring the restrictions against women preaching[3] and the perils of travel for women and free Blacks, Elaw began her extraordinary and extensive itinerant ministry in 1825. After doing some local preaching at outdoor revivals in New Jersey and Pennsylvania, Elaw spent the next fifteen years enduring difficult and dangerous travel from Maine to Virginia and, finally, to England. Less than five months after her 1840 arrival in Liverpool, Zilpha Elaw was a well-known presence among the predominately white, Methodist communities from London to Yorkshire. After five successful years of preaching all over England, Elaw settled into a small boarding room in East London to write her spiritual autobiography, *Memoirs of the Life, Religious Experience, Ministerial Travels and Labours of Mrs. Zilpha Elaw* (1846). After a second marriage in 1850, she was soon widowed again and preaching at a furious pace by 1855.

During the entirety of her celebrity ministry, Elaw was both admired for her ability to attract large crowds and vilified for daring to assert her Black female self as a biblical authority among mostly white audiences. By 1864, the last known press coverage of her ministry, descriptors of her preaching ranged from "excellent," "much admired," and "impressive" to "curiosity," "novelty," and "unseemly." While one reporter praised her sermons, exclaiming that "she is no mean elocutionist" (*Cambridge Chronicle* 5), another denounced her "whining drawl" as "tedious"—noting that "phrenologically speaking, her forehead displayed very little intellectual development" (*Bicester Herald* 6).[4] More than one hundred newspaper accounts, from the rural districts in the far north to the southern metropolis of London, document twenty-three years of Zilpha Elaw Shum's extraordinary ministry after leaving the United States. Because of Elaw's race and gender, her ministry was often met with curiosity, vitriol, or both, even though Christian evangelism was widespread in North American and English culture.[5]

Beginning with the First Great Awakening in the 1700s, Christian revivalism and its outgrowth of spiritual autobiographies were solidified as integral parts of popular culture by the 1800s. Through cheap printing, religious conversion—changing one's spiritual beliefs—could scale up from individual to mass events. Methodism, one of the many new Protestant denominations formed during the First Great Awakening, privileged traveling ministers over local preachers since it fulfilled their mission to bring Christ to all people.[6] Their itinerant preachers were encouraged to keep journals, both for financial records (reimbursement of expenses) and for proof of ministerial efficacy (how many miles traveled and sermons preached yielded how many new members). These journals were sometimes developed into spiritual autobiographies.

Genre, Marketing, and Self-Preservation: The Stories That Could Not Be Told

In spite of the ebb and flow of transatlantic revivalism, the genre of spiritual autobiographies flourished well beyond the nineteenth century as a popular literature. From the earliest years of England's Evangelical Revival, or First Great Awakening, "thousands of women and men went through the travail of evangelical conversion and turned to a certain kind of spiritual autobiography to make sense of their experience, and indeed, to make sense of their lives" (Hindmarsh vii).[7] By the end of the eighteenth century, the evangelical conversion narrative was an established subgenre of spiritual autobiography with a spectacular market spread. During the same periods, a new American leisure class, coupled with the British desire to establish, increase, and record its empire, encouraged a proliferation of travel writing—one of the most popular genres in nineteenth-century Western literary markets.[8] As a renewed desire for spiritual movement gripped large swaths of Western Europe, the Americas, and the United Kingdom, Christian revivalism generated another kind of travel writing—the journals and autobiographies of itinerant preachers and missionaries.

From its inception, spiritual autobiography was a relatively inclusive genre (particularly in the Methodist press) publishing a wide variety of clergy (ordained and lay) and laity across race, class, gender, and age (Hindmarsh 324). As time went on, however, the voices of women were steadily and intentionally diminished. As denominations such as the Methodists and Baptists grew larger, they sought mainstream acceptance. Part of gaining that acceptance meant that by the mid-1800s, most church leadership trended toward male-centered respectability. Just as women's ministry was disenfranchised, so went their support for public spiritual writing. Elaw's 1846 self-publication in London was, indeed, spectacular, given the cultural pressure to ignore, hide, and silence women preachers.[9]

Elaw's narrative follows the model established by early evangelical writers, especially Whitefield and Wesley.[10] Both men were prolific during their lives as "founding fathers" of Methodism. They published serialized journals that could best be described as travel narratives, incorporating the daily life of an itinerant in service to the gospel. Wesley directed early Methodist leaders to keep careful diaries for spiritual improvement and practical record-keeping of conversions, potential conversions and expenses for reimbursement.[11] Thus, these diaries were detailed documentation of their work and often served as the basis for the theological reflections in later publications. They were sometimes published in the evangelical press as serialized narratives of their ministerial travel—where and how they journeyed, who they encountered, and in what conditions.[12] The serial publication of journals was instructive for new preachers, and the format also proved to be a successful way to promote evangelical groups.

Beyond their episodic journals, ministers sometimes published longer, reflective narratives that focused on their conversions and eventual calling to become itinerant preachers. The rhetorical structure of these narratives tended to illustrate four central concerns: (1) the original crisis of conscience, (2) a relief gained from the conversion of faith, (3) a crisis of vocation, and (4) the decision to forsake all and heed the call to preach. The point was not to detail individual conversion and spiritual experience but rather to document the spiritual and physical journey of doing God's work. The narrative purpose was to tell the story of a multitude of conversions over a vast expanse of space and time to verify the evangelical movement (Hindmarsh 228–29). In these books, individual and personal circumstances only matter inasmuch as they develop the story of faith, spiritual growth, and seekers' engagement with divinity. It is a very particular form of autobiography in that it must be not simply a story of the material self but rather a story of the spiritual self.[13] Once the writer has experienced salvation and, in Elaw's case, sanctification, she is an instrument of Christ who works and serves with humility and submission to God.[14] The genre, then, necessitates an authorial tightrope.

The writer cannot be the star nor the prototypical heroine of an extraordinary tale because she is a messenger of God, a faithful servant of her higher power.

In addition to covering the spiritual journeys of conversion and calling, narratives that also detailed the physical experience of voyages to familiar and foreign places were highly desirable. For nineteenth-century readers, the publications of itinerant preachers were quite popular because they crossed two genres in particular demand: religious experience and travel narratives. The audience for spiritual autobiographies included the ever-growing numbers of Christian readers, those who were considering joining a worship community, and the merely curious who found the stories of itinerant life to be exhilarating. Add to these factors that *Memoirs* opens a rare window into the racial and gender differences of itinerancy, and it is clear why Elaw and her patrons felt that her book might enjoy a wide readership in spite of the institutional barriers for women writers.

Unfortunately, by the time Elaw's U.S. ministry had reached its zenith, the Methodist Book Concern, the first Christian publishing house, established in 1789, and primary printer of spiritual narratives, had already decided it would no longer publish anything authored by women.[15] Moreover, the slight encouragement received by some women preachers did not extend to Black women.[16] Notwithstanding her individual popularity, the racial climate coupled with the backlash against women preachers and writers limited Elaw's possibilities in the United States and may have contributed to her eventual move to England. There, several growing Protestant sects, such as the Primitive Methodists and the Bible Christians, were recruiting women preachers with hopes of increasing their membership rolls.[17] Even so, many English congregations had no tolerance for women preachers, and fewer still were interested in a Black woman preacher. In that light, Elaw's ministry was singular enough to warrant attention and extraordinary enough for her to self-publish two editions of her spiritual autobiography, one that sold for two shillings and a "fine" printing that sold for three shillings.[18]

Elaw was selling a story of deliverance—not from bondage but from domesticity and impiety, a salvation she credits to Christ rather than to psychological or physical resistance. In her often dangerous travels, she ministered and prayed with sex workers, substance abusers, and homeless and enslaved people alongside some of the most famous and influential people of the period. Yet Zilpha Elaw's narrative does not deliver the action-driven suspense of a fleeing fugitive—the kind of sensationalism desired and expected by the large British and American readership of slave narratives. There is no Dr. Flint threatening Elaw's childhood innocence as in Harriet Jacobs's journey, no Mr. Covey challenging the manhood of Frederick Douglass.[19] We know that Elaw preached her way through many barriers, countless risks. She managed to survive, but her story did not. We do have her spiritual autobiography, but I propose that it is not *her* story—not really.

Memoirs is a beautifully crafted narrative of itinerant preaching during a Christian awakening that changed American culture from the inside out. We also get to see how Methodism, after its explosive growth in America, was faring back in England, its country of origin. However, we do not get much of Elaw's perspective on the changing culture, how it differed from her past, or what, in fact, her past was like. As most spiritual narratives do, Elaw's book weaves the colorful tapestry of her ministry; it does not invite us into her private world. In general, autobiography conceals as much as it reveals: much cannot or will not be disclosed. In the case of an antebellum Black woman preacher, *most* of the story could not be told if the book were to be sold. Elaw's narrative divulges little about her early life and family. Since the story ends in 1845, it does not include her second marriage, her explosive itinerant ministry in England into the 1860s, and, of course, the circumstances of her 1873 death. Not surprisingly, the events that *are* recorded in her autobiography are veiled tales constrained by genre, audience, race, and gender.

For example, without the endorsement or financial support of any organized church, and risking her own freedom and life, Elaw traveled twice to the U.S. South and preached to all who would listen—enslavers and those they enslaved.[20] When Elaw records her 1828–29 stay in Baltimore, Maryland, Washington, D.C., and Alexandria, Virginia, she does not say much about why she felt moved to go South at exactly that moment. She explains only that she felt it was necessary—even as she relates her ardent fears of being kidnapped and sold into slavery or murdered. As she narrates her time in the region, Elaw declares that it was a successful mission with many souls saved and that she was able to meet some important people.

In actuality, Elaw spent much of the 1828 presidential election cycle preaching to Andrew Jackson's extended circle—some from his infamous kitchen cabinet and most of whom owned Black people.[21] Yet she did not, could not tell *that* story. Instead, in the space of three sentences, Elaw tells her readers that while in D.C. she stayed with "Mrs. Lee" and made such an impression on one enslaver, Naval Commodore Rodgers, that he offered her a permanent position at the chapel he built for Navy officers. The brief anecdote ends with Elaw declaring pleasure that she was able to serve but declining the commodore's offer because God had directed her to move on to other preaching posts (page 50).[22]

Beside discussing these "great" men as enslavers, Elaw may have found her time with the Jacksonian crowd too sordid to relate in a spiritual autobiography.

Impropriety, and perhaps political savvy, might have prevented Elaw from disclosing that "Mrs. Lee," her hostess and the sister-in-law of General Robert E. Lee, was also an opioid addict. Nor does Elaw mention that Anne McCarty Lee was a close friend of President Andrew Jackson's wife, Rachel. Anne and Rachel met and developed a close friendship while they were both in Tennessee trying to heal from deep emotional wounds. Anne Lee was treating her substance abuse, and Rachel Jackson was hiding from Jackson's enemies' public accusations that she was an adulterer and bigamist.[23] We can speculate that Lee's drug use began after her young orphaned sister, Elizabeth, came to live with them. While Anne and her husband, Henry (brother of Robert E. Lee), mourned the accidental death of their infant, Henry had an affair with Anne's sister. The family soon had more to grieve when Elizabeth gave birth to a stillborn baby. Henry Lee, who had been appointed guardian of Elizabeth's estate, was summarily unappointed and sued for mismanagement. Anne Lee, by then suffering from a full-blown opioid addiction, fled to a treatment center in Nashville, where she was befriended by Rachel Jackson, who had retreated to the Hermitage to escape the vicious attacks on her morals.[24] In fact, from Andrew Jackson's perspective, those election cycle character assassinations of Rachel did more than cast aspersions; he declared that they were the direct cause of her death in December 1828, just months before his inauguration. Jackson took office while grieving his beloved wife and desperate to punish those who had maligned her. It wasn't long after Jackson's March 1829 inaugural address before his administration became embroiled in scandal and completely dysfunctional. President Jackson's lingering rage over the sexual policing of his wife as a weapon between men changed the course of political history, and it set the stage for Zilpha Elaw to become a spiritual leader for some of Jackson's closest confidantes, including the beleaguered Lees. Because and in spite of the intersectional realities of her life as a poor, Black preaching woman, Elaw's narrative had to navigate multiple and shifting truths even as it privileged her spiritual mission.

Her rhetorical negotiations are most obvious when she relates opposition to her preaching. Shortly after Elaw's arrival in London, the British Foreign Anti-Slavery Society (BFASS) invited her to speak.[25] The narrative account of Elaw's visit with them illustrates the challenges she faced as a Black woman minister and established her ability to rise above pettiness with divinity. In August 1840 Elaw met with the BFASS Board expecting to provide ministerial service; instead, they received her as if she were a fugitive from slavery—needing aid and available to speak for enslaved Blacks in America. She declined the invitation because they treated her "as the proud do the needy," and she describes the group as "an august assembly; their dignity appeared so redundant, that they scarcely knew what to do with it all" (page 87). It is a textual moment when the reader gets a glimpse of Elaw's racial vulnerability coupled with her biting sarcasm. She dismissively narrates their unwillingness to accept her, on her terms, as a clergywoman.

Off the record, however, her private writing reveals that immediately after making her stand, Elaw's racial consciousness moved her to revisit the board's request in a subsequent letter to one of their officers. Going beyond the text to the archive, I recovered a letter from Elaw to William Tredgold, British diplomat and secretary of the BFASS, that unfolds the hidden complexities of the encounter. The day after Elaw left her meeting with the BFASS, she wrote to Tredgold admitting that although she felt very satisfied with her decision to decline their request, she'd had a restless evening, full of new doubts. After more prayer and consultation with God, Elaw resolved to accept the offer of a speaking engagement rather than delivering a sermon. Elaw made an authorial decision to narrate *only* her initial refusal to speak about enslavement. Not including her reconsideration and subsequent letter to Tredgold confirms that Elaw's purpose was not to advance herself as an abolitionist but rather to establish her evangelical authority. Nonetheless, her "sleepless night" and ultimate decision to "speak for her people," in spite of her righteous rage at the indignities proffered, signal that Elaw acknowledged the cultural work advanced by her ministry even as she privileged her spiritual work. She understood that simply *being* an American woman, born free, and Quaker educated was always a counternarrative to the ubiquitous speaking tours by formerly enslaved Americans (Frederick Douglass, Henry Box Brown, William Wells Brown, William and Ellen Craft, etc.) that were so popular across postslavery England.[26]

Memoirs is one of the most important narratives available to examine a critical period of American and English culture.[27] As one of few Black women who recorded evangelical travels during the antebellum era, Elaw's story is unique and offers a very different evangelical experience than the women who wrote within the African Methodist Episcopal church (AMEC) culture. Some, such as *The Life and Religious Experience of Jarena Lee* (1836, 1849) and *A Narrative of the Life and Travels of Mrs. Nancy Prince* (1850, 1853), were published as narratives. *The Memoir of Old Elizabeth, a Colored Woman* (1863) was published as an evangelical tract, and around 1830 Rebecca Cox Jackson started journaling the religious experiences that led to her dismissal from the AMEC and eventually becoming a Shaker eldress (published in 1981 as *Gifts of Power*, edited by Jean M. Humez).[28] Post–Civil War narratives include Julia Foote's 1879 *A Brand Plucked from the Fire* and Amanda Berry Smith's 1893 *An Autobiography: The Story of the Lord's Dealings with Mrs. Amanda Smith, the Colored Evangelist.* Elaw makes clear in her narrative that she was not connected to the African Methodist Episcopal or AME Zion denominations. Although she ministered to any Protestant denomination and often to African American congregations, Elaw was a member of the predominately white Methodist Episcopal church (MEC) in Bristol, Burlington, Nantucket, and London, and white Protestants constituted the bulk of her audiences. As such, her itinerant experience encompassed a much wider spectrum—mimicking the spectacular spread of American Methodism on the Eastern Seaboard. In contrast, Foote's career started decades after the Second Great Awakening, and Lee's geographic and social domain would have been too narrow to provide substantive perspective on the transatlantic movement. The African American denominations, for obvious reasons, could not establish the same evangelistic itinerancy for their preachers, so their gospel-inspired travels were primarily limited to regional camp meetings and an intraracial circuitry. Likewise, their international travel tended to be as missionaries to Africa; in general, African American women were not traveling alone across the Atlantic to preach in British churches. In effect, Elaw's non-affiliation with the Black churches expanded her purview. Since Elaw joined the MEC in 1808, her 1846 narrative covers both the crest and declining years of the Second Great Awakening over thousands of geographic miles in two countries on opposite sides of the Atlantic.[29] That makes *Memoirs* the most expansive Black female account of nineteenth-century itinerant preaching, covering the longest historical period, and written by the only known Black woman preacher of the MEC.[30] Yet we knew little about the woman at its center.

Because Elaw wrote within a very prescribed literary tradition, we see only small glimpses of the turbulent world she inhabited, and much is left in the shadows. Other than the information attained from her autobiography, not much beyond the general region of her birth has been documented. There is little published research on when or where she died or if she returned from England in 1845 (where the *Memoirs* end). As of publication date, fewer than fifteen journal articles and book chapters included substantive discussion of Elaw's evangelism.[31] This annotated edition of *Memoirs* provides a chronology of Elaw's life: her early life in Bristol, Pennsylvania, and Burlington, New Jersey; her first *chosen* homestead in Nantucket, Massachusetts; her itinerant ministry in Yorkshire, England; and, finally, the years after the publication of her narrative including her second marriage and a long preaching career in the UK until her death in 1873. The archival materials make clear the expanse of Elaw's ministry, its contribution to American and English Methodism, and the significant impact of her travels on nineteenth-century British and U.S. evangelical culture. These newly recovered and essential sources fill some of the biographical gaps, contextualizes her work, and begins to redress one instance of Black women's erasure from American cultural history.

The Known Story

Elaw tells us that she was born in Pennsylvania to free parents and that she, her older brother, Joseph, and younger sister, Hannah, were their only children. Although her mother had given birth more than twenty times, only three children survived infancy. Sadly, the children were separated over the next few years. First, when she was six, young Zilpha's twelve-year-old brother went to live with his mother's parents somewhere in the Midwest. Only six years later, their mother and newborn sibling died during the twenty-second childbirth. Their father sent Hannah to live with an aunt in Philadelphia, and Zilpha, then twelve years old, was indentured to Rebecca and Pearson Mitchell.[32]

While living with the Quaker family, Zilpha could not reconcile herself with their religious practices. She missed the daily prayers and strict rules of her father's household. Elaw felt that the family's silent meditations without formal worship led her to a lack of "religious restraint [which] . . . gave way to the evil propensities of an unregenerate heart" (page 10). Less than two years after the horror of her mother's death and the complete separation of their family, Elaw's father died, leaving her a young Black orphan belonging to a white Quaker family. Elaw describes herself as a mildly rebellious teenager—she used God's name in vain (once) and talked back to her mistress—until she started attending meetings of the Methodist Society, which was making quite a stir in the area. One day while milking a cow, Elaw saw Jesus approaching her with "with open arms," and she felt assured that it was not simply a vision. Declaring her "conscientious veracity and scrupulous adherence to truth," Elaw writes that "the beast of the stall turned her head and looked round as I did; and when she saw, she bowed her knees and cowered down upon the ground. . . . The thing was certain and beyond all doubt" (page 11–12). After experiencing this conversion, Elaw took refuge in her spiritual rebirth and spent her young adulthood developing herself into a model Methodist and redirecting her energies toward Christian salvation. In 1808 she joined a Methodist class[33] and was admitted into the newly established Bristol Methodist Episcopal Society by Rev. James Polemus.[34] Elaw's strict Methodism evoked constant rebukes from her mistress, Rebecca Mitchell, and cruel torment from her teenage peers. This is the extent of Elaw's discussion of her early life.

Indentured women in Pennsylvania were often released from their contracts either through marriage or by a specified age, whichever came first. In

1810 Zilpha married Joseph Elaw when she was between eighteen and twenty years old. When they met, Joseph was also a member of the Bristol Methodist Society. But as a "backslider from religion," he was later disowned by the society and "resolved to use every means to induce [Elaw] to renounce [her] religion" (page 17–18).[35] In 1812 Elaw gave birth to a daughter, their only child. The War of 1812 and the economic depression hindered Joseph's ability to find work, so they moved across the Delaware River to Burlington, New Jersey, where Joseph could pursue his trade as a fuller.[36] In Burlington Elaw was pleased to have a Methodist Society class meeting just a few doors away, and she was able to attend a chapel nearby. Joseph's attempts to stop her from attending meetings only backfired. Elaw disregarded her husband's admonishments and in fact increased her religious fervor by traveling to camp meetings—popular outdoor revivals that were often week-long events attended by thousands of devout evangelicals.[37] For the young wife and mother, leaving her home to travel to spaces temporarily reinvented for worship gave her a heightened sense of purpose. Her narrative suggests that her camp meeting attendance was the primary catalyst for choosing a different path for herself. Indeed, her moment of sanctification occurred at a camp meeting in 1817. Once sanctified, Elaw began exhorting at class meetings and leading prayers at home visits, but she was soon convinced that she had been called to preach.[38] Fearing public ridicule, her husband forbade her preaching, but Elaw preached anyway, citing that he was a nonbeliever and thus disqualified to lead her. In 1823 Joseph Elaw died, and two years later the widow left her eleven-year-old daughter with friends and began her ministry, traveling between Maine and Virginia.

After a decade of itinerant living, Elaw's first chosen home (not selected by her parents or husband) was Nantucket, Massachusetts. Soon after her 1832 arrival on the island, Elaw was confined for eight months with a serious illness. A few kind residents nursed her until her daughter, who had been apprenticed for two years as a dressmaker in New York, came to help. While caring for her mother, Elaw's daughter met and married a local man. During these initial years of Elaw's sickness and then her daughter's first childbirth, Elaw spent her time primarily on the island. By 1835, however, she had resumed her itinerant life and spent most of her time traveling, stopping home for brief periods of respite and rejuvenation with her family.

In the narration of her popular ministry in the United States, Elaw frequently and inexplicably writes of her desire to go to London and that some of her friends strongly supported a mission trip to England. Finally, in July 1840 Elaw began her twenty-four-day journey from New York to London. After Elaw's first five months in Greater London, Mr. Coulson, a superintendent minister, and his assistant, Mr. Crompton, invited her to preach in Yorkshire for the Hull Primitive Methodist Circuit. For the next five years, Elaw ministered mostly for the Primitive Methodists and sometimes for Wesleyan congregations in London and the northern counties of England. Although the spread of Methodism is well documented from its Wesleyan beginnings to the present-day United Methodism, Elaw is not listed among the many women preachers they employed. Within the vast records of the Methodist Archives and Research Centre, Elaw is present but not a presence.

The Backstory

By cross-referencing census records, church journals, and the personal correspondence of prominent white Methodists, I have uncovered much about the life of Zilpha Panco Elaw Shum. Although there is still more to learn about her early life, travels in the mid-Atlantic and New England, and home in Nantucket, this brief biography adds new information to the memoir. Born circa 1792 in Bristol Township, Bucks County, Pennsylvania, Zilpha Panco grew up in a community of free African American families, most of whom were ex-slaves who benefited from Quaker manumissions.[39] In 1758 the Philadelphia Yearly Meeting acted to induce the members of its Quarterly and Monthly Meetings who owned people "to set them at liberty, making a Christian provision for them according to their ages." For the next twenty years, the meeting minutes include voluntary or persuaded manumissions and recorded reparations in the form of payment for previous labor.[40] Quakers who did not voluntarily cooperate were pressured by their peers. Select members formed committees to persuade and warn those who had not started the process of manumission. These committees would make frequent visits to the homes of Quaker enslavers to give "friendly caution."[41] In town and county records, individual Blacks who were formerly referred to only by first names were now grouped and listed together with surnames—thus creating the first public records to recognize them as African American families. In addition to the manumissions, there are several stories in the records of Bucks County that recount the Quakers' active resistance to the various versions of the Fugitive Slave Act.[42] On more than one occasion, town members protected their Black neighbors who had escaped from the South and established homesteads and businesses in the small towns of Bucks County. In at least one instance, when deception did not work to thwart a slave catcher, one fugitive received free legal representation, and when the suit was unsuccessful, the citizens of Bristol took a collection to pay the enslaver for freedom papers.[43] Even though Zilpha Panco's family was scattered by the time she was twelve years old, she lived in the same Bristol neighborhood until she was about twenty years old. Such a community, steeped in the rhetoric of freedom and morality, seems to have significantly influenced her formative years.

During the time Elaw lived in Bristol Borough, Pennsylvania, and Burlington, New Jersey, they were bustling mill towns settled on opposite sides of the Delaware River, a narrow but major shipping highway from the earliest settlements of Dutch, Swedes, and finally the English. Censuses reveal some aspects of where and how these families lived. Elaw's father, Sanco Panco, mother, and three children lived next door to Samuel Panco (presumably Elaw's uncle) and his family of five. The Mitchells, neighbors of the Pancos and members of the Quaker's Middletown Monthly Meeting, were also a family of five during the period they held Elaw's indenture.[44] After marrying, Elaw and her new husband lived a few miles north in Falls Township, another mill town just along the King's Highway, a major thoroughfare commissioned in 1686 (later expanded as U.S. Route 13). When they moved across the river to Burlington, New Jersey, the Elaws and their infant daughter, Rebecca, were part of a small community of African Americans concentrated near the Delaware River on Main and Pearl Streets (Lyght 41–47). During the Elaws' sixteen-year residency, Burlington County had the largest Black population of the state's five southern counties and the largest free Black population in the state of New Jersey. Indeed, Elaw's childhood and marital hometowns were both located in the Delaware Valley, often referred to as the "cradle of emancipation," and must have significantly informed her worldview.[45]

It's not surprising, then, that Elaw's next home was another socially progressive marine town where Black families could prosper. Soon after her arrival in Nantucket, Elaw became gravely ill; she sent for her daughter and began making plans for her funeral. During a prayer vigil, a Quaker woman told Elaw that the "Holy Ghost [had answered]: She shall get better, and in this Island shall hereafter be her home" (page 78). After Elaw's recovery she consented to her Nantucket friends' insistence that she remain on the island. Her decision was cemented when Rebecca married and started a family in Nantucket. While Elaw makes clear how quickly she came to love Nantucket, her memoirs make only cursory mention of her daughter—always only in relation to the progress of Elaw's ministry and travels—and, ironically, does not provide her name. As it turns out, Rebecca Elaw Pierce Crawford's life was integrally intertwined with her mother's, as she shared Zilpha Elaw's first *chosen* homestead on the Island of Nantucket (see appendix A). There, Rebecca met Thomas Pierce, a mariner. Rebecca and Thomas married in 1833 and soon had two boys: Joseph in 1834 and Thomas Jr. in 1837.[46] The Pierce home became a welcome respite for Elaw as she and the daughter from whom she had been separated for eight years chose Nantucket to settle again as a family.

By the time of Elaw's arrival in 1832, Nantucket housed a free Black community of more than five hundred business owners, whalers (mariners and ship captains), teachers, preachers, bankers, seamstresses, domestic workers, laborers, and skilled tradesmen. The island's whaling industry supported many of the Black islanders, some of whom (free and enslaved) began whaling in the early 1700s. The majority of African descendants lived in a geographic area designated by the intersection of the "five corners" and nicknamed "New Guinea," alluding to the African lineage of most of the inhabitants. They built two churches, Zion AME (1832) and the African Baptist Church (1825). The Baptist church was located in the African Meeting House, which also served as a community center and school.[47] Elaw preached at almost all of the Nantucket churches including many sermons in the New Guinea churches. The Black Nantucketers also enjoyed profound and groundbreaking success in legal arenas. They initiated suits to integrate schools; provided successful legal representation to suspend the death sentence for a Black woman convicted of murder; and fought to prevent bounty hunters from kidnapping Black fugitives and their families, even though there was federal law to support the extradition of escapees from enslavement. When Black Nantucketers led the charge to integrate schools, Thomas and Rebecca Pierce were among the first to sign the "Petition of Edward J. Pompey and 104 others of Nantucket for amendment of the Common School Law [to] extend to all children the same educational rights" (Pompey). In short, Elaw and her daughter enjoyed a tight-knit community that took care of its own.

Since Thomas Sr. spent a good deal of time at sea, Rebecca and her mother stayed busy with the children, and both joined the Methodist Episcopal Society. Even though there were two Black churches that welcomed her as a frequent minister in their pulpits, Elaw points out that because she was a "member of the parent stock, or old Methodist Society, [she] possessed an advantage over many other labourers in having access to many pulpits which they had not" (page 80).

When Zilpha Elaw left her daughter's young family to go to London, it is unclear whether she intended to return to Nantucket. In the narrative, Elaw reports a very intense parting with her daughter in 1840. Their emotions may well have been fear of the very real dangers of travel for anyone in the 1800s, particularly women and Black people. However, the narrative description and the realities of evangelical missions suggest that Elaw left Nantucket with no firm plans to return. She was at least forty-five years old and had suffered several near-fatal injuries and illnesses. Given the shorter life expectancy for itinerant preachers and for Black women, coupled with the dangers of travel, both mother and daughter had to acknowledge the probability that Elaw would be living her last days in England. Indeed, after five years of notoriety in England as the Black preaching woman, Elaw wrote of the Nantucket scene: "I rose from the bed on which I had laid for the last time" (page 85). It seems that whatever Elaw and her daughter may have felt about the precarity of the trip to England, by the time she wrote *Memoirs*, it was clear that she no longer considered Nantucket her home. At the end of her narrative, Elaw reports that she intended to return to the United States. It was 1845, the year that Rebecca gave birth to her third son, David. It is possible that Elaw planned to return to go back for this reason, but the trip seems improbable given the events of her life after publishing *Memoirs* in 1846.[48]

For the entirety of Elaw's preaching career in England, she was simultaneously and paradoxically exoticized and ridiculed, yet genuinely respected and admired for her determination to preach. Once Elaw was in London, her notoriety quickly garnered her an invitation to preach in northern England. However much her preaching was welcomed by the people of those districts, that popularity was not shared by the British Methodist church authorities. Elaw's employment, unlike the other women preachers hired to evangelize, was not approved by the church supervisors. There are many records of well-respected women preachers in the minute books of the Primitive Methodist Itinerant Preachers' Friendly Society (PMIPFS), an organization founded to help fund basic needs for the traveling preachers who were central to the mission of the Methodist church. Some of these women began preaching as helpers to their preacher husbands, and many others were single or married women who were responding to their own calling to preach and were hired to do so. Some Methodist sects, such as the Bible Christians and Primitive Methodists, allowed women to preach, but the hiring of a Black woman was another matter altogether. In 1841, when Elaw was living with the Brayshaw family in Addingham, Yorkshire, the PMIPFS Committee sanctioned at least four district clergy for employing Elaw, which they had been told not to do. Fortunately for Elaw, neither Crompton nor Coulson heeded the warnings, and both regularly employed her to preach in their districts throughout the 1840s. In fact, the *Primitive Methodist General Committee Minute Book of 1842* notes in a July entry that "J. Crompton did wrong in obliterating the old accounts of Beele Chapel, and making a fresh and different entry of them, he having had no official authority for doing so" (115). The episode seemed suspect to the supervisors, and he was moved from the district entirely. Given that the account books coincide with the years that Elaw experienced explosive popularity in these districts, the "fresh and different" entries do seem a bit suspicious; it's possible that

Crompton was hiding her pay. Money was clearly a concern for the Methodist leaders, as indicated in a September entry requesting that Yorkshire's Keighley Circuit "must clearly state the amount of the Collections said to have been made by the Black Woman, and also to what purpose those collections were applied" (133). Although Elaw is never named in these minutes, they evidence a sustained and substantive discussion of her working relationship with the Primitive Methodists of England. By the time Elaw returned to London in 1845, she was an established evangelist with significant church sponsors and private patrons.

In a boarding room provided by Thomas Dudley, a bookbinder, Elaw wrote and self-published *Memoirs of the Life, Religious Experience, Ministerial Travels and Labours of Mrs. Zilpha Elaw, an American Female of Colour: Together with Some Account of the Great Religious Revivals in America.*[49] Shortly after the 1846 publication, Elaw was in the Yorkshire Dales, preaching, marketing, and selling her book. In February 1847, the *Kendal Mercury* reported that Elaw preached to "the largest audiences ever witnessed in this chapel," sparking a lively editorial debate (from June through August 1847) about the veracity of her book, specifically the account of her conversion, which involved a cow kneeling before God.[50] After the summer of 1847 debate, news coverage of Elaw seems to pause until the January 15, 1851, *Watchman and Wesleyan Advertiser* included the following marriage announcement: "On the 9th December at Stratford, Bow, Mr. R.B. Shum, of St. Clement Danes, Strand, to Zilpha Elaw, of Somerset-Street, New-road, Whitechapel" (24).[51] In the historical and beautiful sanctuary of Saint Mary, Stratford Bow, Elaw married a white Englishman, Ralph Bressey Shum (b. 1796), four months after he buried his second wife, Ann (see appendix B, fig. 1).[52]

Ralph Bressey Shum was the middle son of John Caspar Shum (b. 1760) and Elizabeth Bressey (b. 1763). John Shum, also a pork butcher, had emigrated from Germany around 1780 and married Elizabeth, a native Englander, in 1791. His family lived in London. The extended Shum (anglicized from Schumm) family emigrated from Neider Stettin, Germany, to Bath, England, and were celebrated for their deep roots in Methodism as class leaders, fundraisers, and staunchly pious pillars of the community.[53] In 1817 Ralph Shum had at least one indentured servant apprenticed with him, and by the time of his death, his estate included two buildings at 12 and 15 Houghton Street. When he married Elaw, Shum was a retired butcher with four grown children: Thomas Casper, Elizabeth Ann, Ralph Bressey (deceased), and Mary.

Elaw's second marriage did not last long because Shum died in September 1854 at age fifty-eight. They were living on 25 Norfolk Street, Whitechapel, and the burial service was performed by Reverend J. Heard.[54] In his will dated August

1854, Shum left his wife an immediate payout of twenty-five pounds, equivalent to a modern sum of approximately 2,500 pounds, and half of the remains of his household, with the other half bequeathed to his daughter Elizabeth. If the two could not agree on the division of items, according to Shum's will, the executor was to make a division, giving Elaw first choice. Shum also set up a ten-shilling allowance for his son, Thomas, and the rest of Shum's estate income was to go to his widow as a weekly allowance.

It's not clear how much, if any, preaching Elaw did during her marriage, but several months after Ralph Shum's death, in the spring of 1855, the *Cambridge Independent Press* reported that "A Female Preacher.—Mrs. Zelpha Shum, from London, a lady of colour, preached twice . . . at the Primitive Methodist Chapel, on the re-opening of the Chapel. The Chapel was filled on each occasion; on Sunday to overflowing. The lady's discourses were listened to with great attention and lively interest" (7). From April to July 1855, at least forty newspapers in England, Scotland, and Ireland confirm that Elaw was busy on the Primitive Methodist English circuits and drawing large crowds. By 1857 she was well known enough that many regional papers no longer explained who she was, referring to her only as "Mrs. Shum." [55] She was so popular, in fact, that she drew the ire of those who denigrated the Methodist "circuit riders" and decried even moreso the advent of preachers who were not white or at least male. In 1863 Elaw was targeted in Philip Cater's *Punch in the Pulpit*, a scathing critique of "reverend jesters"—who he purported were mockeries of Protestant preaching. Cater's book, in which "Mrs. Shum" was one of many examples of "Godly gaucheries" (3), sold enough copies for the London publisher to run at least three editions. Both the live audiences and readers struggled to comprehend the complexities of a Black woman's ministry, which did not fit into their visions of Black American fugitivity.

Yet she persisted, traveling and preaching well into her late sixties, and lived her last days in London. Elaw appears on every UK census from 1841 to 1871, with the exception of 1851, when the Shums may have been on honeymoon travel;[56] she is first listed as living with the Brayshaw family in Yorkshire, then in London as Zilpha Shum, and finally as a mentally infirm widow living with a home health aide.[57] On the 1871 census, she is categorized as "lunatic" and living with a servant/caregiver. Her 1873 death certificate lists her condition as "insane," indicating she probably suffered with dementia before her death (see appendix B, fig. 2). Interestingly, a Nantucket obituary of Rebecca Elaw Crawford (d. 1883) notes the illustrious preaching career of her mother (see appendix B, fig. 6), yet the British announcements minimize Elaw's contributions to the Methodist circuits. There is no mention of her death in the 1873 *Primitive Methodist Magazine* (published in London), and her obituary in the *Methodist Recorder and General Christian Times* only acknowledges that she was "for many years a class leader and a most consistent member of the Wesleyan Society in the St. George's Circuit." [58]

Elaw's Place

The Circuit will not, without our consent, employ the <u>BLACK WOMAN</u>. We sanction Bro. [J.A. Bastow] being the superintendent of the circuit, and Bro. John Lightbody being the circuit book steward.

> *Minute Book of the Yearly Meeting of the Primitive Methodist Itinerant Preachers' Friendly Society, June 1841, Manchester*

—We disapprove of the Circuit having employed a Black woman from America, without having first obtained the Sanction of the general Committee.
—The preparatory Committee judge it wrong to employ the Black woman, as she is a stranger, and professes to belong to another community.
—That the letter from Bradford, with the exception of what is said about the Black woman, is satisfactory, and that they be requested, not to employ her in any way.

> *Primitive Methodist Connexion Journal of the Annual Conference or Meeting held at Reading which commenced on June 11, 1841*

In the objections to Elaw's employment, she is never named. The Primitive Methodists' handwritten journals and minutes evidence Zilpha Elaw's preaching abroad only if one looks for the white men mentioned in her narrative, Reverends James Crompton and John Coulson. In countless yellowed and tattered pages of quarterly and annual, local and regional journals ranging from ten to two hundred pages each, scripted by a variety of men over a ten-year span, only the words "<u>BLACK WOMAN</u>" appear fully capitalized and underlined. The singling out of Elaw all but jumps off the page, but she is never named. Given the increases in membership recorded during the periods she preached in certain districts, Elaw may have been one of the most popular and successful preachers for the Primitive Methodists during her years in the northern counties. But, in the meticulous documentation of their growth and ministerial functions, she is never named.

Elaw's final resting place, an unmarked grave (see appendix B, fig. 7), belies the extraordinary life she lived and the place she has earned in American and English literary and religious history. Written by a "poor, coloured female [with] many things to endure which others do not" (page 42), Zilpha Elaw's *Memoirs* takes its readers on a vicarious journey through the contested borderlands of nineteenth-century Methodism, women's activism, and racial politics in the

United States and England. For the United States in particular, Elaw's *full* story chronicles critical decades of political and social resistance through organized religion. This fully annotated version of *Memoirs* historically situates Elaw's autobiography with contextual footnotes that illustrate the special circumstances under which Elaw provides an expatriate's view of the Second Great Awakening.

Since we now know that over thirty years of Elaw's life and career took place in England, we must reconsider her narrative as one that explains her spiritual journeys as a Black American woman to a British audience. "I was born in the United States of America" (page 9) begins this expatriate account of a Black woman who had been living in England for six years when she published these words. The structure of Elaw's autobiography is framed by her journey across the Atlantic—indicating its central place in her life story. She opens at the close; the dedication is an emotional farewell to the friends and colleagues she has gained during her five-year sojourn in England. The lengthy appeal to her British readers foregrounds for her current readers the extent to which this autobiography is about Elaw's successful travels as much as it is about her success as a minister. In this way, Elaw establishes what is different about her book, and, indeed, her preaching life. Not only has she ministered independently as a female itinerant, but she has also worked abroad extensively and, thus, is sharing a unique story of professional accomplishment as a transatlantic evangelist.

It is precisely her time in England that situates Zilpha Elaw as a particularly interesting lens through which to see the religious, gendered, and social fervor that overwhelmed the United States for much of the nineteenth century. In her narrative, she moves from an antebellum space and makes a place for herself in postslavery England. There, although the practice was hotly debated and vigorously contested, women could and did preach freely. Some, like Elaw, preached as independent evangelists without institutional support, but many others were regularly employed by several prominent denominations.[59] With the issue of her spiritual autobiography, Elaw launched the second half of her public life in the country that she ultimately did not abandon and in which she achieved great success. Even though her book was written as a goodbye to the English, it subsequently functioned as her introduction to a larger evangelical community and career in England. There she would not begin as she did in Bucks County, Pennsylvania— the young wife and Methodist class ingénue attempting to prove her talents and convince others to open doors. Zilpha Panco Elaw Shum was a major contributor to the rapid spread of Methodism, the largest Christian denomination in the United States and Britain.[60] Her narrative functions as an active resistance to those men who did not name her or value her as they wrote their history.

In that spirit of resistance, this edition highlights the international fame of Elaw and takes up the challenge of recovering a woman who was larger than life, yet misrecognized as inconsequential and whose work was (mis)placed at the back of literary shelves. Beyond her own recognition of her important work in *Memoirs*, in Elaw's lifetime she was hyper-visible as a female Black body on public display, yet rendered invisible as a transnational evangelist. Claiming divine authority, Elaw challenged transatlantic racism and rebuked the English abolitionists who diminished and objectified her. She did so by recording her travels, by announcing her ministry, and by self-publishing her narrative, thereby naming her very existence. In Elaw's final, chosen home abroad, *she wrote herself* as the experienced and widely traveled preacher with a book full of souls saved.

NOTE ON THE TEXT

This edition preserves the original spelling, punctuation, and visual format of the original edition. All notes and bracketed text are provided by the editor.

MEMOIRS

OF THE

LIFE, RELIGIOUS EXPERIENCE,

MINISTERIAL TRAVELS AND LABOURS

OF

MRS. ZILPHA ELAW,

AN AMERICAN FEMALE OF COLOUR;

TOGETHER WITH SOME

ACCOUNT OF THE GREAT RELIGIOUS REVIVALS
IN AMERICA.

[WRITTEN BY HERSELF.]

————

PRICE 2s. FINE EDITION, 3s.

————

"Not that we are sufficient of ourselves to think any thing as of ourselves; but
our sufficiency is of God." 2. Cor. iii. 5.

LONDON:

PUBLISHED BY THE AUTHORESS, AND SOLD BY T. DUDLEY,
19, CHARTER-HOUSE LANE; AND MR. B. TAYLOR,
19, MONTAGUE-ST. SPITALFIELDS.

————

1846.

W. AND R. WOODCOCK, PRINTERS,
20½, WARWICK LANE, PATERNOSTER-ROW, AND
BRUNSWICK STREET, HACKNEY ROAD

MRS. ELAW.

DEDICATION.

———————

To the Saints and faithful Brethren in Christ, who have honoured my ministry with their attendance, in London and other localities of England.

Grace be unto you, and peace, from God the Father, and The Lord Jesus Christ.[1]

———————

DEAR BRETHREN AND FRIENDS,

After sojourning in your hospitable land, and peregrinating among you during these last five years; in the course of which period, it has been my happiness to enjoy much spiritual intercourse with many of you in your family circles, your social meetings, and in the house of God, I feel a strong desire again to cross the pathless bosom of the foaming Atlantic, and rejoin my dear friends in the occidental land of my nativity; and, in the prospect of an early departure from your shores, I feel that I cannot present you with a more appropriate keepsake, or a more lively memento of my Christian esteem, and affectionate desires for your progressive prosperity and perfection in the Christian calling, than the following contour portrait of my regenerated constitution—exhibiting, as did the bride of Solomon, comeliness with blackness;[2] and, as did the apostle Paul, riches with poverty, and power in weakness[3]—a representation, not, indeed, of the features of my outward person, drawn and coloured by the skill of the pencilling artist, but of the lineaments of my inward man, as inscribed by the Holy Ghost, and, according to my poor ability, copied off for your edification.

If, therefore, there is anything in the soul reviving and thrilling Christian intercourse we have enjoyed together in the Spirit of Christ, and in the holy communion with which we have so frequently met together in the house of God, mingled our ascending petitions at the throne of grace, unbosomed our spiritual conflicts and trials to one another, and listened with devotional interest to the messages of gospel mercy, and the unfolding mysteries of divine grace, in times now passed over for ever, worthy of your cherished recollections; and, if the poor and weak instrumentality in the gospel of Jesus, of the coloured female, whose labours and sojourn amongst you are hastening to a close, have rendered her an object, not unworthy of your cherished recollections; receive with cordial and generous courtesy, this small token of an esteem and love, which she will continue to cherish on a far distant shore, in another clime, long as life permits its exercise, and resume, on our mutual recognition in that renewed state of existence, which will be characterized by the eternal developments of elevated holiness, blissful immortality, and transcendant glory.

My dear brethren and sisters in the Lord. I gratefully acknowledge the numerous marks of kindness you have conferred upon me during my residence in your land. I intreat your prayers for my preservation from the perils of the deep, whensoever my path may lie through it; and your continued remembrance of my pilgrim course and ministerial labours, at the throne of grace. I affectionately exhort you to walk worthy of the high vocation wherewith you are called, shunning, carefully, the destructive vices which so deplorably abound in and disfigure the Christian community, in this day of feverish restlessness and mighty movement. Remember, dear brethren, that they who will be rich, fall into temptation, and a snare, and numerous foolish and hurtful lusts, which will eventually drown them in perdition. Cease, therefore, from earthly accumulations; but lay up for yourselves treasures in heaven. Renounce the love of money; for it is the root of all evil.[4] Love not the world; for the love of God is not in those who love the world. Look deep into the principles which form the under current, regardless of the artificial surface-polish of society; and abhor the pride of respectability; for that which is highly esteemed amongst men, is an abomination in the sight of God. Deal not in tale-bearing; neither be busy-bodies in other men's matters. Judge not one another, for your Judge standeth before the door. Be not ambitious, ostentatious, proud, haughty, morose, or wrathful; for God resisteth the proud and haughty scorner. Be ye, therefore, clothed with meekness and humility. Shut not your hearts against the poor, but ever remember them; for blessed is he that considereth them; and very unlike Jesus is he who cherishes a lurking prejudice in his heart against the children of need, and stoppeth his ears at their plaints. Take heed what you read: as a tree of knowledge, both of good and evil, is the press; it ofttimes teems with rabid poisons, putting darkness for light, and light for darkness; extolling earthly grandeur and honour, spurious valour and heroism; fixing reputation and character on a false basis; and frequently appearing as the panegyrist of the rankest principles, and the basest vices. Above all, shun an infidel, obscene or disloyal newspaper press, which is the scavenger of slander, and the harlequin of character; the masquerade of morals, and the burlesque of religion; the proteus of sentiment, and the dictionary of licentiousness; the seminary of libertines, and the hot-bed of sedition. Defile not your eyes with the sight of its columns, nor your heart with its proximity. Remember that you are called to be saints, not politicians and news-mongers. Give your cordial preference, therefore, to the Holy Scriptures; carefully read, study, and digest them, especially the title-deeds of the Christian covenant. Endeavour, as far as in you lies, to do the will of God on earth, as it is done in heaven. Imbibe the sentiments and spirit, the temper, disposition and manner of Christ Jesus, your inestimable pattern. Cautiously, diligently, and habitually observe and obey the directions and statutes of Christ and his apostles, that your foundation may be built not upon the sand of current traditions and prejudices, but upon the prophets and apostles, Christ Jesus being the chief cornerstone,[5] and that you may become His true and finished disciples, perfect and entire, lacking nothing, but complete in all the will of God.

And now, dear brethren, I commend you to God and the word of His grace, which is able to build you up, and give you an inheritance among all those who are sanctified. Amen.

Dear Friends, farewell! May the grace of our Lord Jesus Christ, and the love of God, and the communion of the Holy Spirit be with you all.

Amen.

MEMOIRS

OF THE

LIFE, RELIGIOUS EXPERIENCE, MINISTERIAL

TRAVELS, AND LABOURS

OF

MRS. ELAW.

I was born in the United States of America, in the State of Pennsylvania, and of religious parents.[6] When about six years of age, my mother's parents, who resided on their own farm, far in the interior of America, at a distance of many hundred miles, came to visit us. My parents had three children then living; the eldest, a boy about twelve years of age, myself, and a younger sister. On his return, my grandfather took my brother with him, promising to bring him up to the business of his farm; and I saw him not again until more than thirty years afterwards.

At twelve years of age I was bereaved of my mother, who died in child-birth of her twenty-second child, all of whom, with the exception of three, died in infancy. My father, having placed my younger sister under the care of her aunt, then consigned me to the care of Pierson and Rebecca Mitchel, with whom I remained until I attained the age of eighteen. After I had been with the above-mentioned persons one year and six months, it pleased God to remove my dear father to the world of spirits; and, being thus bereft of my natural guardians, I had no other friends on earth to look to, but those kind benefactors under whom my dear father had placed me.

But that God whose mercy endureth forever, still continued mindful of me; but oh, what a change did I experience in my new abode from that to which I had been accustomed. In my father's house, family devotion was regularly attended to morning and evening; prayer was offered up, and the praises of God were sung; but the persons with whom I now resided were Quakers, and their religious exercises, if they observed any, were performed in the secret silence of the mind;[7] nor were religion and devotion referred to by them in my hearing, which rendered my transition from home the more strange; and, being very young, and no apparent religious restraint being laid upon me, I soon gave way to the evil propensities of an unregenerate heart, which is enmity against God, and heedlessly ran into the ways of sin, taking pleasure in the paths of folly. But that God, whose eyes are ever over all His handy works, suffered me not unchecked to pursue the courses of sin. My father's death frequently introduced very serious reflections into my mind; and often was I deeply affected, and constrained to weep before God, when no human eye beheld my emotion. But, notwithstanding these seasons of serious contrition, my associations with the juvenile members of the family were too generally marked by the accustomed gaities of a wanton heart.[8] Our childish conversations sometimes turned upon the day of judgment, and our appearance in the presence of the great God on that portentous occasion, which originated in my breast the most solemn emotions whenever I was alone; for I felt myself to be so exceedingly sinful, that I was certain of meeting with condemnation at the bar of God. I knew not what to do; nor were there any persons to whom I durst open my mind upon the subject, and therefore remained ignorant of the great remedy disclosed by the plan of salvation afforded by the gospel, and incapable of religious progress. I was at times deeply affected with penitence, but could not rightly comprehend what it was that ailed me. Sometimes I resolutely shook off all my impressions, and became more thoughtless than before; one instance, in particular, is so rivetted on my memory, that I shall never forget it when ever I glance back upon my youthful life. On this occasion I was talking very foolishly, and even ventured to take the name of God in vain, in order to cater to the sinful tastes of my companions; it well pleased their carnal minds, and they laughed with delight at my profanity; but, whilst I was in the very act of swearing, I looked up, and imagined that I saw God looking down and frowning upon me: my tongue was instantly silenced; and I retired from my frolicsome companions to reflect upon what I had said and done. To the praise of divine mercy, that God who willeth not the death of a sinner, but rather that all should turn unto him and live,[9] did not even now abandon me, but called me by an effectual call through the following dream. It was a prevailing notion in that part of the world with many, that whatever a person dreamed between the times of twilight and sunrise, was prophetically ominous, and would shortly come to pass; and, on that very night, after I had offended my heavenly Father by taking His name in vain, He aroused and alarmed my spirit, by presenting before me in a dream the awful terrors of the day of judgment, accompanied by its terrific thunders. I thought that the Angel Gabriel came and proclaimed that time should be no longer; and he said, "Jehovah was about to judge the world, and execute judgment on it."[10] I then exclaimed in my dream, "Oh, Lord, what shall I do? I am unprepared to meet thee." I then meditated an escape, but could not effect it; and in this horrific dilemma I awoke: the day was just dawning; and the intense horror of my guilty mind was such as to defy description. I was now about fourteen years of age; and this dream proved an effectual call to my soul. I meditated deeply upon it, my spirits became greatly depressed, and I wept excessively. I was naturally of a very lively and active disposition, and the shock my feelings had sustained from this alarming dream, attracted the attention of my mistress, who inquired the reason of so great a change. I related my dream to her, and also stated my sentiments with respect to it: she used every endeavour to comfort me, saying that it was only a dream; that dreams have nothing ominous in them; and I ought not to give myself any more concern respecting it: but she failed in her attempt to tranquillize my mind, because the convictions of my sinfulness in the sight of God, and incompetency to meet my Judge, were immoveable and distressing. I now gave myself much to meditation, and lisped out my simple and feeble prayers to God, as well as my limited apprehensions and youthful abilities admitted. About this time, the Methodists made their first appearance in that part of the country,[11] and I was permitted to attend their meetings once a fortnight, on the Sabbath afternoons, from which I derived great satisfaction; but the divine work on my soul was a very gradual one, and my way was prepared as the dawning of the morning. I never experienced that terrific dread of hell by which some Christians appear to have been exercised; but I felt a godly sorrow for sin, in having grieved my God by a course of disobedience to His commands. I had been trained to attend the Quaker meetings; and, on their preaching occasions, I was pleased to be in attendance, and often found comfort from the word ministered by them; but I was, notwithstanding, usually very much cast down on account of my sins before God; and in this state I continued many months before I could attain sufficient confidence to say, "My Lord and my God." But as the darkness was gradually dispelled, the light dawned upon my mind, and I increased in knowledge daily; yet I possessed no assurance of my acceptance before God; though I enjoyed a greater peace of mind in waiting upon my heavenly father than at any previous time; my prayer was daily for the Lord to assure me of the forgiveness of my sins; and I at length proved the verification of the promise, "They that seek shall find;"[12] for, one evening, whilst singing one of the songs of Zion, I distinctly saw the Lord Jesus approach me with open arms, and a most divine and heavenly smile upon his countenance. As He advanced towards me, I felt that his very looks spoke, and said, "Thy prayer is accepted, I own thy name." From that day to the present, I have never entertained a doubt of the manifestation of his love to my soul.

Yea, I may say further than this; because, at the time when this occurrence took place, I was milking in the cow stall; and the manifestation of his presence was so clearly apparent, that even the beast of the stall turned her head and bowed herself upon the ground. Oh, never, never shall I forget the scene. Some persons, perhaps, may be incredulous, and say, "How can these things be, and in what form did He appear?" Dear reader, whoever thou art, into whose hands this narrative may fall, I will try to gratify thee by endeavouring to describe his manifestation. It occurred as I was singing the following lines:—

"Oh, when shall I see Jesus,
     And dwell with him above;
And drink from flowing fountains,
     Of everlasting love.
When shall I be delivered
     From this vain world of sin;
And, with my blessed Jesus,
     Drink endless pleasures in?" [13]

As I was milking the cow and singing, I turned my head, and saw a tall figure approaching, who came and stood by me. He had long hair, which parted in the front and came down on his shoulders; he wore a long white robe down to the feet; and, as he stood with open arms and smiled upon me, he disappeared. I might have tried to imagine, or persuade myself, perhaps, that it had been a vision presented merely to the eye of my mind; but, the beast of the stall gave forth her evidence to the reality of the heavenly appearance; for she turned her head and looked round as I did; and when she saw, she bowed her knees and cowered down upon the ground. I was overwhelmed with astonishment at the sight, but the thing was certain and beyond all doubt. I write as before God and Christ, and declare, as I shall give an account to my Judge at the great day, that every thing I have written in this little book, has been written with conscientious veracity and scrupulous adherence to truth.

After this wonderful manifestation of my condescending Saviour, the peace of God which passeth understanding was communicated to my heart; and joy in the Holy Ghost, to a degree, at the least, unutterable by my tongue and indescribable by my pen; it was beyond my comprehension; but, from that happy hour, my soul was set at glorious liberty; and, like the Ethiopic eunuch, I went on my way rejoicing in the blooming prospects of a better inheritance with the saints in light. [14, 15]

This, my dear reader, was the manner of my soul's conversion to God, told in language unvarnished by the graces of educated eloquence, nor transcending the capacity of a child to understand.

The love of God being now shed abroad in my heart by the Holy Spirit, and my soul transported with heavenly peace and joy in God, all the former hardships which pertained to my circumstances and situation vanished; the work and duties which had previously been hard and irksome were now become easy and pleasant; and the evil propensities of my disposition and temper were subdued beneath the softening and refining pressure of divine grace upon my heart.

In the year 1808, I united myself in the fellowship of the saints with the militant church of Jesus on earth; and I can never forget that memorable evening on which I went up formally to present my hand to the brethren, and my heart for ever to the Lord.

I was received by the travelling preacher, the Rev. J. Polhemos.[16] After sermon, he conducted the class; in the course of which he inquired if there were any persons present who desired to join the society: I then arose from my seat, and replied, "Yes, bless the Lord, here is one." He fixed his eyes upon me for a short time, and said, "Well, this seems a bold champion indeed." He then asked me the reason of my hope in Christ; if I enjoyed the evidence and witness of the Holy Spirit; if I calculated that I should be able to hold out to the end; and many very important questions besides; cautioning me against the deceptive imagination that the testimony I had given before the brethren, which had been witnessed by angels, or my union with the church, would alone be sufficient for my salvation. He then inquired if there existed any objections against my admission as a member of the Methodist Episcopal Society; and there being none, he entered my name into the class book of the society. I then returned home, meditating on that which I had heard and done, and praying that God would bestow on me sufficient grace to enable me to perform all his righteous will. Truly, in those days, my peace flowed as a river, and the light of God's countenance continually shone upon me; my path grew brighter and brighter, and my soul was stayed upon his gracious word and promises.

But, notwithstanding this tide of divine comforts so richly replenished my soul, Satan, my great adversary, frequently assailed me with various trials and temptations, and the young folks often derided me as being a Methodist: it was my happiness to be such, and I thanked God who counted me meet to be a partaker of the heavenly calling.[17] I sometimes met with very severe rebukes from my mistress, and I endured her reproofs without the exhibition of my former resentments and saucy replies: whatever storm arose, I was hid in the cleft of the rock until it was blown over. How vast a source of consolation did I derive from habitual communion with my God; to Him I repaired in secret to acquaint Him with all my griefs, and obtained both sympathy and succour. At such times, an overflowing stream of love has filled my soul, even beyond my utmost capacity to contain, and I have thought, when in such ecstasies of bliss, that I should certainly die under them, and go to my heavenly father at once, from an earthly to an heavenly transport; for I could not imagine it possible for any human being to feel such gusts of the love of God, and continue to exist in this world of sin.

But it was with me as with the great apostle of the Gentiles; when I was a child I thought as a child, I spake as a child, I understood as a child; but when I attained to maturity, I put away childish things. For as an earthly father pitieth his children, so does our Heavenly Father pity those who fear Him: they who serve Him in the time of peace, He will not abandon in the times of war and conflict, which in our probation here it behooves us to pass through. He has promised to carry the young Lambs in His bosom; and He verified that promise, in my experience, in the day of my trouble. Many were the tears which overflowed my eyes, and indicated the sorrows of my heart, and which none but God was the witness of. There were no persons in the house in which I resided, to whom I could at any time open my mind; for the knowledge of God was possessed by none in that family with the exception of my master, and amongst them I dwelt as a speckled bird;[18] but the want of suitable associates, and the singularity with which I was treated, drove me to God my refuge, and proved very congenial to increased intimacy of communion with Him.

Prior to my experience of the life and power of godliness, my mistress frequently charged me with pertness and insolent behaviour; but after I had imbibed somewhat of the meekness and gentleness of Jesus, and had been instructed by his religion not to answer again when chided, then she frequently charged me with sullenness and mopishness. This treatment often sent me to the throne of grace, to seek the sympathy of Him who is touched with the feeling of our infirmities. I now felt, bitterly, the loss of my dear mother, whose earthly remains had long since been consigned to the house appointed for all living, and her spirit made meet for the inheritance of the saints in light, in which I hope to meet her at the right hand of God. Oh, how often do I think of the advantages enjoyed by many young people, who are blessed with devout and godly parents, and of the little estimation they are held in by too many perverse and giddy children, who, instead of greatly prizing the grace conferred upon them, resent the kind restraints of family worship and attendance at the house of God. Some of them, perhaps, may ultimately be led as I was, when their parents are gathered to the generation of their fathers, to pine after the privileges which they had once despised and finally lost. See ye to it, ye careless, giddy, perverse young folks, while the light of parental godliness yet illumines the house; prize it, imbibe it, conform yourselves to and profit by it, that the fervent petitions of your pious parents, in your behalf, may be prevailingly successful, by the production of a spirit of prayer in yourselves, and the bowing of your souls to God.

Before I knew the power of real religion, I was timid and fearful when alone in the dark; and if I had recently heard of the death of any person, even if it had occurred at a distance of twelve miles, I durst not go out of doors at night alone, from the superstitious dread of seeing their apparition, and to pass a grave-yard alone was terrible indeed; but when the Lord had spoken peace to my soul, by the manifestation of Christ, my fear was removed; and my heavenly Father instructed me in reference to departed spirits, that if they slept in Jesus they would have no desire again to visit this world of sorrow; and if, on the other hand, they had died under the power and dominion of Satan, he would surely retain them safely in his custody, and not allow of their enlargement. I thus was freed from the terror by night, and dwelt secure under the protection of the Almighty.

The place of meeting for the class I was connected with, was two miles distant from my abode, and my way thither lay near two grave-yards; but, thanks be unto God, I had no dread upon my mind as I passed them continually on my way to and return from the class meeting; and I counted this as strong evidence of a great privilege to a heart renewed by divine and omnipotent grace; to God be all the praise! It is to be considered that a two miles journey in the more rural territories of the United States, is very different from the same distance along the streets or well frequented roads of England: across the lonely fields, and through the dark and hazy woods at night, the way is awfully silent and frightfully wild; but these nocturnal walks were to me seasons of sweet communion with my God: I went on my way rejoicing; fervent prayers and heavenly meditation were to me the very elements of life; my meat and drink by day and night. My delights were to follow the leadings and obey the dictates of the Holy Spirit, and glorify with my body and spirit my Father who is in heaven. I enjoyed richly the spirit of adoption: knowing myself to be an adopted child of divine love, I claimed God as my Father, and his Son Jesus as my dear friend, who adhered to me more faithfully in goodness than a brother: and with my blessed Saviour, Redeemer, Intercessor, and Patron, I enjoyed a delightsome heavenly communion, such as the world has never conceived of.

Thus I passed three happy years after my conversion, growing in grace and in the knowledge of God. At the commencement of my religious course, I was deplorably ignorant and dark; but the Lord himself was graciously pleased to become my teacher, instructing me by his Holy Spirit, in the knowledge of the Holy Scriptures. It was not by the aid of human instruments that I was first drawn to Christ; and it was by the Lord alone that I was upheld, confirmed, instructed, sanctified, and directed.

The persons who become members of the Methodist societies in America are first introduced to the class, which they attend for six months on probation; at the expiration of which, if their conduct has been consistent with their professions, they are baptised, and accounted full members of the society.[19] After I had completed my six months probation, I was baptised by the Rev. Joseph Lybrand;[20] and I shall never forget the heavenly impression I felt on that joyfully solemn occasion. Truly the one Spirit of Jesus doth by means of His ministers, baptise us into the one body of Jesus. 1 Cor. xii. 13. When he said, "I baptise thee into the name of the Father, Son, and Holy Ghost, Amen," I was so overwhelmed with the love of God, that self seemed annihilated: I was completely lost and absorbed in the divine fascinations. The Rev. Divine then added, "Be thou faithful unto death, and thou shalt receive a crown of life; and, 'Whatsoever thy hand findeth to do, do with all thy might;' for this is the will of God in Christ Jesus concerning you." I was now accounted a full member of the society, and privileged with the communion of the Lord's Supper. In this happy home I continued nearly seven years, and only parted from it when I left my situation.

In the year 1810, I surrendered myself in marriage to Joseph Elaw, a very respectable young man, in the general acceptation of the term, but he was not a Christian,—that is, a sincere and devoted disciple of Christ, though nominally bearing His name. Oh! let me affectionately warn my dear unmarried sisters in Christ, against being thus unequally yoked with unbelievers. In general your lot would be better, if a millstone were hung about your necks, and you were drowned in the depths of the sea, than that you should disobey the law of Jesus, and plunge yourselves into all the sorrows, sins, and anomalies involved in a matrimonial alliance with an unbeliever. This mischief frequently emanates from the delusive sentiments in which the female portion of the Christian community is steeped. Young ladies imagine themselves their own mistresses before they are able to shift for themselves; and especially when they attain the legal maturity fixed by the civil law. Pride, consequential haughtiness, and independent arrogance in females, are the worst vices of humanity, and are denounced in the Scriptures as insuring the severest retributions of God. Isaiah iii. 16–24. The laws of Scripture invest parents with the trust and control of their daughter, until the time, be it early or late in life, when the father surrenders her in marriage to the care and government of a husband: then, and not till then, the guardianship and government of her father over her ceases; and then, formed as she is by nature for subordination, she becomes the endowment and is subject to the authority of her husband. The boastful speeches too often vented by young females against either the paternal yoke or the government of a husband, is both indecent and impious—conveying a wanton disrespect to the regulations of Scripture: the fancied independence and self-control in which they indulge, has no foundation either in nature or Scripture, and is prolific with the worst results both to religion and society. That woman is dependant on and subject to man, is the dictate of nature; that the man is not created for the woman, but the woman for the man, is that of Scripture. These principles lie at the foundation of the family and social systems; and their violation is a very immoral and guilty act. These remarks will not, I trust, be out of place here. I now observe, in reference to the marriage of a Christian with an unbeliever, that there is not, there cannot be in it, that mutual sympathy and affectionate accordance which exists in the marriage lives of devoted Christians, when both parties are cordially progressing on the king's highway. How discordant are the sentiments, tastes, and feelings of the Christian and unbeliever, when unequally, and I may say, wickedly allied together in the marriage state. The worldly man displays his settled aversion to the things of religion, and especially against the sincerity and tenacity with which his believing partner adheres to them; and on the other hand, the believer displays his settled abhorrence of the things of the world, to which he is crucified and dead: nor can the strength of any carnal attachment betwixt the parties, or the utmost stretch of courtesy on both sides, ever reconcile the radical opposition of their principles. If the saint winks at the worldly course pursued by his partner, he evidences the weakness of Christian principle in himself, is unfaithful to his profession, and perfidious to the King of kings; if he reproves it, he involves the household in strife, his own soul in vexation, and perils it by wrath. Besides, the wife is destined to be the help-meet of her husband; but if he be a worldly man, she cannot, she dare not be either his instrument or abettor in worldly lusts and sinful pursuits; if he be a saint, and she a child of wrath, she is not his help-meet, but his drawback and curse; and in either case she possesses the title or name of a wife without the qualification, viz. that of a help-meet. By the Jewish law, the marriage of a Jew with a woman of a prohibited nation, was not accounted marriage, but fornication, Ezra x. 11, Hebrews xii. 16; and it is a very serious impropriety also under the Christian dispensation. I am aware that when once the carnal courtship is commenced, the ensnared Christian fondly imagines that he shall soon be able to persuade his unregenerate companion to think as he does, and also to love and serve God with him; and on the other hand, the carnal suitor accounts religion as mere whimsy and pretense, and flatters himself that he shall soon divert the object of his desire from so melancholy and superstitious a pursuit; and thus both of them are miserably deceived, and miss of that happiness they so fallaciously had dreamt of. I am sorry to say, I know something of this by experience. My dear husband had been a member of the society to which I belonged, and had been afterwards disowned by them; but I could not regard him as a backslider from religion, for I am of opinion that he had never tasted of the pardoning love of God through the atonement of Jesus Christ. He made me many promises that he would again unite with the Church, and try to devote his life to the service of God; but they were never fulfilled. After we had been married about a year, he resolved to use every means to induce me to renounce my religion, and abolish my attendance at the meeting-house. It was then that my troubles began, and grew so severe, that I knew not what to do; but that God who is a present help in every time of need was with me still, and enabled me to endure every trial with meekness; and when suffering his keenest chidings for my attendance at the meeting-house, I kept my mouth as with a bridle, and sinned not with my tongue. He was passionately fond of music and dancing, and determined to introduce me to such amusements; thinking that I should be as delighted as himself with the merriments of the world, and hoping thereby to accomplish his object: but that God whom I served night and day, preserved me in the hour of temptation, and shielded me from harm. We resided about twenty miles from Philadelphia, a city of great note in America, and which I had never yet seen. An opportunity at length was presented for us to repair thither; and my dear husband projected my introduction to his favourite resort—the ball-room, on our visit to this great city. We accordingly travelled to Philadelphia; and after we had been there a few days, we went to take a walk and view the different edifices and parts of the city: he then conducted me into a place which I quickly recognised as a ball-room; for the violin struck up, and the people began to caper the merry dance, and take their fill of pleasure. The tones of the music and the boundings of the people were to me like awful peals of thunder; and all I could do was to weep before God. I often think and say,

"Where'er I am, where'er I move,
I meet the object of my love."

Although I was then in a ball-room, I think that I never heard a sermon that preached more impressively to me than the display I witnessed there, in the din and scenery of that vapourish bubble of worldly gaiety and pleasure. Well might the wise man exclaim, "All is vanity and vexation of spirit!"

From the ill success of this wretched experiment, my dear husband found his expectations disappointed, and he never after urged me to accompany him to such places,—to God be all the praise! We soon returned home; and I continued on my course, blessing and praising God for his kind preserving care of me in the perilous hour of temptation.

My husband was a fuller by trade; and when the embargo was laid on British vessels, all traffic ceased betwixt the two nations: the cloth manufacturers in the States enlarged their business very extensively, and the demand for hands was urgent.[21] By this turn of affairs we were induced to remove our place of residence to the city of Burlington, in the state of New Jersey, which was to me a happy removal indeed; and I plainly read the indications of the Lord's goodness in it: for the class assembled at a house but a few doors from mine; the chapel was also near, and I more plentifully enjoyed the means of grace, and grew thereby. Highly did I prize these precious privileges, for I grew in grace daily, and in the knowledge of the truth as it is in Jesus. With cheerful gratitude and paramount peace could I sing these lines—

> "How happy every child of grace,
> Who knows his sins forgiven;
> This earth, he cries, is not my place,
> I seek my rest in Heaven."

I am compelled to omit much interesting and important matter relative to my religious experience and life, and pass to the more strikingly eventful points, lest I should swell these pages beyond my present limited means for the press.

In the year 1817, I attended an American camp-meeting. Oh, how I should like our dear English friends to witness some of our delightful camp meetings, which are held in the groves of the United States. There many thousands assemble in the open air, and beneath the overspreading bowers, to own and worship our common Lord, the Proprietor of the Universe; there all arise and sing the solemn praises of the King of majesty and glory. It is like heaven descended upon an earthly soil, when all unite to

"Praise God, from whom all blessings flow."

The hardest hearts are melted into tenderness; the driest eyes overflow with tears, and the loftiest spirits bow down: the Creator's works are gazed upon, and His near presence felt around.

In order to form a camp meeting, when the place and time of meeting has been extensively published, each family takes its own tent, and all things necessary for lodgings, with seats, provisions and servants; and with wagons and other vehicles repair to the destined spot, which is generally some wildly rural and wooded retreat in the back grounds of the interior: hundreds of families, and thousands of persons, are seen pressing to the place from all quarters: the meeting usually continues for a week or more: a large circular enclosure of brushwood is formed; immediately inside of which the tents are pitched, and the space in the centre is appropriated to the worship of God, the minister's stand being on one side, and generally on a somewhat rising ground. It is a scaffold constructed of boards, and surrounded with a fence of rails.

In the space before the platform, seats are placed sufficient to seat four or five thousand persons; and at night the woods are illuminated; there are generally four large mounds of earth constructed, and on them large piles of pine knots are collected and ignited, which make a wonderful blaze and burn a long time; there are also candles and lamps hung about in the trees, together with a light in every tent, and the minister's stand is brilliantly lighted up; so that the illumination attendant upon a camp-meeting, is a magnificently solemn scene. The worship commences in the morning before sunrise; the watchmen proceed round the inclosure, blowing with trumpets to awaken every inhabitant of this City of the Lord; they then proceed again round the camp, to summon the inmates of every tent to their family devotions; after which they partake of breakfast, and are again summoned by sound of trumpet to public prayer meeting at the altar which is placed in front of the preaching stand. Many precious souls are on these occasions introduced into the liberty of the children of God; at the close of the prayer meeting the grove is teeming with life and activity; the numberless private conferences, the salutations of old friends again meeting in the flesh, the earnest inquiries of sinners, the pressing exhortations of anxious saints, the concourse of pedestrians, the arrival of horses and carriages of all descriptions render the scene portentously interesting and intensely surprising. At ten o'clock, the trumpets sound again to summon the people to public worship; the seats are all speedily filled, and as perfect a silence reigns throughout the place as in a Church or Chapel; presently the high praises of God sound melodiously from this consecrated spot, and nothing seems wanting but local elevation to render the place a heaven indeed. It is like God's ancient and holy hill of Zion on her brightest festival days, when the priests conducted the processions of the people to the glorious temple of Jehovah. At the conclusion of the service, the people repair to their tents or other rendezvous to dinner; at the termination of which prayers are offered up, and hymns are sung in the tents, and in the different groups scattered over the ground; and many precious souls enter into the liberty of God's dear children. At two o'clock, a public prayer-meeting commences at the stand, and is continued till three, when the ministers preach again to the people. At six o'clock in the evening, the public services commence again as before; and at the hour of ten, the trumpet is blown as a signal for all to retire to rest; and those who are unprovided with lodgings, leave the ground. On the last morning of the camp meeting, which is continued for a week, a solemn love feast is held; after which, all the tents are struck and every thing put in readiness for departure; the ministers finally form themselves in procession, and march round the encampment; the people falling into rank and following them. At length the ministers turn aside from the rank, stand still, and commence singing a solemn farewell hymn; and as the different ranks of the people march by, they shake hands with their pastors, take an affectionate farewell of them, and pass on in procession, until the last or rear rank have taken their adieu. This farewell scene is a most moving and affecting occasion. Hundreds of Christians, dear to each other and beloved in the Spirit, embrace each other for the last time, and part to meet no more, until the morning of the resurrection; and many a stout-hearted sinner has been so shaken to pieces at the pathetic sight, as to fall into deep conviction of his depravity before God, which has ended in genuine repentance and saving conversion to Christ. I, for one, have great reason to thank God for the refreshing seasons of his mighty grace, which have accompanied these great meetings of his saints in the wilderness. It was at one of these meetings that God was pleased to separate my soul unto Himself, to sanctify me as a vessel designed for honour, made meet for the master's use. Whether I was in the body, or whether I was out of the body, on that auspicious day, I cannot say; but this I do know, that at the conclusion of a most powerful sermon delivered by one of the ministers from the platform, and while the congregation were in prayer, I became so overpowered with the presence of God, that I sank down upon the ground, and laid there for a considerable time; and while I was thus prostrate on the earth, my spirit seemed to ascend up into the clear circle of the sun's disc; and, surrounded and engulphed in the glorious effulgence of his rays, I distinctly heard a voice speak unto me, which said, "Now thou art sanctified; and I will show thee what thou must do." I saw no personal appearance while in this stupendous elevation, but I discerned bodies of resplendent light; nor did I appear to be in this world at all, but immensely far above those spreading trees, beneath whose shady and verdant bowers I was then reclined. When I recovered from the trance or ecstasy into which I had fallen, the first thing I observed was, that hundreds of persons were standing around me weeping; and I clearly saw by the light of the Holy Ghost, that my heart and soul were rendered completely spotless—as clean as a sheet of white paper, and I felt as pure as if I had never sinned in all my life; a solemn stillness rested upon my soul:

> "The speechless awe that dares not move,
> And all the silent heaven of love."

Truly I durst not move, because God was so powerfully near to me; for the space of several hours I appeared not to be on earth, but far above all earthly things. I had not at this time offered up public prayer on the camp ground; but when the prayer meeting afterwards commenced, the Lord opened my mouth in public prayer; and while I was thus engaged, it seemed as if I heard my God rustling in the tops of the mulberry-trees. Oh, how precious was this day to my soul!

I was after this very frequently requested to present my petitions to the throne of grace in the public meetings at the camp; and to my astonishment, during one of the services, an old gentleman and his wife, whose heads were blanched by the frost of time, came to me, fell upon their knees, and desired me to pray for them, as also many others whom I expect to meet in a happier world: and before the meeting at this camp closed, it was revealed to me by the Holy Spirit, that like another Phœbe, or the matrons of the apostolic societies, I must employ myself in visiting families, and in speaking personally to the members thereof, of the salvation and eternal interests of their souls, visit the sick, and attend upon other of the errands and services of the Lord;[22] which I afterwards cheerfully did, not confining my visits to the poor only, but extending them to the rich also, and even to those who sit in high places in the state; and the Lord was with me in the work to own and bless my labours. Like Enoch, I walked and talked with God: nor did a single cloud intervene betwixt God and my soul for many months after.[23]

But Satan at length succeeded in producing a cloud over my mind, and in damping the delightful ardours of my soul in these blessed labours, by suggesting, that I ought not to make so bold a profession of an entire sanctification and holiness of spirit, lest I should be unable at all times to maintain it; and to this evil suggestion I sinfully acceded, and dilated chiefly in my visits on the goodness of God; and much ceased to enforce that high attainment, and to witness to the indwelling presence and superintending sway of the Holy Spirit in a clean and obedient heart, which I had so powerfully experienced; but alas! I soon proved that to God must be cheerfully ascribed the glory, or he will not vouchsafe to us a continuance of the happy enjoyment.

I write this as a warning to others who may be attacked with the same temptation, that they may be careful not thus to grieve the Holy Spirit of God: but ever remember, that we are witnesses of that gracious passage of Scripture, "This is the will of God, even your sanctification." "For this the Saviour prayed on behalf of his disciples, 'Sanctify them by thy truth, Thy word is truth:' " and Peter says, "Ye have purified your souls in obeying the truth through the Spirit:" and "As he which hath called you is holy, so be ye holy in all manner of conversation." As, therefore, this blessed doctrine is most certainly believed by us Methodists, it is both our high privilege and bounden duty to manifest it to those around us; and, in default thereof, we shall bring clouds of darkness upon our souls.

I shall here narrate a very extraordinary circumstance which occurred in the family of Mr. Boudinot, one of the richest gentlemen in the city of Burlington.[24] The Lord bade me repair to this gentleman's residence, and deliver a gospel message to him. I was astounded at the idea of going to such a man, to talk to him of the condition of his soul; and began to reason with myself as to the propriety thereof. Satan also suggested that a man of his rank and dignity would not listen to such a poor, ignorant creature as myself. I therefore concluded, that possibly I might be mistaken about this message, and that it might have arisen in my imagination merely, and not have come from God. I accordingly decided in my mind that I would not go to him. But oh! how soon did my heavenly Master show me that I had disobeyed his high commands, given me by the impression of his Spirit upon my heart; for I habitually enjoyed so clear an illumination of the divine presence and glory upon my soul, a conscience so pure, and an eye so single, that the slightest omission would produce the intervention of a cloud and an obscuration of the divine ray upon my spirit; and thus I felt on this occasion, being deprived of the divine ray, and of the peculiar zest and nearness of divine intercourse I had hitherto enjoyed with my heavenly Father. I endeavoured to search out and ascertain the reason, why the lustre of my Father's countenance was obscured upon my soul; for so manifest was the gloom on my spirit, that even my class leader said, "Why, how is this Zilpha, that you appear less lively than you did a week or two since?" yet I still remained ignorant of the cause thereof; but on the next class evening, one of the itinerating ministers presided, and he gave forth the following lines to be sung—

> "Jesus, the hindrance show,
> Which I have feared to see;
> And let me now consent to know,
> What keeps me back from Thee."

While singing these lines, I was led to discover that I had not obeyed the call of the Lord, by refusing to go to Mr. Boudinot's, as I had been directed.

> "In me is all the bar,
> Which God would fain remove:
> Remove it; and I shall declare,
> That God is only love."

I then laid open my case before my dear minister; and I shall never forget the kind and excellent advice he gave me upon that occasion. I never durst take any important step without first consulting my superiors; and having informed him of the painful exercises of mind I had passed through, and of the disregard I had paid to my heavenly direction, he advised me, by all means, to go whither I had been directed, and no more confer with flesh and blood; but proceed in the course of duty and obedience, leaving the event to God, before whose judgment-seat we shall all stand to give an account of our stewardship. Upon this, I again sought my heavenly Father at the throne of grace, promising that I would go in His name, whither he had sent me, if He would be pleased to restore to me the light of his countenance and Spirit; and He graciously favoured me with the request of my heart.

I then went to the residence of Mr. Elias Boudinot, and had access to all who were in his house; and it was a day for ever to be remembered; for such an out-pouring of divine unction took place, as I never witnessed in all my life. All other matters were laid aside but that of religion; and little was to be seen but weeping and mourning. Some of us were occupied in praising the Lord, but most of the household were weeping the penitential tear for their sins. There were company visiting at the house at the time, and when dinner was ready, there were none to come and partake of it; we had quite a search to find, and some trouble to induce them to come to dinner. One lady, who was then on a visit there, had shut herself up in her apartment to read the New Testament; another was shut up in another apartment; one of the servants had locked himself up in the pantry, and there he cried aloud upon God for mercy. It was a day of wonders, indeed! Oh, that so gracious a visitation might come upon thousands of families in England! How sweet is the path of obedience! God will bless while man obeys; "for what his mouth hath said, his own almighty hand will do." I again enjoyed a full measure of the Holy Spirit, and kept that sacred, hallowed fire alive in my soul; to God be all the praise!

I thus attended to my Master's business in this and similar spheres of effort for the space of five years; during which period, much good resulted from the attempts of so simple and weak an instrument as myself; because directed by the wisdom, and sustained by the mighty power of God. Five happy years, on the whole, were they indeed to me; notwithstanding that I had many sorrows and grievous trials to endure and contend with.

> "Trials must and will befal;
> But with humble faith to see,
> Love inscribed upon them all,
> This is happiness to me." [25]

The bitters of my cup were continually sweetened by the smiles of Jesus; and all things went on easy, because my heavenly Father took the heaviest end of the cross and bore it with me: thus the crooked was made straight, and the rough became smooth.

In 1816, I had a presentiment on my mind of a speedy dissolution; and felt so confident in this expectation, that, when in the class-meeting, I could not forbear from speaking in a strain which implied my speedy departure. My leader inquired if I was about to leave Burlington? Upon which, I opened my mind to him, and the train of my feelings; he made no comment upon it at the time; and in the week following, I accidentally met with a severe fall, by which I was so injured internally, as to allow no presage of recovery; my medical attendant pronounced it impossible that I could live, and my friends for many days looked to see me breathe my last; but God ordered it otherwise to every expectation.

While I was thus lying with but one step betwixt me and death, a dear lady, who was a preaching Quakeress, came to see me, and take a last farewell, not expecting to see me again in this life, as she was about taking a religious tour in the country. She affectionately told me she hoped that all would be well with me, and that we should again meet in a better world, though we might meet no more in the flesh. But though my recovery was very gradual indeed, yet it pleased God to raise me up again; and then, with what renewed pleasure did I sit under the sound of the glorious gospel of our Lord and Saviour Jesus Christ, and resume the work of my heavenly Master, going forth in his great name from day to day, and holding sweet converse with my God, as a man converses with his friend. This family or household ministry, as I may call it, was a particular duty, a special calling, which I received from the Lord to discharge for the space of five years; at the expiration of which, it was taken from me, and consigned to another sister in the same class with myself. How wonderful are the works of the Almighty, and his ways past finding out by the children of men! I was often so happy in this work as to be quite unable to contain myself; sometimes I cried out, "Lord, what wilt thou have me to do?" for it seemed as if the Lord had yet something more in reserve for me to undertake.

I had at this time but one sister living, who resided in Philadelphia, about twenty miles distant from Burlington; she was the only sister, who with myself arrived at years of maturity; a very pious woman, and she conducted herself very strictly and exemplarily in all her movements: she was so sanctified and devoted a Christian, that some persons have informed me, that they have sat with her in their meetings, and received much edification from beholding the earnest devoted-ness of mind she manifested in the house of God; thus, "as iron sharpeneth iron, so doth the countenance of a man his friend."

This dear sister of mine was at length attacked with a mortal disease, and intelligence of her illness was communicated to me. I therefore repaired to Philadelphia; and on entering the room, I found her so emaciated and altered in appearance, that I scarcely knew her; but in so happy a frame of mind, that the body seemed almost unable to detain so heavenly a spirit. As I stood by her bed-side weeping, she said,

"I'll take my sister by the hand,
And lead her to the promised land."

Thus I found her; and after staying with her a few days, thus I left her, and returned home to Burlington. But being pressed with concern for her, I could not long rest at home; I therefore arranged my affairs there, and taking my little daughter with me, set off again for Philadelphia. When I arrived at the house of my brother-in-law, I went directly into the chamber where my sister was lying; and the first thing she said to me was, "My dear sister, I am going to hell." I had not either spoken or sat down in the house; but upon hearing this, I kneeled down and tried to pray; but she instantly exclaimed, "Oh, do not pray, for you will only send me the sooner to judgment!" My astonishment was immense at finding her in such an altered condition of mind; for only a fortnight previously she was exulting in the high praises of God, completely weaned from all things of an earthly nature, and longing to depart to the world of spirits. Many kind brethren and sisters visited her, and prayer was made day and night unto God for her, that her soul might be released from the bonds of darkness; but she remained in this horrible state for nearly a week after my arrival. Some of the ministers bade me not to be discouraged on her account; saying that for they had witnessed others who had been in a similar condition, and had afterwards experienced a most powerful deliverance. I had never before heard of such a case, much less witnessed one; and it was equally as surprising as it was afflictive to me; but the Spirit of God at times whispered in my heart, "Be of good cheer, thou shalt yet see the glory of God." My faith and hope were thereby strengthened; yet the sorrowful sight of my poor dear sister opposing every effort of the friends to pray with and for her, did not a little, at intervals, deject and cast me down. Thanks be unto God, the hour at last arrived when he was pleased to burst through the gloom, and set the captive free. A number of the friends had assembled in the house, and we joined in prayer together; after several friends had prayed, in a moment such a spirit of prayer came upon me, as seemed to shake the whole place, as at the memorable apostolic prayer-meeting. Acts v. 31. I immediately commenced praying; and while thus engaged, my dear sister exclaimed aloud, "Look up, children, the Master is coming!" and she shouted, "Glory to God in the highest, and on the earth peace; for I again have found Jesus, the chiefest among ten thousand. Honour and glory, and majesty and power, be given to Him for ever and ever." "Now," said she, "turn me round, and let me die in the arms of Jesus; for I shall soon be with Him in glory." We then turned her over on her other side, as she requested, and awaited the event; she then swooned away, and lay for some time to all appearance dead.

What will infidelity say to this? It surely will not attempt to charge a sincere and godly Christian on her death-bed with hypocrisy; nor can it be consistently attributed to fanaticism. The antagonising conflicts of Christian faith, and its triumphs through the aids of the Holy Spirit over the powers of darkness, as exemplified on such occasions, are very remote from the whimsical vagaries of an over-heated and incoherent imagination; such experience, under certain circumstances, is the natural cause and effect of exercise of Christian faith, in collision with forces asserted by the gospel to be engaged in hostile action to it; and it is a fact worthy of extensive observation, that the vast variety of mental exercises and religious experiences of all true and lively Christians, in every grade of society, in all ages, and in all denominations and sections of the Christian Church, are of too uniform and definite a character to be ascribed to the wild and fluctuating uncertainties of fanaticism: so widely spread an uniformity as that which exists in the genuine pilgrim's progress of Christian experience, can never be philosophically shewn to be an attribute of fanaticism; an uniformity, like that of the human constitution, admitting of the greatest variety of individual features, yet all governed by the same laws; and it may be retorted also, that stubborn facts continually prove, in other countries as well as in modern Gaul, that no fanaticism is more luxuriant, bewitching, and arrogant, than that which inscribes on its ensign—"The Age of Reason," and roots itself in the soil of infidelity.[26]

After my dear sister had laid in a swoon for some time, she revived, and said, amongst other things which I could not remember, "I have overcome the world by the kingdom of heaven;" she then began singing, and appeared to sing several verses; but the language in which she sung was too wonderful for me, and I could not understand it. We all sat or stood around her with great astonishment, for her voice was as clear, musical, and strong, as if nothing had ailed her; and when she had finished her song of praise, (for it was indeed a song of praise, and the place was full of glory,) she addressed herself to me, and informed me, that she had seen Jesus, and had been in the society of angels; and that an angel came to her, and bade her tell Zilpha that she must preach the gospel; and also, that I must go to a lady named Fisher, a Quakeress, and she would tell me further what I should do.[27] It was then betwixt one and two o'clock in the morning, and she wished me to go directly to visit this lady, and also to commence my ministry of preaching, by delivering an address to the people then in the house. I cannot describe my feelings at this juncture; I knew not what to do, nor where to go: and my dear sister was pressingly urgent for me to begin and preach directly; and then to go and see the above-named lady. I was utterly at a loss what to say, or how to move; dear heart, she waited in silence for my commencing, and I stood in silence quite overwhelmed by my feelings. At length, she raised her head up, and said, "Oh, Zilpha! why do you not begin?" I then tried to say something as I stood occupied in mental prayer; but she said, "Oh! do not pray, you must preach." I then addressed a few words to those around me, and she was very much pleased with the attempt: two of the sisters then took me by the arm, and led me into another room; they there informed me they expected to see me sink down upon the floor, and that they thought my sister was perhaps a little delirious. The next day when I was alone with her, she asked me if that hymn which she had sung on the previous night was not beautiful; adding, "Ah, Zilpha! angels gave it me to sing; and I was told that you must be a preacher; and oh! how you hurt me last night by not going where I told you; but as soon as you moved, I was released." She continued in this happy frame of mind until her soul fell asleep in Jesus. The whole of this sick-bed scene, until its termination in death, was as surpassingly wonderful to me, as a Christian, for its depths of religious experience and power, as it was afflictively interesting to me as a relative. I have, however, since learnt that some other Christians have occasionally been known, when in the very arms of death, to break forth and sing with a melodious and heavenly voice, several verses in a language unknown to mortals. A pure language, unalloyed by the fulsome compliment, the hyperbole, the tautology and circumlocution, the insinuation, double meaning and vagueness, the weakness and poverty, the impurity, bombast, and other defects, with which all human languages are clogged, seems to be essential for the associations of glorified spirits and the elevated devotions of heaven, are, doubtless, in use among the holy angels, and seems to be a matter of gracious promise on the part of Jehovah, on behalf of his redeemed people. Zephaniah iii. 9.[28]

I have been very careful, and the more minute in narrating the experience of my dear sister during her illness and death, in hope that it may possibly meet the cases of others tempted in a similar manner; that they may take encouragement from her happy and triumphant end. She had evidently grieved the Holy Spirit in some way or other, and He had withdrawn from her His comforting presence for a time; but He returned to her again with abundant mercy and comforting grace. After receiving a little refreshment, the last words she spoke were, "Now I want a good prayer;" her husband then commenced prayer; and during the exercise, her happy spirit bade adieu to the frailties and sorrows of this mortal life, prepared for, and assured of, her title to a jointure in the ever-blooming glories of the inheritance of the saints in light.

Notwithstanding the plain and pointed declaration of my sister, and though the Scriptures assert that not many wise, rich, and noble are called; but God hath chosen the foolish things of this world to confound the wise, and the weak things of the world to confound the mighty, I could not at the time imagine it possible that God should select and appoint so poor and ignorant a creature as myself to be his messenger, to bear the good tidings of the gospel to the children of men.

Soon after this, I received a visit from a female who was employed in the work of the ministry, who asked me if I did not think that I was called by the Lord to that work? to which I replied in the negative; she then said, "I think you are; now tell me, do not passages of Scripture often open to thy mind as subjects for public speaking and exposition? Weigh well this matter and see; for I believe that God has provided a great work for thy employment."

But still I could not believe that any such line of duty was enjoined upon me. Though one intimation came after another, and I had warning after warning, to prepare me for and urge me to it, I went on from one degree to another, without seriously and earnestly entertaining the subject; yet I often reflected on that which had been expressed by this kind friend, and especially on what had fallen from the lips of my dear sister Hannah but a short time previously to her death; but I kept these things very reservedly to myself, and pondered them in my heart, as did Mary the mother of Christ. Besides all this, I continually endured such sore trials from my poor unconverted husband, as powerfully operated to deter me from the thought of such an undertaking; but on the other hand, when I had been contemplating the wonderful works of creation, or revelation of the mind and truth of God to man, by the inspiration of his prophets, I have been lost in astonishment at the perception of a voice, which either externally or internally, has spoken to me, and revealed to my understanding many surprising and precious truths. I have often started at having my solitary, contemplative silence thus broken; and looked around me as if with the view of discovering or recognising the ethereal attendant who so kindly ministered to me, Heb. ii. 14;[29] not, indeed, with the slightest alarm, though with much wonder; for I enjoyed so intimate and heavenly an intercourse with God, that I was assured He had sent an angel to instruct me in such of His holy mysteries as were otherwise beyond my comprehension. Such communications were most gratifying and delightful to me; yet I had not sagacity sufficient to discern, that, gifted with such an aid as this, I had a sufficiency from God for the proclamation of his gospel. 2 Cor. iii. 5.[30] Every thing failed to convince me that God had destined me for the ministry; intimation and qualification were alike unheeded by my unbelieving ignorance of the will and ways of God; and thus I continued, for several years after my sister's death, unmindful of the allurements as well as the precepts of God.

As all other means had failed to move me to proceed upon my appointed duties, the Lord used other means to move me; for when gentle means do not answer, the rod must be applied to bring us into subjection to our Master's will. In 1819, it pleased God to lay me upon a bed of affliction, with a sickness which, to all appearance, was unto death; an internal inflammation wasted my body, in defiance of all the means and remedies which were resorted to; and I grew worse and worse. The medical gentleman who attended me said, he could do no more for me; he was a very pious Christian, and his visits were very precious to me; for we often held much sweet counsel together about the things of God. Real religion is very seldom to be found amongst the medical profession; but thanks be to God, there are some to be met with, occasionally, who can administer comfort to the soul while relieving the ailments of the body; and thus it was with him.

I had many persons come from far and near to visit me, because God was with me; my soul was preserved in great peace and tranquility; but, on one occasion, when in conversation with my husband about my death, which seemed to be fast approaching, I could not forbear from weeping, from the thought of leaving behind me, in this evil and stormy life, my poor little girl who was then about seven years of age. It then occurred to my mind, that this natural anxiety which I felt, did not comport with an absolute submission to the will of God; and evinced the inordinate strength and force of those ties by which I was still bound to this earth. I then, in prayer, pledged myself afresh to God, begging that he would effectually wean me from all the excesses of nature's ties; and that my affections and will might be brought into due submission to the will of my heavenly Father. I wrestled in prayer against my insubordinate affections, for about two hours, and the Lord graciously bestowed upon me the victory; and I became so dead to this world, that I felt no anxiety to give any directions as to what should be done for the child after my decease. I was perfectly resigned to the will of God, and willing either to live or die as he thought best; though I could rather have preferred to depart and be with Christ, which is far better. While thus awaiting the divine disposal, my doctor came in one morning, and said, "There is but one thing more that I can try for you, and it is a very severe operation; nor can I say how it will affect you; but if you wish to try it, I will apply it in the name of God;" adding, "that it is our duty to try every means for the restoration of health, leaving the event to God." I therefore consented to submit to the operation, which was, to have my side burnt with caustic, and have an issue inserted therein. I complied, and the thing was done; but it well nigh proved the breaking asunder of the slender thread of life. A kind Quaker lady, who much visited and attended to me during my illness, being unable to witness the operation, was absent from me on that day: when she came on the morrow, I had scarcely power left me sufficiently to recognise her; and my exhaustion was so extreme, that I could not even raise my hand. I was many weeks ere I recovered from this painful operation, and my debility was long protracted; but at times the presence of the Holy Spirit was so powerful within me, that I seemed quite invigorated and strong; and in this illness, I received another striking communication in reference to my future employment in the ministry; it occurred after the renewed dedication of my soul to God as above related. About twelve o'clock one night, when all was hushed to silence, a human figure in appearance, came and stood by my bed-side, and addressed these words to me, "Be of good cheer, for thou shalt yet see another camp-meeting; and at that meeting thou shalt know the will of God concerning thee." I then put forth my hand to touch it, and discovered that it was not really a human being, but a supernatural appearance. I was not in the least alarmed, for the room was filled with the glory of God, who had permitted the veil to be removed from my mortal vision, that I might have a glimpse of one of our heavenly attendants,—of one who had a message to deliver to me from God. There are many sceptical persons who conceitedly, rashly, and idly scoff at the idea of apparitions and angelic appearances; but they ignorantly do it in the face of the most extensive experience, instinct, belief, and credible testimony of persons of every nation, and of all ages, as well as the inspired statements of the Scriptures. The universal belief of mankind in the separate existence of the soul after death, is sustained, not by fanciful speculations, but by matters of fact; from facts of this class, this belief derives more substantial support and confirmation than from all the cold deductions of metaphysical ratiocination. Ocular proof is its own demonstration, and commands a far more extensive currency than logical influence. Seldom do the juries of our criminal courts establish their verdicts on evidence equally abundant and express, with that which is furnished by every locality to facts of this description; and the number of such facts in the possession of the present generation of mankind, or even of each hamlet or parish in the world, is astonishingly greater than ever meets the ear of the public, or enters into the conceptions of the headstrong, heroic, and unreasoning sceptic. From that moment I was assured of my ultimate recovery; nor could any human assurances or arguments have persuaded me to the contrary. Soon after this, one of our ministers having heard of my illness, and of the happy frame of my mind, travelled a distance of several miles to see me; he informed me, that he longed to be in such a situation as mine—so near to the gate of heaven. I replied, "Brother, it seemeth to me that I shall yet see another camp-meeting." He then addressed me in a manner that implied, that in his judgment it was quite impossible, and out of the question. But from the very hour in which the kind celestial messenger delivered to me that comforting and assuring announcement, I began to amend; though my recovery was very gradual, and it was a long time ere I was able to sit up. Thanks be unto the Lord, my sickness was not unto death, but for the glory of God. So sturdy had been my unbelief that my merciful and indulgent God was thereby induced to adopt more severe and extraordinary means to bring me into subjection to his holy will. My spirit and temper were now subdued, and resigned to do the will of God, which I was desirous to ascertain, but my hour was not yet come; I therefore waited patiently until the time when it was to be revealed to me, often, in the mean time, saying, "Lord, what wilt thou have me to do? whatever seemeth good unto Thee, give me the ability, and I will do it."

Eight months had passed away since I had been permitted to attend in the sanctuary of God; but the happy day arrived at last, when I was sufficiently recovered to repair thither again. My kind friends came to assist me to go to the chapel, by supporting me on each side; and I arrived there very comfortably. A minister occupied the pulpit on that occasion, who was unknown to me, and preached on the nocturnal visit of Nicodemus to Jesus. He spoke with much power, and the glory of God filled the house; the people shouted for joy, and the whole place seemed in motion. Glory for ever! Glory be to God! for his presence was manifested on earth. After an interval of fifteen months from the time when I received the angelic announcement, I heard it published in the meeting, that there was to be a camp-meeting in five weeks from that time. At the moment when I heard the notice proclaimed, I felt a sensation as if I had received a blow on the head, or had sustained an electric shock. So singular a feeling surprised me, and gave rise to much thought; but I could not account for, or explain its cause.

The spot where the camp-meeting was announced to be held, was at a great distance from my home; and as my long indisposition had borne heavily on my earthly resources and entirely exhausted them, I knew not how I should be furnished with sufficient means to undertake such a journey. My poor husband was extremely hostile to religion, and had an extravagant prejudice against camp-meetings; the bare mention of them usually irritated him, excited him to treat me with much bitterness and urged him to denounce them as pregnant with all manner of evil. However, on my return home, I informed him of the projected camp-meeting, and of my desire to be present at it; and contrary to my expectations, he spoke not a word in reply. I was surprised at this, but I regarded it as springing from the restraining power of that God, who, on one occasion, would not permit even a dog to move his tongue against the children of Israel as they passed by.[31]

I had been ill nearly two years, and was even then unable to help myself; nor had I any apparel suitable for me to go into the grove with; and much clothing was requisite for such an occasion. I knew not therefore what to do; it would have been useless to have applied to my husband for assistance for such a purpose: go without more apparel I could not; I was therefore quite at a stand to know how to proceed. But God took the cause in hand, and made the way plain and pleasant; for my dear old master Mitchel, under whom I had been brought up, had heard a year back that Zilpha was very sick; and though he had received no subsequent intelligence as to whether she lived or died, yet he thought if she was living, she must by this time be in need of some pecuniary assistance; he had been inclined, therefore, to send her a supply of money, but knew not how to effect it from want of opportunity.

However, in the month of August, the society of Friends hold their quarterly meetings in Burlington, New Jersey; and they are in the practice of taking long journeys to attend these meetings; so he encouraged his son and daughter to come over to the meeting at Burlington; desiring them when there, to search after and if possible find out the residence of Zilpha, present his kind love to her, and hand her a donation which he committed to their care. When the quarterly meeting of the Friends came on in our city, to my great astonishment who should come to see me, but William and Achsah Mitchel, the former companions of my youthful days, with whom I had been reared; and as we not seen each other for several years, it was indeed a happy meeting; and they came to me with presents, as did the wise men who came to the infant Jesus and his mother, and presented them with frankincense and myrrh; to God be all the praise! Then I might have said with Job's friend, "The Almighty has been my defence; and now I have plenty of silver." Being thus supplied, I was enabled to make preparations for going into the mount of God, to hear his holy word; and during all my preparations, my husband, contrary to his usual manner, preserved a perfect silence. Thus all went on easily and calmly, it being the Lord's doing, and it was marvellous in my eyes.

As the time drew near, we ascertained that a considerable number of coloured people were about going thither from our parts; and the members of our class arranged for all of them to sojourn together in one tent. But we were as yet unprovided with one, nor did we know where or how to procure it. My heavenly Father then put it into my heart to go to a friend of mine, and ask for the loan of his tent, and I obtained it at my request without the least hesitation; and thus all things were provided in readiness for the projected journey.

I have been particular in narrating these circumstances, to show the ever-mindful care of God for us; and how he disposes our matters even when we are unable to discern any possible way, or to provide for the exigencies, which clog up and embarrass our paths. How remarkable was it that my dear father Mitchel, who had brought me up from my childhood, should, after an absence of ten years, be stirred up in his mind to send me such a timely relief; and the more especially as it was the first favour of the kind that I received from him. Oh! let all the powers within me unite in fervent adoration of the God I love.

At length the auspicious morning arrived for us to proceed on our journey to the holy mount of God; the carriage soon drove up to my door, and I bade farewell to my dear husband. We started off, and it being a delightful day, we had a very pleasant journey, and arrived on the camp ground in the afternoon of the same day. I was very cordially received by the dear friends, and the dear brethren in the ministry joyfully hailed my appearance on the camp ground; and I was promptly handed to a seat to take refreshments after my journey. There were thousands already assembled; but the best of all was, God was there; and much good was accomplished in the name of Jesus. Friday and Saturday were two heavenly days indeed; the mighty power of God was greatly displayed, and His ministers were like a flame of fire; so animated with godly zeal. I never saw so much godly effort and evangelic exertion displayed in all my life as on that occasion. On the Lord's-day morning, the presiding Elder stepped forth in the might of the Holy Spirit, like Joshua, when he went to meet the angelic captain of the Lord's hosts, and said, "Let this day be entirely spent in holiness to the Lord; let no table be spread; but let us abstain as much as possible from food, and see what the Lord will do for us this day; for this is the great day of battle against the old dragon and the powers of darkness." Oh! what a memorable day was this. The public prayer-meeting commenced at seven o'clock in the morning; and at half-past eight o'clock, dear Mr. Potts preached a powerful sermon, under which many souls were awakened to a concern for their eternal interests.[32] At ten, the trumpet sounded again for preaching, and the presiding Elder preached from 2 Cor. v. 20. "Now then we are ambassadors for Christ; as though God did beseech you by us; we pray you in Christ's stead, be ye reconciled to God." When he came to the application of his discourse, there seemed not to be one person on the spot, whose eyes were not suffused with tears; both high and low, rich and poor, white and coloured, were all melted like wax before the fire. In every part of that vast concourse, the number of which was estimated at seven thousands, there were heaving bursts of penitential emotion, with streaming eyes; and the mighty action of the Holy Spirit, and the quickening energy of God was so obvious and exhilirating, that all the sons of God shouted for joy. At the conclusion of this lively and interesting meeting, the people returned to their tents to pray with, and direct and comfort those who were in the distresses of godly sorrow. A number of persons were collected in our tent, who were in great distress, earnestly imploring the mercy of God. We engaged in fervent prayer with and for them; and a great noise being made from the mingling of so many voices, and of such various tones of sorrow and rejoicing, of despair and exultation, of prayer and praise, hundreds were attracted to the place, and came round to witness the scene, and ascertain what was going forward. One of the brethren manifested some uneasiness and dissatisfaction at the eagerness with which the people came rushing into our tent; and I said to him, "Oh, never mind, my brother; let them come in and see the wonderful works of God;" and I was in the act of pressing through the crowd to open the back part of the tent, which I was just about to do, when I felt, as it were a hand, touch me on the right shoulder; and a voice said to me, "Go outside of the tent while I speak with thee." I turned myself round to see from whom the voice proceeded; but there were none near me but those of our own company; and not any of them were addressing me. I immediately went outside and stood at the door of the tent; and in an instant I began as it were involuntarily, or from an internal prompting, with a loud voice to exhort the people who yet were remaining near the preacher's stand;[33] and in the presence of a more numerous assemblage of ministers than I had ever seen together before; as if God had called forth witnesses from heaven, and witnesses on earth, ministers and members, to witness on this day to my commission, and the qualifications He bestowed on me to preach his holy Gospel. How appropriate to me was the text which had been preached from just before, "Now, then, we are ambassadors for Christ." Our dear ministers stood gazing and listening with wonder and astonishment; and the tears flowed abundantly down their cheeks while they witnessed the wonderful works of God. After I had finished my exhortation, I sat down and closed my eyes; and there appeared a light shining round about me as well as within me, above the brightness of the sun; and out of that light, the same identical voice which had spoken to me on the bed of sickness many months before, spake again to me on the camp ground, and said, "Now thou knowest the will of God concerning thee; thou must preach the gospel; and thou must travel far and wide." This is my commission for the work of the ministry, which I received, not from mortal man, but from the voice of an invisible and heavenly personage sent from God. Moreover, this did not occur in the night, when the dozing slumbers and imaginative dreams are prevalent, but at mid-day, between the hours of twelve and two o'clock; and my ministry was commenced in the midst of thousands who were both eye and ear witnesses of the fact. Oh, adorable Trinity! dispose me to do thy holy will in all things. This was my experience on the Lord's day on the camp ground; a day wherein the energies of the Holy Spirit were amazingly exerted, and His presence circulated; and on which hundreds drank into, and were filled with the Spirit. It was such a day as I never witnessed either before or since. On the Monday came the solemn parting time, of bidding farewell to the brethren and sisters, who were about to proceed to their different stations and places of residence, never to meet again until they meet before the throne of Jesus. Many hundreds of them have doubtless, since then, gone to their final rest; and will sing the praises of their Redeemer in that world of immortality to which we are all hastening; may we then hail their happiness; and with them share the bliss of the blood-bought myriads around the glorious throne in heaven. Having taken our farewell of the dear friends on the camp ground, we started for Burlington; and happily and safely returned home more spiritual and heavenly minded, and stronger in the Lord, than when we came. On my arrival at home, I found all well, and things peaceful and quiet; and for a short time, I went on my way rejoicing.

But Satan, my unwearied adversary, did not suffer me long to remain exempted from conflict and trouble. Soon after my return, I laid my case in reference to my call to the work of the ministry before the ministers; and they greatly encouraged me to proceed, and to preach wherever and whenever opportunities offered. They saw no impropriety in it, and therefore advised me to go on and do all the good I could. I first broached the subject to Mr. John Potts, the beloved brother who preached at the camp-meeting on the morning of the day on which the heavenly commission was delivered unto me: and I obtained the approbation and sanction of all the ministers and of the society. But some of the members of our class soon began to betray a little jealousy, lest I should rise into too great estimation; for a prophet is not without honour, save in his own country; and they began to discover many faults and imperfections in me; for three years previously there had not been a single jarring string amongst us; and nothing could be done without my opinion being first given: in every thing I suited them exactly, and we were a very loving and happy band: but after I commenced the work of the ministry, I was a person of no account, and ever had been; and I became so unpopular, that all our coloured class abandoned me excepting three. Like Joseph, I was hated for my dreams; and like Paul, none stood with me.[34] This treatment, however painful, by no means damped my ardour in the work to which I had been called. I still continued in my Master's work, and great crowds assembled every Lord's day to hear me: the Lord was with me and strengthened me in my feeble labours; the number of white brethren and sisters who flocked to my ministry increased daily; the work prospered amazingly; and thus I had gone on for two months before my husband knew any thing about it; for he never went to a place of worship. At last the tidings came to his ears, and were tauntingly disclosed by one who said to him, "Josh, your wife is a preacher:" this important announcement he met with a direct negative; but when he returned home, he asked me if it was true; and I informed him that it was. "Well," said he, "I'll come and hear you, if I come barefoot:"[35] at these words my heart leaped for joy; and I indulged in sanguine hopes that he might thereby be converted to God. He came according to his word; and I think that conviction of the sinfulness of his state strongly fastened on his conscience, for he became much troubled in mind: he was also apprehensive that I should become a laughing-stock for the people; and this also grieved him considerably: sometimes he said to me, "Now child, we are undone:" it appeared to him so strange and singular a thing, that I should become a public speaker; and he advised me to decline the work altogether, and proceed no further. I was very sorry to see him so much grieved about it; but my heavenly Father had informed me that he had a great work for me to do; I could not therefore descend down to the counsel of flesh and blood, but adhered faithfully to my commission; and very soon after, all my friends who had forsaken, me, returned to me again, for they perceived that God was with me; and many were added to our numbers, whom I hope to meet in the realms of immortality.

My poor husband's health about this time began visibly to decline; and his disorder soon settled into an intractable consumption: the amount of care which now devolved upon me was very great;[36] I was compelled to work very hard to keep my little family and household comfortable in this time of affliction; and it was frequently with great difficulty that I balanced my income and expenditure; but thanks be to God, he opened my way before me, comforted, cheered and strengthened me, and conducted me through all my difficulties far beyond my expectations: it is true, I diligently used every means in my power, and my exertions were sanctified and blessed by the Lord. The worst feature of this affliction was, that my dear husband yet remained a stranger to the precious blood of atonement, and to the Lamb of God who taketh away the sins of the world. A short time prior to his death, he indicated a better state of mind than formerly: he even confessed the misconduct with which he had behaved towards me; requested my forgiveness, and expressed his hope of meeting me in the better world; he acknowledged that my behaviour had ever been irreproachable; and hoped that the Lord would ever sustain me: many other things he uttered of much importance; and his countenance assumed such a calmness and sweetness, that the neighbours who visited him observed the change, and spake of it with great satisfaction. Glory be to God, who doeth all things well; who is too wise to err, too good to be unkind.

"Above the rest this note shall swell,
My Jesus hath done all things well." [37]

The fatal hour came at last when the brittle thread of life snapped asunder, and his spirit fled to an invisible world. This mournful event took place on the 27th day of January, 1823. It was a day never to be forgotten. Although my poor husband had suffered under so protracted an illness, and I had had so much time to prepare for the solemn hour, I found my strength very inadequate to sustain the awful scene; my strength, alas, was perfect weakness; but God was my strong tower and my refuge in the day of distress. Some kind friends came forward, and offered to undertake the interment of the corpse and defray the expences of his funeral; but as it was the last thing I could do for him, I declined their generous offer, and chose rather to do it myself; and though it involved me in considerable expense, my creditors waited patiently, until by the Lord's blessing I was enabled pay it all off to the uttermost farthing; to God be all the praise!

After my dear husband was buried, and I had become a little settled, instead of submitting myself in all things to be led by the Spirit, I rather leaned to my own understanding, and procured a situation of servitude for my little girl, and another for myself,[38] judging these the best means I could adopt for the liquidation of my debts; and I remained in service until my health was so impaired that I was compelled to relinquish it; nor did the blessing of my heavenly Father appear to prosper this course; for I was constantly obliged to be under medical treatment, and yet grew worse and worse. I therefore left my situation, and went back to my house, which I had still reserved in case I should want it. I then opened a school,[39] and the Lord blessed the effort, and increased the number of my pupils, so that I soon had a nice little school; many of the society of friends came and visited it, and assisted me with books and other necessaries for it. They were also much pleased with the improvement of the children; and when any strangers came to visit Burlington, they introduced them to me; and it was gratifying to many of them to see a female of colour teaching the coloured children, whom the white people refused to admit into their seminaries, and who had been suffered formerly to run about the streets for want of a teacher. The pride of a white skin is a bauble of great value with many in some parts of the United States, who readily sacrifice their intelligence to their prejudices, and possess more knowledge than wisdom. The Almighty accounts not the black races of man either in the order of nature or spiritual capacity as inferior to the white; for He bestows his Holy Spirit on, and dwells in them as readily as in persons of whiter complexion: the Ethiopian eunuch was adopted as a son and heir of God; and when Ethiopia shall stretch forth her hands unto him, their submission and worship will be graciously accepted.[40] This prejudice was far less prevalent in that part of the country where I resided in my infancy; for when a child, I was not prohibited from any school on account of the colour of my skin. Oh! that men would outgrow their nursery prejudices and learn that "God hath made of one blood all the nations of men that dwell upon all the face of the earth." Acts xvii. 26.

But my mind was not long at rest in this situation; for the remembrance of the commission which I had received from the Lord very strongly impressed me; and as the Lord had said, "Thou must preach the gospel, and thou must travel far and wide," so He was about to bring it to pass, but I knew not in what manner. I was not as yet out of debt; and with an empty exchequer, I felt myself but ill adapted to set out on an excursion for preaching the gospel.[41] I was not as yet sufficiently broken in nor bent enough to the discipline of heaven, entirely to live and walk in the Spirit; but projected many schemes and ways for the Lord to act by; yet He did not stoop down to my wretched conceptions, nor avail Himself of my short-sighted plans: for He hath said, "I am God, and besides me there is no Saviour." "For as the heavens are higher than the earth, so are my ways higher than your ways, and my thoughts than your thoughts." Isaiah lv. 9. I appointed many opportunities in my own mind, on which to venture on a journey into the country to preach the gospel in far distant places, if the Lord would beforehand furnish me with the necessary supplies for such an undertaking; but I thought it a sin to undertake such a journey while I remained indebted to any man. And here Satan bound me down for two years; at the expiration of which, I possessed no more accumulation of funds than before; and notwithstanding that my school was greatly improved, yet I was hedged up on every side; as it is written, "Cursed is every one that continueth not in all things written in the book of the law to do them."

I then began to question the reality of my call to the ministry; and endeavoured to bring it to the test by laying my heart before the Lord, and solemnly praying to the God of my salvation, that if it were His will for me to go out to preach the gospel, He would give me a token thereof by opening my way before me at the end of three months; and, if otherwise, that He would remove from my mind the weighty impression, which clogged me with care, kept me as a prisoner on parole, and blighted every other prospect in life. I accordingly waited very quietly until the time was nearly expired, watching carefully the signs of the time; but all was still dark; and not only so, I was also attacked with a severe fit of sickness, and rendered unable to attend to my school. I then concluded that I had been mistaken, and endeavoured to attribute my past impressions to the zeal of imagination; for I thought, if it had really been the design of God to send me forth to preach His gospel, He would have disposed my affairs so as to open my way, and suitably replenish my purse for the journey; but instead of this being the case, my situation became more and more irksome, and hemmed in with difficulties. Oh! how amazingly difficult is it for the Christian, when decoyed by erratic gleams, or delusive principles, he misses his way, wanders from his proper compass point, and flounders amongst the marshy reeds of worldly principles and proprieties, to detect his error, espy the gospel beacon, and regain his path: thus it was with me; and in prayer I said to my heavenly master, in reference to my ministry, "Now I know that I am mistaken; and I am not going out at all."

I had no sooner uttered these words, than a dreadful and chilling gloom instantaneously fluttered over, and covered my mind; the Spirit of the Lord fled out of my sight, and left me in total darkness—such darkness as was truly felt; so awful a sensation I never felt before or since. I had quenched the Spirit, and became like a tormented demon. I knew not what to do, for I had lost my spiritual enjoyments; my tongue was also silenced, so that I was unable for speak to God: and though my congregation continued to meet every Lord's day, I had no power whatever to preach to them. The members of the class inquired why I did not preach to the people? "You see," said they, "how the people flock to hear you, and yet you do not preach to them." This went like a dagger to my heart; for it was evident to all that I had displeased my God, and therefore He had withdrawn His Holy Spirit from me; nor had I any life or power whatever in prayer. I then laid my case before some of the church; but none of them could administer any comfort to me. I also consulted some of the Society of Friends, but they could give me no instructions, because my business was not with mortal man, but with the living God. The anguish of my soul continually increased; every thing went contrary with me, and I fretted and repined, and found fault when there was no occasion, except in myself. I shall never forget the reproof I received from my little daughter on account of the irritability of my temper. She looked at me one day, and said, "Mother, what does ail thee? why, I never saw thee so before; I believe thou art going to be like some of the queer old women." I received this reproof as sent from God, who, I believe, had put it into the mind of the child to utter it; and, from that day, I solemnly pledged myself to the Lord, that if He would again bestow on me the aids of His Holy Spirit, I would go forth in His ministry just as I was, not waiting for any further provision or preparation, but trusting alone in His holy word; and I prayed that He would enable me again to preach to my people in Burlington; and that on such and such day of the month, I would obey His holy commands, whatever might become of me. The Lord accepted of my proposition; and on the next Lord's day, my tongue was set at liberty, and my heart was enlarged; and I was enabled to preach with more fluency and copiousness than ever before. I then informed my audience, that I must leave them, and go out into the vineyard of the Lord; and announced to them on what day I should preach my farewell address to them. It was a Bochim, a day of weeping indeed with them, but they said, "the will of the Lord be done." [42]

I had been under this dark cloud for more than three weeks; and the time appeared to me more than three months; but it now retired, and my captivity vanished. Heaven again opened to my eyes and ears, because I was at last led to discern the path of obedience, and hearken to the counsel of the Almighty, saying, "This is the way; walk ye in it." The chastisement of God is often more profitable than His indulgence would be; His correction is kindness, and His severity mercy.

My peace again flowed as a river on a calm summer's day; and I began to draw my school to a close. About three weeks prior to the time appointed for the dismission of my scholars, some friends who resided in the direction my mind was disposed to take, and with whom I had been previously acquainted, came to Burlington; and they, together with some of my dear people thought it advisable for me to accompany them on their return; but I saw no possibility of doing this, because they were about to take their departure before I could arrange my affairs, and receive the accounts due to me at the end of the current quarter. I therefore informed my kind friend that I should not be ready to go with him; but he insisted upon it, and enforced it with many arguments. I replied, "It is utterly impossible for me to be ready to go with you;" at which he seemed somewhat offended; and his wife then said, "Why, Zilpha, if thou feelest that thou art bound to go, and if it is thy wish to go, and if thou canst not get ready at this time, never mind, go as soon as thou canst, and thou wilt get along somehow, and thou wilt hardly understand how; if thou art sent, He that sends thee will take care of thee." This filled my heart with tenderness, and my eyes with tears, and I replied, "Oh, neighbour Hull, this is a word of consolation indeed now I will return home and weep before the Lord, and all will be well." I returned home, and my little daughter seeing the tears flowing down my cheeks, said to me, "Now, mother, what is the matter?" for she was aware of the great anxiety of mind I had so long been labouring under, and said all she could to comfort me; and added, "If I were you, I should not mind what any person said, but I should go just as I had arranged to go, and do not think any thing about me, for I shall do very well." By this time my scholars had gathered, and the school business commenced; and for the Bible class, the lesson was in the Psalms; one of the little boys commenced the 125th Psalm, which begins thus, "They that trust in the Lord shall be as Mount Zion, which cannot be removed, but abideth for ever." While the psalm was being read, it seemed as if I had never seen it before; but the Almighty had sent it as a special message from heaven to me: those words so filled my heart, that all my tears were dried away, and I could only exclaim, "Glory be to God!" My soul rejoiced in God my Saviour, yea, the God of my salvation. No more foreboding fears assailed me; every circumstance readily converged to its proper point, and all things were prepared exactly to the appointed hour. I took my little girl, and placed her under the care of a dear relative of mine, and proceeded on my way to the City of Philadelphia, commenced my Master's business, and strange to relate, when I arrived in that large city, every one appeared to be acquainted with my situation. I preached in a great many chapels, and every congregation voluntarily made a collection for my aid; and every person at whose house I visited, gave me something for my journey. Oh! how astonishing was this to me. I had been for several years striving to provide myself with necessary supplies for my Master's work, and without success; nor did I ever think of obtaining any money in my travels. It never occurred to me that I should receive a single penny in this work: but when I was willing, I ought to say—made willing to go just as I was, as the apostles of old, without purse or scrip, then the Lord made my way straight before me, and dealt bountifully with me; then was that blessed promise verified, "Seek ye the kingdom of God, and His righteousness, and all other things shall be added unto you."[43] In the first three weeks I obtained every particle that I wanted, and abundance of silver to proceed on my journey with. Oh! what mercy and what goodness was manifested to such a poor, unbelieving, weak, and unworthy instrument as me. How often have I said, "Lord! send by whom thou wilt send, only send not by me; for thou knowest that I am ignorant: how can I be a mouth for God!—a poor, coloured female: and thou knowest we have many things to endure which others do not." But the answer was, "What is that to thee? follow thou me."

Thus I left my child and ventured on my journey, not knowing whither I should go. From Philadelphia I started for New York; and on my journey passed within three hundred yards of my own home, yet did not call there, but pursued my journey and arrived in New York; and there the Lord rendered my ministry a blessing to many precious souls—glory be to His name. I was absent from home seven months; and when I returned, I was able to meet my creditors and pay my debts, which was an unspeakable indulgence. Hallelujah. Praise the Lord.

I returned home in April, 1828, and remained there a few days. During my stay at home, I was one day exercised with devout contemplations of God, and suddenly the Spirit came upon me, and a voice addressed me, saying, "Be of good cheer, and be faithful: I will yet bring thee to England and thou shalt see London, that great city, and declare my name there." I looked round to ascertain from whence and from whom the voice proceeded, but no person was near me; my surprise was so great that my very blood seemed to stagnate and chill in my veins: it was evidently the Spirit of the Lord whose I am, and whom I serve, who had spoken to me; and my soul responded to His word, saying, "The will of the Lord be done in and by me on earth, as it is by His servants in Heaven." My mind was at this time very much perplexed as to what was the will of God concerning me: I was in doubt as to what I ought to do; but, after a few days, I took my journey again to Philadelphia, with the intention of visiting the southern or slave-holding states of America; here I saw my dear daughter, and remained with my friends during some few weeks; but the confusion of my mind still continued, and whenever I opened a bible, wherever I visited, as well as at my apartments, the book of the prophet Jonah was perpetually presented before me. I mentioned to my friends the uncertainty of my mind as to what the Lord required me to do, the propriety of a voyage to England, and my repeatedly opening in the Bible at the book of Jonah; and they assured me that if it was God's will that I should then visit England, He would make it appear, and smooth the way for me in His own good time. I therefore rested upon this assurance; and while I yet abode in Philadelphia, I dreamed one night, that I saw two ships cleared out of the docks there, bound for England, and I was not on board either of them. I then concluded that the time for my journey to England had not yet come; and being now satisfied on this matter, I started off for the southern territories of the United States, where slavery is established and enforced by law. When I arrived in the slave states, Satan much worried and distressed my soul with the fear of being arrested and sold for a slave, which their laws would have warranted, on account of my complexion and features. On one occasion, in particular, I had been preaching to a coloured congregation, and had exhorted them impressively to quit themselves as men approved of God and to maintain and witness a good profession of their faith before the world, &c. I had no sooner sat down, than Satan suggested to me with such force, that the slave-holders would speedily capture me, as filled me with fear and terror. I was then in a small town in one of the slave states; and the news of a coloured female preaching to the slaves had already been spread widely throughout the neighbourhood; the novelty of the thing had produced an immense excitement, and the people were collecting from every quarter, to gaze at the unexampled prodigy of a coloured female preacher. I was sitting in a very conspicuous situation near the door, and I observed, with very painful emotions, the crowd outside, pointing with their fingers at me, and saying, "that's her," "that's her;" for Satan strongly set before me the prospect of an immediate arrest and consignment by sale to some slave owner. Being very much alarmed, I removed from my seat to a retired part of the room, where, becoming more collected, I inquired within myself, "from whence cometh all this fear?" My faith then rallied and my confidence in the Lord returned, and I said, "get thee behind me Satan, for my Jesus hath made me free." My fears instantly forsook me, and I vacated my retired corner, and came forth before all the people again; and the presence and power of the Lord became greatly manifested in the assembly during the remainder of the service. At the earnest request of the friends, I consented to preach there again on the following Lord's-day morning, which I accordingly did. Some of the white brethren in connexion with the Methodist Society were present on that occasion; at the conclusion thereof, they introduced themselves to me, and wished me to preach for them in the afternoon; to which I agreed; and they obtained permission of the authorities to open and use the courthouse; and therein I obtained a very large auditory; and God gave forth proofs that my ministry was from Him, in giving me many seals to it on that day; thus was I relieved from my fearful forebodings, and pursued my course with increased energy, rejoicing in the prosperity and success with which the Almighty crowned my efforts.

After this, I visited Baltimore in the State of Maryland, and attended a conference of the coloured brethren, by whom I was very kindly received;[44] a large field of labour was provided, and a great and effectual door of utterance opened to me by the Lord. After labouring there for some weeks, I proceeded to the City of Washington, the capital of the United States, and the seat of government: here also I laboured with much success; many souls obtaining the knowledge of salvation by the remission of their sins, with the gift of the Holy Spirit, through the instrumentality of so feeble an earthen vessel. I continued my travels southward into the State of Virginia, and arrived at the City of Alexandria, where the Lord rendered my labours effectual to the conversion of many from darkness to light, and from the power of Satan unto God. I abode there two months, and was an humble agent, in the Lord's hand, of arousing many of His heritage to a great revival; and the weakness and incompetency of the poor coloured female but the more displayed the excellency of the power to be of God. There were some among the great folks whom curiosity induced to attend my ministry; and this formed a topic of lively interest with many of the slave holders, who thought it surpassingly strange that a person (and a female) belonging to the same family stock with their poor debased, uneducated, coloured slaves, should come into their territories and teach the enlightened proprietors the knowledge of God; and more strange still was it to some others, when in the spirit and power of Christ, that female drew the portraits of their characters, made manifest the secrets of their hearts, and told them all things that ever they did.[45] This was a paradox to them indeed: for they were not deficient of pastors and reverend divines, who possessed all the advantages of talents, learning, respectability and worldly influence, to aid their religious efforts; and yet the power of truth and of God was never so manifest in any of their agencies, as with the dark coloured female stranger, who had come from afar to minister amongst them. But God hath chosen the weak things of the world to confound the mighty. Divine goodness raised me and honoured me as an angel of God; yet my bodily presence continued weak; the passions, frailties and imperfections of humanity abounded in my own consciousness; the union of such meanness and honour rendered me a riddle to myself. I became such a prodigy to this people, that I was watched wherever I went; and if I went out to tea with any of the friends, the people would flock around the house where I was; and as soon as they judged that the repast was finished, they came in and filled the house, and required me to minister to them the word of life, whether I had previously intended to preach or not. The people became increasingly earnest in their inquiries after truth; and great was the number of those who were translated out of the empire of darkness into the Kingdom of God's dear Son.

At this place, resided a gentleman named Abijah Janney,[46] belonging to the society of friends, at whose house I spent many delightful hours. One day he requested to speak with me alone; and having accompanied him to another apartment, when we were seated, he said to me, "Now Zilpha, I perceive that thy visit to this place will be attended with much good, if thy deportment amongst the whites, and especially amongst the slaves, be prudently conducted; for there seemeth in reference to the great topics of thy ministry to be much interest felt by the people generally." This was a well-timed and salutary caution, and most prudent advice to me, situated as I was in connexion with two distinct communities, so opposite in condition, so contrasted in intelligence, and so antipodal in their feelings and prejudices. These words at such a time were to me as apples of gold in pictures of silver.[47]

During my continuance in this city, I had a very severe attack of the fever which is endemial in that climate;[48] but I was attended by a physician of first rate eminence, and by several most kind and anxious nurses; and the Lord was pleased speedily to raise me up again; most kind and affectionate were this people to me: before I was able to sit up an hour, Mr. Janney sent his carriage morning and evening to take me out, that I might be benefited by the refreshing breezes, and be regaled by the sweet zephyrs which gently fan over the verdant plains of that genial clime. It was the Lord's doing; and to him be all the praise.

On my recovery, I again resumed my Divine Master's work; and going to my physician to discharge his demands for his skillful care and kind attendance upon me during my illness, he refused to receive any remuneration, assuring me, the reflection that he had been instrumental, through the blessing of God, of contributing towards my recovery, afforded him much pleasure; that it was his desire his past services to me should be free of cost; and expressed his hope that I might long be spared to do the will and work of the Lord.

Although I had been sick and laid aside for a time, I lost nothing, except the dross of earthly affections: it was merely a furnace, in which my heavenly father saw the necessity of my being placed for a time: and I believe that I was thereby weaned still more from the world, separated to my God and purified in holiness. The methodist preacher at that station, Mr. J. Gess, behaved to me with very great kindness; he much promoted my labours in that neighbourhood, and I proceeded throughout the vicinity of Alexandria, preaching the gospel with the happiest results. On one occasion, I took an excursion with some ladies, a few miles into the country, to preach at a distant farmhouse occupied by a Mr. Marifield; and as is usual with the farmers there to keep very savage dogs for the protection of their premises, this gentleman had three of those animals; very fierce and ferocious creatures, which met us at the door; but, as the family were present, without giving us any molestation; yet as the people soon came flocking to the meeting, the inmates were concerned on account of the ferocity of the dogs, and tried to fasten them up, but could not succeed; but God restrained the savage beasts and they were very quiet, though the assemblage was so large, that we were compelled to resort to the orchard, and hold our meeting beneath the spreading apple trees. When I took my position, the three dogs came and laid down, one on each side, and the other behind me; and there they remained till the conclusion of the service; and as the people shook hands with me and bade me adieu, they rose, wagged their heads, and brushed me as if to welcome my visit there. It was a most interesting and profitable season; and the presence and power of God were greatly manifested: there were several youth in attendance, who were reputed to be very wild and giddy, but they appeared to be struck with awe at the religious fervour manifested, and conducted themselves with reverence and solemnity.

I had also another engagement, arranged by some friends, for me to go into another part of the country, about twelve miles distant, and preach in the grove; but I was prevented by heavy rains from fulfilling it for three Lord's days successively: at length, the weather becoming more favourable, I was published to preach there on the following Lord's day: as the time drew near, I was in much perplexity through inability to fix on any passage of Scripture as a text to preach from, or rather, because the Lord had not as yet presented a passage to my mind or fastened one upon my spirit; but as I was speaking to the dear friend at whose house I was then visiting, of the dilemma I was in, the following passage powerfully flashed upon my mind, "Set thine house in order, for thou shalt die and not live." In meditating upon this passage, my soul was barren. I was oppressed by a complete dearth of suitable ideas, and unable to obtain any spiritual opening or discernment of this text; I then foolishly endeavoured to abandon it; and as if I possessed the right of self direction, or liberty to select what messages I pleased, searched the Scriptures for another text; but to no purpose; for every other was sealed up from me, though I continued my search until twelve o'clock on the Saturday night, and resumed it in the morning at the dawning of light; but I learned that when the Lord impresses a text on the minds of His servants, that He will not be tempted by our solicitations to have another one substituted. Having such a distance to go, we started off at nine o'clock in the morning; and I went as reluctantly as a criminal goes to the bar: as we approached within a few miles of the selected spot, we observed the people from every direction over the face of the country repairing thither; which rendered the distress of my mind the more poignant. It is a weighty matter for a well-furnished preacher to address a numerous auditory in the name of the Lord of Hosts; but to go as I then did, destitute of a topic whereon to preach, was a mental affliction indeed. When we arrived at the place, it was already like a camp-meeting; the platform was erected, hundreds of persons assembled, and all things in readiness. I directly ascended the stand, and read forth a hymn, which was sang by the congregation, offered up prayer, and gave out another hymn. Whilst the congregation were singing, I was anxiously searching for a text to preach from; but no other could I find than that which had been given me. When, therefore, the singing was finished, I arose and read the passage before referred to, which I had no sooner done, than my mind took a comprehensive grasp of the subject; a region of truths were unfolded to my view, such as I had never previously conceived of; and it occupied me an hour and a half to exhaust the fund of sentimental treasure, which the Divine Spirit poured into my mind. It was, indeed, a time of refreshing from the presence of the Lord.

At the conclusion of my discourse, I inquired if there were any ministers present; intimating, that if this was the case, an opportunity was offered them of further addressing the audience; and a minister being present from George Town, who had arranged to preach a funeral sermon at a neighboring spot, and the relatives of the deceased being all present, it was agreed that he should preach it there from the platform; and it constituted an appropriate sequel to my sermon; we enjoyed quite an heavenly day in the grove, and returned home in the evening in peace.

Among the number of persons who were introduced into the fold of our God, in the city of Alexandria, was Miss Butts, a young lady who found peace with God through our Lord Jesus Christ, and manifested remarkable piety. In the correspondence with which she subsequently favoured me, she indicated an affectionate desire to see me again in the flesh; and assured me of the happiness and freedom she enjoyed in the service of the Lord. The work of the Holy Spirit was greatly manifested in this city; both high and low, rich and poor, white and coloured, all drank out of the living streams which flowed from the City of our God. Every day brought me tidings of souls newly born of God. Even the angels in heaven rejoice over the repenting sinner, and much more should the redeemed on earth! Oh, the depth both of the riches and knowledge of God! How unsearchable are His judgments, and His ways past finding out!

Before I took my leave of this city, Lady Hunter, the wife of Major Hunter, came to Alexandria; being a member of the Methodist Society, she invited me to spend a few days at her house, and preach on the Lord's day. I accepted the invitation, and enjoyed my visit greatly. The Major was not a religious man; and as the ministers frequently visited his Lady, he was in the habit of attacking them with controversial cavils against their faith. As he displayed but little respect to persons, when he came home from the city, accompanied by several other gentlemen, the Bible was produced, the family summoned to evening prayers, and I was required to officiate as chaplain. As I prayed, read, and commented upon the Scriptures, he mustered his interrogatories, and produced his objections. I had no more desire for a mental collision than ambition for or prospect of a triumph in a contest for intellectual pre-eminence with such an antagonist; but as He who sent me, helped my infirmities, and was ever ready to succour me, I was enabled to reply to all his questions and quibbles, and maintain the truth. Indeed, he appeared highly gratified that my answers were such as in no way put the cause of religion to the blush before his friends, who had been introduced for the purpose of testing my poor feminine abilities. The Lord directed his servants on such emergencies, to take no thought or premeditation for the framing of their speech; and promised them a suitable inspiration of his Holy Spirit; and he richly assisted me on this occasion; to Him, therefore, be all the renown!

Taking my departure, amidst the regrets of many, from Alexandria, I returned to Washington: my visits were very numerous there among the people; and my company was desired by many of the great folks, even by the friends and associates of the President of the United States. Some religious gentlemen, friendly to the cause of missions, proposed for me to go out to Africa,[49] and labour among the native tribes; but I declined their proposal; telling them, my heavenly Father had given me no such direction; and I dared not go thither unless sent by his Divine Majesty; but if God had required me to go thither, I should not have ventured on a refusal: they therefore urged this matter no further. I was continually visited by ladies from all parts of the city and its vicinity; many of them informed me they had heard their friends relate, with most lively interest, the astonishing wonders of divine grace and power, which had attended our meetings in the groves; and what seasons of refreshing and spiritual edification they had experienced at those meetings. When on a visit at the residence of General Van Esse, I was invited by Lady Lee, the wife of General Lee, to a visit at her residence; and to preach at a chapel the ladies had erected at Green-leaf point, for the use of the missionaries who came thither.[50] On the day appointed, her carriage came for me, and I went accordingly: after tea, a great number of her friends met there, who were going to the meeting; and among them was Commodore Rogers and his Lady, with many others who came from a distance.[51] When the time came, Mrs. Lee and myself went on first; and she took the opportunity to caution me against the supposition that the bulk of those ladies and gentlemen were religious persons; assuring me they were merely coming from motives of curiosity to hear what I might say, and witness my performance. If I had gone confiding in my own poor abilities, this information would, doubtless, have utterly disconcerted me; but I depended on the faithful promise of my Master, that he will be with me even unto the end; nor was I disappointed. A large congregation assembled, composed of persons of all grades of society. I commenced the service by reading a portion of the Scriptures; when I gave forth my hymn, the ladies assisted to sing it, and the service was thus far sustained with propriety. I based my discourse on the Gospel of St. John v. 25. The Lord was pleased to give efficacy to the word of His grace, and to apply it with saving power to the mind of Lady Rogers. I perceived in the course of my sermon, that she was greatly interested and powerfully affected by it: indeed a mighty religious awe and solemnity rested upon the entire assembly. During the service, and for several days afterwards, the spiritual welfare of Mrs. Rogers was a theme, which, as it were, involuntarily occupied a very prominent interest in my mind; and I felt strongly assured that the Lord would endow her with the rich blessings of his salvation. In a few days after, I proceeded on my travels, and heard nothing further of the results of this meeting.

My next visit was to Baltimore, and from thence I went to Annapolis, where I continued during a great part of the winter. Here, also, the Lord gave forth to the people His gracious attestations that my ministry was from Him; for my speech and my preaching were not with enticing words of man's wisdom, but in demonstration of the Spirit, and in power: it was mighty through God, to the pulling down of strongholds; and became the power of God to the salvation of many. On one Lord's-day evening in this place, I was led by the Spirit to discourse very impressively on mortality and death; so much so, that my sermon might have been well suited to a funereal occasion; I was succeeded in the pulpit by a local preacher, a coloured brother and a slave; this poor brother seemed to manifest an undue anxiety for his freedom. Certainly, freedom is preferable to bondage, as saith the apostle Paul, 1 Cor. vii 21; who bade the Christian brethren in bondage to be unconcerned about it, unless an opportunity arrived of their attaining freedom; in which case, they were to avail themselves thereof. This poor brother in bonds, however, was very impatient of slavery, and anxiously sighed for liberty. Alas! his life and spirit, his body, his bones, and his blood, as respects this life, were legally the property of, and at the disposal of his fellow man. But his sighs were heard in heaven by Him who looseth the prisoners, and the time of his release arrived. In that same week he was taken ill, and finally fell asleep in Jesus, departing to be "where the wicked cease from troubling, and the weary are at rest. There the prisoners rest together; they hear not the voice of the oppressor; the small and great are there, and the servant is free from his master." Job iii. 17–19. His interment was a remarkably afflictive occasion: his corpse was brought into the chapel during the time of service, and the wailings of the congregation grew so intense, that the officiating minister was unable to proceed with the service. The suddenness of the stroke was surprising; and the loss of their beloved minister appeared to his sorrowful flock more like a dream than a fact. Oh, the abominations of slavery! though Philemon be the proprietor, and Onesimus the slave, yet every case of slavery, however lenient its inflictions, and mitigated its atrocities, indicates an oppressor, the oppressed, and the oppression.[52] Slavery in every case, save those of parental government, criminal punishment, or the self-protecting detentions of justifiable war, if such can happen, involves a wrong, the deepest in wickedness of any included within the range of the second table.[53]

In the Slave States of America the law sanctions the arrest of any person of colour, within their territories; and unless such person can produce the most unexceptionable papers in proof of his freedom, the legal officers may sell him on behalf of the State, into perpetual captivity. Blessed for ever be the Lord, who sent me out to preach his gospel even in these regions of wickedness, He preserved me in my going out and my coming in; so that the production of the documents of my freedom was not once demanded during my sojourn on the soil of slavery. While staying at Annapolis, I was engaged to preach at a place some miles distant in the country, and while proceeding thither in a one horse chaise, we were obliged to cross a river, and were about to get into the ferry-boat, together with our horse and chaise, when the horse fell down and put us in danger of drowning; but by the dexterity of the men who assisted us, and the blessing of God, we safely landed on the other side, still further in the interior of the Slave States. On another occasion, I went from Annapolis to preach on the Lord's day at another station in the country. Many hundreds were collected together, to whom I preached from these words, "Behold the Bridegroom cometh; go ye out to meet him." An elderly gentleman sat in a very conspicuous seat just before me, greatly agitated; the restraint of his emotions was evidently a matter of great difficulty, for his soul had deeply adopted the prayer of the publican, "God be merciful to me a sinner." When I retired from the pulpit the people rushed eagerly forward to salute me; they appeared to be quite overpowered by their penitential feelings, and in an agony of self-abasement. The multitude of repenting sinners on that occasion doubtless exhilirated many an angel-mind, and caused heaven itself to thrill with joy. That my mission was from God was manifest to them by His communication of the Holy Spirit, through my ministry, to those who received my testimony; the power of the Lord was present, indeed, to pull down some of the strongholds of Satan, and to set up Christ in the hearts of the people. On my return to Annapolis, I was thrown out of my chaise, and so much injured that I was unable to preach in the evening, in the city. I was very ill in consequence for some time, but the Lord raised me up again and restored me to health. On my recovery I resumed my work; and being on a visit at the house of one of our ministers, I heard tidings of Lady Rogers of Washington, through the medium of a minister who had recently been there. Being on a visit to Commodore Rogers, the latter inquired if he knew anything of the preaching woman, adding, that he hoped God would bless every lane of her life; for that his wife was become a very pious woman through attending a meeting held by her, at Green Leaf's point; and further, if she would come and reside in that neighbourhood, he would make a suitable provision for her subsistence. A gentleman residing in the city of Annapolis, offered to give me a house and a plot of ground on condition of my residing there; but it was not meet for me to depart from my Master's work, from considerations of worldly interest. I dared not, like Demas, forsake my itinerating ministry, to love this present world: nor was filthy lucre the object I had in view in the service of the gospel.[54] The cheerful liberality of grateful affection is one of the evidences of sincere discipleship to Jesus; but the love of mammon has no place in the hearts of his true ministers, who love the flock rather than the fleece.

Before I left Annapolis a gentleman, named Watson, residing in the city, one of the local preachers, earnestly desired me to accompany him to Mount Tabor, about ten miles distant, and preach for him in his appointment; I had no desire for this journey on account of my remaining weakness, and the severity of the season, it being winter: but as he would take no denial, coming repeatedly to solicit my compliance, I reluctantly consented, and a dreary journey we had; the cold being intensely rigorous, the roads bad, and travelling dangerous. On our arrival I found that the people had not been apprised of my coming, but Mr. Watson ascended the pulpit and introduced me to the audience; he then retired and I occupied his place, very much to the astonishment of the people. A young man was present who behaved very indecorously, and as the people came in he pointed with his finger to me, tittering and laughing. Poor young man; before that meeting was terminated, his laughter was turned to weeping. This place was on that day a Mount Tabor indeed, not celebrated by the visit of Moses, but blest with the presence of Christ.[55] After the service the brethren requested me to preach for them again on the 25th day of December, commonly called Christmas day; but Mr. Watson thought it best to decline another journey in so inclement a season; it was therefore arranged that I should abide at the house of Mr. Beard, one of the trustees of the chapel, till after the 25th instant; and I accordingly returned with him and his family to their house to dinner. At this place I was still further in the interior of the Slave States, and now left without an earthly protector. During the dinner time, the young man above referred to formed the topic of conversation. It appears that he was a slave-driver, accounted the most profligate drunkard in that vicinity, and habituated to every vice; and it was remarked that he had never been previously known to evince so much serious attention to a sermon as he had paid to my discourse, in the morning: and that his kneeling during the concluding prayer was a matter of surprise to them; however, my mind was greatly moved with evangelic interest for this young man: and, like Paul, for the Galatians, I travailed in birth for him.[56]

On the appointed morning of the 25th instant, I said to one of Mr. Beard's sons, who was a member of the society, "Now, brother, let us go to meeting, having our swords sharpened, and who knows but God will give us this young man?" "Oh!" he replied, "he is far enough off from here by this time, and has swallowed many bowls of drink ere now." On hearing this, I gave up all expectation of seeing him; but when we entered the chapel, to my great surprise he was there, clothed, and in his right mind. I preached that morning from Luke ii. 10;[57] and, under the sermon, every heart was melted, nor was one person to be found in the entire assembly, whose eyes were not suffused with tears. The gallery of the chapel was occupied by the slaves, and the body of the building with proprietors; and all were alike affected. Mr. Beard requested the congregation to restrain the expression of their feelings; but the powerful operation of the Holy Spirit disdained the limits prescribed by man's reason, and bore down all the guards of human propriety and order. The presence of the Holy Ghost filled the place, and moved the people as the wind moves the forest boughs. Mr. Beard's cautions were unavailing; the coloured people in the gallery wept aloud, and raised vehement cries to heaven; the people below were also unable to restrain their emotions; and all wept beneath the inspirations of the Spirit of grace. I was obliged to stop in my discourse, and give vent to my own feelings, and leave it to God to preach in His own more effectual way. Oh, what a memorable day was this! Saints and angels poured their little current of holy and benevolent sympathies into the volume of mercy, love, and grace, which streamed from the compassions of the Infinite Eternal into our little earthly sanctuary, to staunch the bleeding heart, remove its guilt, reform its character, and give new impulse to its powers. At the conclusion of the service, several of the gentlemen present collected a sum of money amongst themselves, which they presented to me, with great expressions of gratitude for the faithful and warning discourse I had preached to them in reference to their spiritual interests; the brethren, also, cordially invited me to come again, offering me the use of the chapel whenever I thought fit to come and occupy it: they wished me God's speed, and we took our farewell of each other, probably to meet no more until the gospel dispensation and its ministry is closed for ever.

I then returned to Annapolis, and received the kind welcome of my dear friends there; and from thence I proceeded on my journey homeward, through Baltimore and Philadelphia, to Burlington; and thus closed with me the year 1829, amid scenes of usefulness and godly revivals and conversions to Christ, the memory of which will be cherished with the most lively interest by thousands of persons.

I will mention, in this place, that many months after my visit to Mount Tabor, I received a letter from the young man whose conversion is above narrated; in which he earnestly desired me to come and visit them again, offering to defray all the expenses of the journey; but the Lord had directed my steps in another direction, and kept my conscience tender and fearful of offending him; so that I durst not step aside from the path of His guidance for any private interest, personal gratification, or earthly gain. Whatever of sorrow or difficulty I met with in the paths of the Lord, I was enabled to sustain, and cheerfully to bear the cross after my loving Lord and Master; but the privilege of self-direction the Lord did not permit so ignorant and incompetent a servant as I was, to exercise. It was one of the crying provocations of ancient Israel, that "they did every man that which seemed right in the sight of his own eyes," and "walked after the imagination of their own hearts." May I ever be preserved to "trust in the Lord with all my heart, and not lean to my own understanding." Lord! ever teach me the way wherein I should go.

> "Oh, may thy Spirit guide my feet,
>   In ways of righteousness;
> Make every path of duty plain
>   And straight before my face.
> Since I'm a stranger here below,
>   Let not my path be hid;
> But mark the road my feet should go,
>   And be my constant guide."

When I was a child, I thought as a child;[58] and often wondered how the ancient servants of the Lord knew the will of God in reference to their movements in life; and how they understood when and whither the Lord required them to go; but when I had fully dedicated myself to the service of the Lord, I experienced "the secret of the Lord to be with them that fear him." When our souls are in a right position before God, the will of the Lord, in reference to our future movements, is always made manifest and plain to us in the Lord's own time. It is only when we are carnal, wayward, neglectful, and disobedient, that our mental vision becomes obscure, and we fail of reading the Lord's indications, or that he ceases to bless us with His guidance. In all the errands on which the Lord has been graciously pleased to send me for the proclamation of His gospel, my work has been attended with the witness of His Spirit, and He hath given seals to my ministry, and souls for my hire.

My mind was at this time directed to the northern States of America; and I accordingly took my daughter with me, and went to New York, where I abode some few weeks, and then went, accompanied by many of the brethren, to Oyster Bay, to attend a camp-meeting held there, which proved a very blessed season to many hundreds of persons; and numbers were, on that occasion, savingly converted to God.[59] On the second time of my appearing in public at that place, I preached from Deut. v. 29, "Oh, that there were such an heart in them, that they would fear me, and keep all my commandments always, that it might be well with them, and with their children for ever;" and under this discourse, it pleased God to capture my own daughter in the gospel net; she cried out aloud, during the service, and exclaimed, "Oh, Lord! have mercy upon me, for I can hold out no longer. Oh, Lord! have mercy upon me." This occurred in the midst of listening hundreds, and it produced a most thrilling sensation upon the congregation; for, said they, "It is her own daughter!" and their emotions of sympathy were still more excited, when they learnt that she was my only child. Many a mother strongly felt with me on that occasion; and though my position would not allow me to leave the pulpit, to go and pour the oil of consolation into her wounded spirit, yet, thank God, there were abundance of dear friends present who were ready for every good word and work. The conversion of a soul is not to be effected by the mere effort of man; none but God can communicate a full pardon to the guilty soul; but, ere that meeting dissolved, the glorious work was accomplished, and Christ, the chiefest of ten thousand and the altogether lovely, was manifested in her heart, the hope of glory: thus she experienced the knowledge of salvation by the remission of her sins, being called out of darkness into God's marvellous light; the Spirit of adoption was imparted to her; she rejoiced in the Lord with all her soul; and His love was shed abroad in her heart by the Holy Ghost.

We then returned to New York, where I apprenticed her to the dress-making business; and taking my leave of her and the friends there, I departed for Newhaven, in the State of Connecticut, being richly replenished by Him who hath said, "I will never leave thee nor forsake thee;" and as I went to and fro in the earth, from place to place, embracing a scope of space and effort too vast for minute detail, the Lord blessed my labours wherever I went, to the conversion of sinners and the edification of saints; but I was not wholly exempted from those trials and persecutions, which are the common lot of the servants of Jesus. The principalities and powers of evil spirits, (Ephes. vi. 12) which Christians have to contend against, which Christ despoiled, (Colos. ii. 15) and which constitute the strength of the empire of darkness, the world of evil spirits, the right hand of the prince of the power of the air, (Ephes. ii. 2) who is the god or deity of this world, (2 Cor. iv. 4); these principalities occasionally obstructed me much; and, by blinding and infatuating the sons of men, inspired them with a hostile zeal against me.[60] This was particularly the case at Hartford; in which city some of the most influential ministers of the Presbyterian body greatly opposed me; and one of them, a Mr. House, resolutely declared that he would have my preaching stopped; but he, like Sanballat, imagined a vain thing;[61] for the work was of God, who made bare his arm for the salvation of men by my ministry. Thanks be unto God who always caused me to triumph in Christ; and made manifest the savour of his knowledge by me in every place.

While the opponents of my ministry were pursuing their plans of opposition, it happened that I was sent for one day to visit a Mr. Freeman, who was dangerously ill; I accordingly went to see him: and while occupied in praying with him, his medical attendant, a physician of the first eminence, and moving in the highest rank in society, came into the chamber; he waited patiently until my supplications were concluded, and I had withdrawn; he then inquired into the condition of his patient, and finding him much better, he exclaimed with surprise, "It is the woman who has made you better." No, dear reader, it was not by my power or holiness that the sick man was benefitted, but the power of God through faith in the name of Jesus; for the Scriptures say, that "the prayer of faith shall save the sick." On my departure from the house, the doctor inquired who I was, and from whence I came; and expressed his wish to hear me himself, desiring them to inform him when and where I should next preach. It appeared that he had previously heard many reports respecting me, for my ministry had been attended by persons of every rank in life.

The time soon arrived for my appearance again in the pulpit, and many of the great folks were present, and amongst them, the physician; and the Spirit of the Lord was there also, to direct and bless and own his word, or the efforts of a poor weak female would have been feeble and insipid indeed: but on that occasion a very great interest was excited in the minds of the audience, for greater and mightier is He that is in us, than the spirit which directs the world; and the more we live and walk in the Spirit, the more the might of God dwells in us and breathes in our words. The doctor then visited his minister, the Rev. Mr. House, the very gentleman who had declared that he would stop me from preaching in that city, and spoke of me to him in such terms as induced the clergyman to exclaim, "Well, if God has sent her, I bid her God's speed." The work of the Lord spread throughout the city, and amongst people of every denomination; and such a revival took place as filled the city with astonishment; and Mr. House, my former opponent, seeing the wonderful works of God, exhorted his congregation to be sober and stand at their posts, "for," said he, "I perceive that God is about to do a great work in this city, therefore be ye still, and know that it is of God." Being encouraged by the smiles of my heavenly Father, and animated to increased zeal in his holy cause, I went from house to house and preached Christ and Him crucified to the people; I even ventured into houses of ill fame, and exhorted the debased inmates to repent of their sins and turn to Jesus Christ: and many of these unfortunate females became the genuine disciples of Jesus. I also penetrated into the alleys and courts, and the different outskirts of the town, where vice and immorality abounded; and it pleased God to effect a mighty change in the morals and habits of the people, especially in the south quarter of the town. I met with many persons here, who called themselves Universalists; but they might more properly be named Deistical Sceptics; they pretended to believe that the whole human family would eventually be saved, irrespectively of their principles and conduct. Many of these gentlemen came to hear me preach, at the house of a friend, in the skirts of the city, to which I had been invited, but very little to their satisfaction; they much approved of my prayers, because my intercessions included all the human family: but they were unable to reconcile them with my preaching, in which I insisted on salvation by the remission of sins, through genuine faith in the crucified Redeemer; described the lost condition of mankind, and exhorted men to flee from the wrath to come. Blessed be the Lord, there were several of these very persons who believed and turned to Him with all their heart; and among them was Mrs. Spring, a lady connected with the third Presbyterian chapel in the city, who attended at that meeting with three of her daughters; they were attired in mourning for another daughter, who had recently died: and, as I was expatiating, on the attendance of kind angels on the death bed scenes of the saints, I observed these ladies weeping with great emotion. In a few weeks afterwards, I was again invited to spend a few days at the same house; and I was then informed that this lady and her three daughters had, from that evening, evinced a saving conversion to God, having been under that sermon convinced of sin, of righteousness and of judgment to come. Mrs. Spring stated that she felt more under that discourse, in reference to the death of her daughter, than she did at the time of her decease: and from that time they had no rest until they obtained the assurance of peace with God, through our Lord Jesus Christ: they were soon after introduced to me, and I received much kindness from them.

I met with a young woman in the course of my ministry in Hartford, who was very unsteady and depraved in her habits; her mother was a member of the Methodist Society, and at that time ill; she wished me to be sent for to visit her, but the daughter insisted that I should not come there; or, if I did, she threatened to swear and dance in my presence during my visit, and to treat me with all possible disrespect. However, this young woman was by some means or other induced to come and hear me preach; and the Lord was pleased to open her heart, that she attended unto the things that were spoken; at the conclusion of the service, she came to me and invited me to come and visit her mother; and the next morning she called upon me again. I exhorted her, prayed with and for her, and she became so attached to me, that my company was continually sought by her: she was soon after admitted into the household of faith, and I afterwards preached in their cottage: thus one of my enemies became my child in the gospel, and my sister in the Lord.

Intending to take my departure from this city, I went to the coach office, and paid my fare, was booked as a passenger for the next day, leaving directions for the coach to call for me on the following morning; but so eager were the people for my further stay amongst them, that some of the brethren went and took up my fare at the coach office, and would not listen to any proposition for my departure. I therefore resumed my labours among them, being constantly engaged by day and night in the work of the Lord, without an intervening cloud, for the space of three months, preaching in the chapel on the Lord's-day, and on one evening in the week.

On one occasion, a number of persons, amounting to between twenty and thirty, presented themselves in the chapel, in great distress, and deep penitence on account of their sins. The excess of their emotions were such, that the order of worship was suspended; for some were calling upon the name of the Lord, some were groaning to receive the atonement of Jesus, while others were rejoicing in his salvation and giving glory to God. Our services were not unfrequently interrupted by scenes of this description; for the operations of the Holy Ghost can no more be circumscribed within the limits of man's arrangement, than the wind and rain and sunshine can be restricted to man's times and opportunities. Order in divine worship and in the house of God is graceful and appropriate; but the life and power of religion is not identified with, nor in proportion to, the polish of the minister, the respectability of the congregation, or the regularity and method of its services: the most abrupt and extraordinary vicissitudes of weather are frequently productive of more benefit than the nicest graduated scale of temperature; and had it not been for some of these instances, in which the Almighty displayed the wonders of his victorious grace, even though the accustomed proprieties and regularity of divine service were at the time abruptly trenched upon and suspended, there are many churches now lively and flourishing, which, notwithstanding the exactness of the order of their worship, and the beauty of their arrangements, would now be but little more than so many religious automata. Our duty is humbly to submit to, rather than attempt to limit, the Holy One of Israel; and when God is at work, though the ark may seem to rock with irregular motion, let not men pretend to more wisdom than their Creator, lest, like Uzzah, they fall themselves in their attempts to direct His energies, and regulate His movements.[62]

My mental hemisphere soon after this became obscured and cloudy, and my mind became exceedingly heavy and sorrowful; satanic spirits also gained access to my soul and harassed me much, and I seemed oppressed with fearful forebodings of some impending evil; I knew not any cause in myself for this reverse of my spiritual condition, and was wholly unable to account for, and comprehend the reason thereof. The following words constantly ran through my mind during this affliction:

> "Lord, what are all my sufferings here,
> If thou but make me meet,
> With that enraptured host to appear
> And worship at thy feet."

I waded through much gloominess and sorrow; the dial of my spirit was beclouded with great darkness, and I wept much and frequently; but the cause was beyond my comprehension.

The chapel in which I had been preaching was called an union chapel, and was not the property of any particular sect of Christians; but the majority of the persons worshipping therein were Presbyterians; and by them, at length, a great jealousy against me was excited, fostered and hatched under the influence of the rulers of the darkness of this world, professedly on account of my being a Methodist. The chapel was to some extent involved in debt; and this Presbyterian faction came forward before the managers with a proposition to procure a minister to supply the pulpit for three months free of expense; requesting, at the same time, that I might not be informed of their proposal: the volunteer preacher was accordingly introduced and tendered his services to supply the pulpit every Lord's-day; and as the chapel was in debt, the proposition was accepted, and the matter arranged and settled. Upon this, one of our friends came and informed me, that it had been arranged by the managers, that Mr. A. should preach on next Lord's-day, in the morning, myself in the afternoon, and Mr. B. in the evening: this somewhat enlightened my understanding into this mystery of iniquity. I attended the morning service on the next Lord's-day, and heard Mr. A. preach; and in the afternoon, as I was proceeding to the chapel, one of the managers met me and informed me he had learnt that Mr. C. was appointed to preach there on that afternoon, and advised me not to enter the pulpit: thus instructed, I took my seat with the congregation: soon afterwards the deacons entered the chapel, and seeing me setting in a private seat, they came and desired me to ascend the pulpit according to the recent arrangements: I then related to them what the manager had said to me; they assured me his statement was untrue, and urged me to take the pulpit; having been informed of all the circumstances, when I appeared in the pulpit I was obliged to vent my feelings in a shower of tears, before I could utter a word; and my dear flock were very much affected at the sight; but we afterwards enjoyed a very blessed meeting. In the evening, I went again and heard the Rev. Mr. B.; there were many of the officials present; and on the conclusion of the service the congregation still kept their seats, none offered to leave, but maintained a profound silence, and the eyes of many of them were fixed in expectation upon me; I felt called forth by the assembly, and rising to my feet, I said, If there are any present who feel anxious about their souls, and will come forward, we will hold a prayer-meeting. A great number then came forward; and when they were seated, the preacher descended from the pulpit, and with the official gentlemen present, without deigning the least notice of me, went and conferred with the persons who were seeking the salvation of their souls, and instructed them in the way of life; after which, they announced that their minister would preach again on Wednesday evening, and closed the meeting, without giving me an opportunity of saying a word: this conduct seemed much like gospel rival-ship, a thing which unhappily too greatly prevails amongst Christians: the apostle Paul intimated that some in his day preached Christ of contention, for the purpose of increasing his affliction; and I cannot but think that this treatment was intended for my affliction;[63] it was too plainly marked to be mistaken; for they all sat waiting in mute silence, until I had invited the inquiring souls to come forward; and then coolly obtruded their grave admonitions on those who had been pricked in their hearts, and were become impatiently violent to grasp the kingdom of heaven; shutting me out entirely, and concluding with a notice that their new minister would preach on the following Wednesday evening, and the next Lord's-day; directing those who wished for further instructions to apply to them at their several residences. My affections were, however, very strongly attached to my little flock; and on the Wednesday evening, I went again to hear the new minister; but the Lord said unto me, "It is enough; I will take thee away from them, and I will put bands upon thee, and thou shalt not go out amongst them; and I will make thy tongue cleave to the roof of thy mouth, that thou shalt be dumb, and shalt not be a reprover to them, for they are a rebellious house. But when I speak unto thee, I will open thy mouth, and thou shalt say unto them, Thus saith the Lord God, He that heareth, let him hear; and he that forbeareth, let him forbear: for they are a rebellious house." Ezek. iii. 25–27. Thus it was partly with me, for on that very night, I was suddenly attacked with a very severe fit of illness, and confined by it for five weeks, so that I became dumb to them indeed. After I had been ill three weeks, the Rev. Mr. Moffit, one of our principal Methodist preachers, came to Hartford;[64] and, under his ministry, the revival which the Lord had began by my instrumentality was renewed again; the chapel became completely deserted, the new minister became discouraged, and shortly withdrew altogether.

Mr. Moffit spent several weeks in Hartford, and preached every evening in the week for the greater part of the time; the people flocked, from every part of the town, to his ministry; and many people were turned unto the Lord. Many of the Methodists and many of my congregation also experienced, under him, a great revival of the work of the Lord in their souls. Before he left the city, it pleased God to raise me up and enable me to go and hear him, and render my thanksgivings to God for His great goodness and tender care towards me in my illness: before I was able to go abroad, those very persons who had treated me so unhandsomely called to inquire after my health; and expressed their hope that God would bless and restore me to health, that I might soon resume my labours among them again, saying, that I had already effected much good to many souls; but as the Lord had said unto me, "when I speak, thou shalt hear: and I will put words in thy mouth and thou shalt speak;" on my recovery, I left the city for a short time; when I returned again, these people were extremely anxious for me to preach to them, and by the grace of God, I resumed my former station and continued my labours amongst them for some time without interruption; the Lord having made it increasingly manifest that He had sent me, and that my ministry was from Him.

A few weeks before I finally left this city, I learnt that Mrs. Adams, the wife of a gentleman in the legal profession, had been dangerously ill for a long time, and had expressed a great desire to see me; I, therefore, without an invitation, called at her residence, but I was so weak at the time, that when I arrived there I fainted, and was taken to bed; when I recovered, I was conducted into her chamber, where Mr. Adams, and all the family were collected, expecting to see her breathe her last; she had been ill so long a time, and wasted so much, that her skin had been broken through by the pressure of the bones. After a little conversation, I inquired if I should pray with her; consent being given, I bowed down before God, and lifted up my heart in supplication to Him on her behalf. It was a time of much power; and all the family were bathed in tears. Mrs. Adams' sister accompanied me to the door on my retiring, and asked me if I did not think her sister was very near her end. I said, 'no: I think she will recover, for God showed me this in the time of prayer.' She then sent one of the servants to lead me home; the next morning I was so ill as to require medical aid; and the physician who attended Mrs. Adams was sent for. He seemed much pleased to communicate to me the intelligence that Mrs. Adams was vastly better; and before I left the city, she was down stairs, at the head of the family. This circumstance made a great impression on the inhabitants of the city, who thought it strange, indeed, that God, in answer to my prayer, should heal the sick: the intelligence flew from street to street, that Mrs. Adams was recovered; and those reverend gentlemen, who had so strenuously exerted themselves to silence my ministry, were themselves completely disconcerted, and their objections silenced. I might add many more of the kind and condescending corroborations, the Lord was pleased to manifest on my behalf in that city; but I forbear narrating any further instances, and leave them to be further revealed in the disclosures of another life.

The wonderful revivals of the work of God, some of which I have attempted to describe, were not done in a corner; but extended throughout the greater part of the vast territory of the United States: many were the labourers, zealous and devoted their spirits, and indefatigable their exertions, whom the Lord raised up, and sent forth to achieve these blessed conquests, the reports of which have long since reached the ears even of British Christians, and excited amongst them some searchings of heart, and some curiosity to have further information respecting them; insomuch that I have understood that men of high repute for learning and wisdom, have been sent over to ascertain the nature, as well to investigate the means and extent of those great transatlantic revivals: what report of the good land they returned with, I have not been informed, but generally I have found that the wise and learned have seldom experienced much of the heavenly discipline of God's Holy Spirit; "the world by wisdom knew not God;" and though many Christians are at immense pains to acquire the wisdom of this world, God bringeth it to nought, and taketh them in their own craftiness; He hideth His counsel from the "wise and prudent, and revealeth it to babes." The man who would judge of so high a matter as a revival of the kingdom of heaven upon earth, must be spiritual (he need not be learned) himself; for the spiritual man judgeth all things; yea, even the deep things of God, yet he himself is judged of no man, for no man can fathom the sacred Urim and Thummim, or as St. John says, the holy anointing or unction which abides in his soul.[65]

I left Hartford for Boston, in the state of Massachusets, in company with a lady, who was from the latter city: and the Lord went before me and cleared up the way; for, in the city of Boston, many doors were opened for my reception; and the Lord wrought wonderfully among the people. Many of the brethren were going to a camp meeting at Cape Codd, about sixty miles from Boston, and invited me to go with them, which I did with great pleasure, and we had very pleasant weather. Many thousands attended at that meeting, and the Lord manifested forth his glory and his grace. Hundreds came to that camp-meeting, to make sport and derision of the saints, and of their worship, who returned home themselves rejoicing in God their Saviour. A band of young gentlemen, connected with the highest families in the town of Lynn, chartered a large vessel, brought their tent, provisions, and every other necessary for a week's sojourn on the camp ground, with the wicked intention not only of greatly annoying us, but of dispersing the camp meeting altogether: the manner in which they approached the encampment rendered it but too evident what kind of persons they were, and for what purpose they came. When these wanton young gentlemen arrived upon the ground, they went from tent to tent, and appeared to be greatly struck with astonishment at the novel appearance of the scene; for the Lord had set the hearts and consciences of the people in motion; some of them were weeping with godly penitence; others were rejoicing in the salvation of Christ, manifested to their souls; in the public services, the ministers were as a flaming torch, and their words as a two edged sword;[66] and the powerful discourses they preached from the platform, made a wonderful impression on these giddy young men, and their conduct became greatly altered. On the Thursday, between twelve and two o'clock, matters were so changed that they prepared their tent for religious service, and sent for me to come and preach to them; I went accordingly, and commenced the meeting, and some of our ablest preachers followed soon after and assisted me, and the Lord owned and blessed our message, and many of these young gentlemen became deeply affected, and cried to God for mercy. The ministers evinced the greatest attention and tender care of them; but they more particularly desired to hear, "the woman:" and the next day I was sent for to preach to them again; after which, we all attended the prayer meeting at the preachers' stand; and many of them found mercy with God. When the camp meeting broke up, all of them with the exception of four, together with many others both white and coloured, manifested the triumphs of redeeming grace, and evinced a saving conversion to God; and the happy result of that meeting was, that, in a short space of time, in the town of Lynn alone, upwards of two hundred persons were added to the Methodist Episcopal Church.

The brethren residing at the Cape having strongly solicited me to tarry for a time with them, I consented, and instead of returning with the brethren to Boston, went home with the Cape friends, and travelled with the itinerating preachers on the different circuits of the Cape district, and with great success; for the glorious camp meeting we had just before attended, had laid the foundation for an extensive and continuous revival: the fields were indeed white, already to harvest; and we went to reap them, and receive the rich wages of souls for our hire.

In the course of my excursions, I went into the Haverich circuit, and entered one of their chapels. After the service had commenced, I observed a young man in the assembly who appeared to idolise himself, and to soar very high into the regions of self-conceit; his excessive self-complacency very much attracted my attention, and I felt a desire to have some conversation with him; not suspecting that there was any probability of its coming to pass; but God overrules and arranges matters for His people, that they may glorify His name. It happened that we went that day to dine with this very young gentleman's father-in-law; and during the time of dinner he came in. Some one at the table then asked him if there were many persons in attendance at the meeting in the morning; to which he replied, no; adding, that he was a fool in going, for it was complete folly to attend those meetings. These words came very painfully to my heart; but as I was to preach in the afternoon, and required much self-composure, I passed over his remarks in silence; when the service of the afternoon was over, I returned to tea with the family, and being now at liberty, having no sermon before me to preach, I was not indisposed for a colloquy with him; he was also desirous of having some conversation with me, and had prepared himself for that purpose; after tea, he came again, and brought many others with him to witness his feats of prowess: so he promptly commenced an attack upon me, worked himself into a great fury, and spouted away for a time; but his ammunition was quickly exhausted; his creed, if he had any, was that of modified deism; looking for a future paradise to be enjoyed by all men indiscriminately; he was, however, deplorably ignorant of the Scriptures; I replied to him according to the ability the Lord gave me; and conviction of the truth went with the word, so that he became of the number of believers in Christ, and subsequently behaved to me with very great kindness—to God be all the praise for ever and ever.

My ministry every where, on the Cape, was very numerously attended: there were but few buildings that could contain the numbers who flocked to hear the word of the Lord; as I journied from place to place, many an open waggon became my pulpit, from which I preached in the open air to listening multitudes, the candidates for immortality, and directed them to the Lamb of God who taketh away the sins of the world.[67] My own soul was filled with heavenly hope, which maketh not ashamed; my affections were set upon things above; my treasure was in heaven; my hope bloomed with the glories of immortality and eternal life: it was the anchor of my soul, sure and steadfast; I rejoiced in hope of the glory of God; and in my ministry, I determined to be conversant with no other topic, to know nothing amongst men but Jesus Christ and him crucified.[68] The divine treasures which God imparted into my earthen vessel I freely poured out; and the Lord constantly replenished me with more; so that I was always being exhausted and ever being filled with the heavenly treasures of divine knowledge; and became more and more able to bring out of the good treasure in my heart things new and old. The Lord enabled me to keep my heart with all diligence; and having my own soul right with God, I was enabled to set others right also. I affectionately press it upon the attention of every minister of the gospel, who really desires that his ministry may be effectual to convert and sanctify men, to attend to himself first, to see that the work of genuine conversion be perfected in his own heart; that he is truly born again of the incorruptible seed of the word of God, which liveth and abideth for ever; that he is thoroughly cleansed from his old sins; enjoying the remission of sins and justification to life; that the word of God abideth in him, and is fruitful; that he enjoys the spirit of adoption; is sealed with the Holy Spirit of promise; that the Holy Ghost dwelleth in him; that he comes to the light in every thing; is pure in heart, and hath his eye single to the glory of God; that he is sanctified by the truth; purified by obeying it; that he abideth in Christ the true vine; dwelleth in God and God in him; that he hath continual communion with the Father, and with his Son Jesus Christ; that he lives and walks in the Spirit; is led by the Spirit; that he is not proud of these attainments, but simple and of a childlike disposition; that his heart is preserved in a state of transparency, and so free from guile and sin, that he would not be reluctant to have it probed by a truly godly-experienced and judicious Christian of like attainments. Let him see to it that he is meek, lowly, patient, contrite and humble, habituated to self-denial, filled with charity or love which is the bond of perfectness; that his will is entirely submitted and resigned to the will of God; that his meat and drink is to do the will of his Father in heaven; that his attitude is that of a self-devoted, living sacrifice, utterly at the disposal of his God, taking up every cross placed before him; that he meekly and practically regards the sayings of Jesus and the precepts of the Christian Scriptures, aiming at a perfect observance of them all, that he may become a finished disciple of Jesus Christ, exercised in all parts of Christian duty and practise, and copying the pattern set by his Lord, devoting soul and body, time and opportunities, money and means, his entire all to the service of Jesus; not wedded to this life, but holding it as loosely as possible, rejoicing in hope of the glory of God, and seeking an increased knowledge of Christ, the fellowship of His sufferings, and the spiritual might of His resurrection. Such a man as this, if called and sent by Christ into His vineyard, is able to make men wise unto salvation; and is the kind of minister whose labours Jesus will deign to bless. Such ministers have adorned and blessed the church in all ages; and such ministers occasionally adorn it still. It is an axiom which holds good in Christianity, as well as in common life, that whatever man has borne, been, or done, man may bear, be, or do; and there is no more impossibility of attaining eminent saintship in the present day, than there was two thousands of years since: with the Scriptures in our hands and the Holy Spirit in our hearts, we possess advantages even beyond those Christians who enjoyed the living ministry of the apostles. He who would be a master in Israel should possess such an experimental knowledge of the Christian religion, as an university cannot bestow, but which is the exclusive endowment of the Holy Ghost. A well-disciplined minister is a father in Christ; an elder in the Christian church; and happy is that flock over which the Holy Ghost hath made him an overseer: who are fed by him, not with college lore, nor with orations such as are emitted by divines not yet out of their teens; but with such instructions as the Holy Ghost teacheth, comparing spiritual things with spiritual. When ministers aim at revivals in their flocks, they must first obtain them in their own souls; for he who has left his first love, is in no condition to communicate the glowing flame to others: he must first remember from whence he has fallen, and repent, and do his first works; strengthen the things that remain; stir up the gift of God in himself; obtain the pure gold of true faith, well tried in the fire, and anoint his mental eyes with the illuminating eye-salve of divine unction; render his body a temple for the Holy Ghost, and equip himself with the whole armour of God,[69] and then he may efficiently contribute to the health and prosperity of the souls of others; being a discerning, faithful watchman, and a good shepherd to them. I have witnessed such ministers, (who are rightly named 'Great Grace,') lay open the heart, cast down imaginations and every high thing that exalteth itself against the knowledge of God: and with the Spirit's two-edged sword, divide the sinner from his sins, slay the lion, and bring him a lamb-like penitent to the feet of Jesus; then take the new creature by the hand, lead him by the side of still waters, in paths of righteousness; comfort, exhort, warn, instruct, and build him up in our most holy faith, that he may eventually have the joy to present him faultless and perfect in Christ Jesus.[70] Oh! that every leader of souls in Britain may speedily become a Joshua, to bring all the Lord's Israel into the promised rest of faith.[71]

In the course of my travels on the Cape, I one day met with a young lady recently married, whose pride and self-consequence were superlatively high; her parents, brothers and sisters were decidedly religious; but her vanity and haughtiness had hitherto resisted the humbling impressions of true godliness. I felt my mind much drawn after this young lady, but she rejected every advance of mine, and contemptuously avoided my conversation. I spent a day at her father's house; during which time she was with us; but she sat as a queen, and maintained all the dignity of haughty reserve to every religious topic; at night, we had family prayer; and I followed the impressions of my mind, in fervently praying for her; and took my leave of the family. In about two years afterwards, I again met with her mother, who informed me that, on that evening, this young lady was brought to repentance towards God: she was afflicted with penitential anguish to an extraordinary degree, ere she was enabled to exercise faith in our Lord Jesus Christ; since that time, she evinced as great anxiety to see and unbosom her mind to me as she had previously to shun and repulse me. Verily, God doeth all things well: all praise to His glorious wisdom and power; His rich and free mercy, and adorable grace.

Having reaped a rich harvest of souls on the Cape, I returned to the city of Boston, where I remained for a few months; the Lord having made my way prosperous, many doors were opened to me, the word of God had free course and was glorified; many who sat in darkness there saw the great and the true light, and turned to the Lord with all their heart; from thence I proceeded to the city of Salem, and laboured amongst the Methodists with much attendant prosperity. The coloured people had a chapel in course of erection, and stood in great need of assistance; the Methodist brethren therefore, in conjunction with several gentlemen in the city, subscribed a considerable sum of money, with which they furnished them with a pulpit and seats for the chapel. When the building was got in readiness, I delivered the first discourse therein, from Zech. ii. 10, "Sing and rejoice, O daughter of Zion; for I come, and I will dwell in the midst of thee, saith the Lord." [72] The Lord graciously manifested and recorded His name there on that occasion; and many considered their ways, and turned from their vanities to serve the living God. The Lord was pleased also to apply a portion of His word with much power to my own soul, as it was delivered by His angel. Zech iii. 7. "Thus saith the Lord of Hosts, if thou wilt walk in my ways, and if thou wilt keep my charge, then thou shalt also judge my house and shalt also keep my courts, and I will give thee places to walk among these that stand by."

In that city, the ladies who were connected with the several Christian denominations, were in the habit of holding a monthly union prayer-meeting together; and as this brought the different denominations into closer contact with each other, it caused a rich intercourse of sanctified gifts and graces amongst them, for the edification of the general body; it also greatly promoted Christian love, for the pure, genial currents supplied by genuine gospel faith, purified the disciples from party bigotry, and caused them to love one another for the truth's sake. It was delightful indeed to hear Episcopalians, Presbyterians, Baptists, and Methodists, avow the rich enjoyments they had in the spirit of adoption from God, who gave forth the corroborating testimony of His divine witness with their spirits to their heavenly filiations. The Christian church should manifest one fold and one shepherd; one body and spirit; one hope, one Lord, one faith, one baptism; and one God and father of all who is above all, and through all, and in all. O that the Christian community in Great Britain were all of one heart and one soul; only, but earnestly, contending for the faith once delivered to the saints; that there were no divisions among them, but all were speaking the same things, and perfectly joined together in the same mind, and in the same judgment; none being puffed up one against another, knowing that ministerial partizanship, doctrinal divisions, and sectarian prejudices flow from sheer carnality, and savours nothing of the grace of God. Rom. xvi. 17. 1 Cor. iii. 3.[73] During my stay in Salem, a great alteration was effected in the morals of the colored friends; I hope to be forgiven by my English brethren, in saying, that it is not an uncommon thing for white Christians to reprobate the morals of their sable brethren, without an adequate occasion; the intelligence, the circumstances, and the habits of the two races are widely different; and it is the part of a moted eye and biased heart to require the same standard tale of bricks from the Ethiopean family! Or, in other words, an observance by them of all the proprieties attached to the refined Christian morals of the more cultivated Saxon stock; the illiterate colored Christian is competent to, and ought, practically, to carry out the precepts of the Christian religion to the utmost extent his circumstances admit of; but Christian charity will not rashly judge him, for an imperfect conformity to the politer standard of morals and tasteful delicacy, which have been superadded to the Christian precept, by the supererogative pride of high-toned sensibility and civilization; a more perfect exemplification of Christian morals than that which characterized the apostolic era has never been attained by any later age; but its simplicity and want of polish would have presented a very rude and vulgar exhibition in contrast with the whited exterior, the artificial delicacy and current respectability or pride of life of much of the present-day Christianity. The immoralities of the Abyssinian brethren, when they occur, are obvious and glaring, and are easily visited and purged by the discipline of the church; but those of more polished Christians too often flow in a deep and mighty under current: no principles are more vicious, no practices more immoral and debasing, than covetousness and worldly pride; the Scriptures exclude those who are guilty of them from any inheritance in the kingdom of God and Christ; yet it is a fact but too well known, that these vices have an unrestrained course throughout the more civilized Christian communities; and that an attempt to expel these immoralities from those communities, by subjecting all such offenders to the discipline of the church, would fill with confusion, and crumble to ruins every denominational superstructure in Christendom.

The Lord's blessing on my visit to Salem was made apparent by the improvement which followed in the morals and habits of the colored population; many of whom became truly devout, righteous, holy, godly, spiritual, and heavenly-minded: by devout, I mean, devotional and religious; righteousness consists in being and doing right; holiness is purity internally and practically. Godliness is an assimilation of the human character to that of our heavenly Father; spirituality is such a practical acquaintance with spiritual things, and abiding sense of the existence and agency of spiritual and invisible beings, and converse with them, as gives a complete ascendancy to the moral and mental powers over the animal propensities; but it more especially consists in a discernment of the presence and operations of the Holy Spirit, fellowship with God and his Son Jesus Christ, and the communion of the Holy Spirit, together with an habitual and deep consciousness, and a blooming prospect of the momentous realities of a future life. Heavenly-mindedness consists in having our mind and hope fixed upon the things above; on the mercy-seat and throne of grace, the heavenly Jerusalem; the mansions which Jesus is preparing for us there; the heavenly Mount Zion;

the general assembly and church of the first-born; the innumerable company of angels; the blood of sprinkling; the mediator and high-priest of the new covenant; and upon God the judge of all. Many of my sable brethren became eminently spiritual, having ceased to be led by their animal appetites and worldly lusts, they were led by the Holy Spirit of God which dwelt in them, and whose temples they were. In the Methodist connexion, also, I had an extensive circle of young ladies who were constant attendants upon my ministry, and who were in an especial manner my charge in the Lord; these manifested great diligence in their pursuit of the higher attainments of experimental spirituality. The love of God being richly shed abroad in their hearts by the Holy Ghost, many of them attained to considerable eminence in the apprehension of, and conformity to, the love of Christ, which passeth knowledge; abiding in Christ, dwelling in God, and walking in the light as God is in the light, they experienced that perfect love which casteth out fear; the holy vigour and zeal with which they pressed forward after the life of God, the avidity with which they drank until they were filled with the Spirit, and the wonderful revelations God was pleased to manifest to them, provoked me to run forward in the heavenly race with increased earnestness, lest they should overtake, and leave me behind them: but as the Lord set me as their leader, He sustained me as such; and an abundance of grace was given to me as His commissioned servant, to maintain my leadership. I abode in Salem throughout the winter, and a most delightful winter it was.

I also paid a visit to the friends at Lynn; a town to which reference has already been made; the Rev. J. Melvill was the minister stationed there, who invited me to preach in his pulpit, which I did to an overflowing audience: on that occasion, I had the happiness to see many of those dear young men who had attended the camp-meeting as before narrated. On the conclusion of the service, they formed themselves into two ranks down the aisle of the chapel, in order to salute me as I passed betwixt them; and we parted in the hope of a joyful meeting on the morning of the resurrection.

From Salem I again returned to Boston, which city I left in May, 1830, in company with a Mrs. Ruby, who had been thither on a visit, and was now returning to Portland, in the State of Maine, in the north-eastern part of America. We had a pleasant passage by water; the night was calm, and we reached Portland about eight o'clock in the morning. It is a beautiful city, situated on the sea coast; built on a considerable elevation, and the houses being white, it presents a very conspicuous and fine appearance from the sea.

On my arrival, I found the friends to be a very benevolent and kind-hearted people: they gave me a very cordial reception; we quickly became well acquainted and at home in each other's company, and it was a blessed visit to my own soul and to their souls also. The Abyssinian chapel, a very neat and pretty erection, was appropriated to my service:[74] and the news of a female being about to preach therein, attracted a great number of persons from all parts of the city; the Lord applied my message to the hearts of many of them, and they cried to Him for mercy, they sought Him with their whole heart, and He was found of them to be a God merciful and gracious, pardoning iniquity, transgression, and sin; and like the eunuch, they went on their way rejoicing.[75] The chapel was constantly filled during my stay, amongst them: many were made happy in the love of God, enjoyed a sense of His approbation and the witness of His Spirit with their spirits that they were the children of God; many strangers were continually attracted to the chapel; and on one Lord's day, a gentleman was present whose emotion was so strong as to excite much attention; he at length retired to the lobby where he vented his feelings in sobs and tears: he stated to one of the brethren that he was a sea-captain, a stranger to earthly fears, that his heart was attracted and rivetted by the discourse which was in the course of delivery, so that he could not retire from the place; but being unable to repress his feelings, and desirous of evading observation, he preferred standing in the lobby. Another person was there also under similar circumstances, who called upon me the next day, and informed me that he had been a sailor during the last forty years, and had encountered every form of marine danger: that he had belonged to a ship of war, and been accustomed to the roaring of cannons, and all the tragic horrors of naval warfare, but never had felt dismayed by any accumulation of peril; he now wept bitterly, and we both knelt before the Lord in supplication, and the Lord heard and spoke peace to his soul. Many other instances of the Lord's especial favour to me, and blessing upon my ministerial labours in that city I might relate; but the limits I am compelled to assign to the compass of this volume require their omission.

After remaining a few months in Portland, I was moved to travel further into the State of Maine, and I journied in company with Mr. Black, a Baptist minister to the town of Brunswick; a town eminent in the State for its literary institutions. Mr. Black preached there on the Lord's-day, and I was invited to occupy the pulpit of the Baptist chapel on the Monday evening; which I did, and preached to a very crowded auditory, of whom a large number were collegians: at the close of the meeting, I was invited to preach there again.[76] After this, my mind was impressed that I must go to Bath; a town about ten miles distant; though I had received no invitation, possessed no introductory means to any one, neither knew any person there, and had been informed that the town was not inhabited by one person of colour; my mind was therefore somewhat saddened on account of this impression; I knew not how to proceed in it; and committed my way unto God, who in His own way and time brought it to pass.

In a few days I went to preach at a small country village; and, a female from Bath being present at the meeting, I sent a message by her to the religious people of Bath, requesting permission to come and preach to them; this was the first time in my life that I had ever requested as a favour to myself, that which in the nature of things is the communication of a favour. In a few days I received an answer from them, intimating that they neither knew nor had heard of me previously; but that they regularly held a prayer-meeting at certain times at a certain house about a mile from the town, at which I might attend if I thought proper.

Although this reply seemed rather uncourteous and grating to the feelings, yet the matter was from the Lord, and I durst not refuse even an invitation so uncouth. Accordingly a kind sister conveyed me in her chaise to the place on the day of their next prayer meeting: having alighted, we inquired of the housewife if that was the meeting-house; she admitted that it was; 'but,' says she, 'who asked you to come here?' Having given her the name of the friend who had sent to me, she added, 'Oh! then go to him, go to him, he will tell you all about it.' It is to be deplored that some Christians have 'Nabal' so prominently inscribed upon their tempers, that they display an equal moroseness with the canine snarlers: such are unmindful of the authority and disobedient to the laws of their Master, by which they are required to be courteous, gentle and kind; and they greatly disgrace the Christian profession by their churlishness.[77] We departed from that surly abode, and went into the town, but were unable to find one person belonging to the society or who knew anything of our coming; nor could any of them accommodate us with a night's lodging: we therefore rode back to the house where the meeting was to be held, and the time for its commencement was nearly arrived. We again alighted and knocked at the door, and it was opened by the female before mentioned, who, when she saw us, shut it again in our faces and turned away. As she did not lock the door, I opened it and entered into the house. A great many people and the preachers were already assembled; I sat down in the meeting and reflected on the repulsive reception I had met with; and conscious that I had now discharged my duty before God, I resolved, if not requested to preach, to sit in silence and wait before Him.

When the time for service arrived, one of the preachers came to me and said, 'Sister, I suppose you wish to address the meeting,' to which I assented: and as he stated that the assembly were desirous of hearing me, I went into the desk opened the meeting, and preached from Isaiah xlviii. 18, "Oh, that thou hadst hearkened to my commandments! then had thy peace been as a river; and thy righteousness as the waves of the sea."[78] The audience were very numerous and attentive; much feeling was excited and many tears were shed, for the Lord was with me in the work, to give efficacy to the word of His grace. At the conclusion of the service, the society were detained to consult on matters of their own; and I retired to prepare for my departure. When we were ready to enter the chaise, some of the sisters came to us, and informed me that I might be accommodated with a lodging at the residence of a lady in the neighbourhood; but as they did not assign any object for my further stay with them, I declined the offer, and departed. I afterwards learnt that they had been consulting about my preaching in the town on the next Lord's day, and had arranged for me so to do; though they did not then inform me of it. After the sermon, my soul was filled with an inexpressibly sweet serenity and heavenly peace. On our way home we called at a house on Brunswick plains, which is midway betwixt the two towns, where one of our friends resided; and as they were preparing supper for us, I sat in thoughtful meditation on the varied goodness of God towards me; and looking upwards, the Lord opened my eyes, and I distinctly saw five angels hovering above and engaged in the praises of God: the raptures of my soul were too awful and ecstatic on that occasion for human description: the sensual world are unacquainted with the overwhelming fascinations which thrill through every instinct of the spiritual mind under the complacent manifestation of etherial intelligencies and their enchanting influence. I concluded that this wonderful manifestation was a token for good, and a proof that the Lord was well pleased with the course I had taken; and I was encouraged to hold several meetings throughout the week, and preached on the Lord's day twice on the plains, and once in Brunswick. I learnt, in the meantime, that a great curiosity had been excited in Bath on account of my visit to that place, and that I was anxiously expected there again. On the Lord's day morning, immediately after I had commenced the service, one of the Bath preachers came in, and when the service was over, informed me that he was directed to conduct me to Bath to preach there in the evening; but being then engaged to preach in Brunswick in the evening, he was much disappointed at my declining his invitation; however, I promised to call and preach there when on my journey to Bangor, to which town I purposed shortly to go: in a short time, taking leave of the friends at Brunswick, I went to Bath, and was very kindly received by Mr. Wilkinson, one of the preachers: in the evening I preached in their spacious chapel to a very large and attentive audience: after service they made a collection, the whole of which they generously presented to me; being a larger sum than I had received from any other congregation in the State of Maine; they then earnestly requested me to remain a few days with them, and preach again ere I proceeded on my journey, to which I was constrained to consent. As the immense concourse retired from the chapel, the noise of so many hundreds of feet unbroken by any human articulation was very remarkable, and excited the surprise of some of the friends as being very unusual in that town; but the people obviously had

"A while forgot their earthly cares,
And soared above this vale of tears,
To yon celestial hill."

I attended the different meetings of their classes during my stay there, and enjoyed a very pleasant visit among them; and, having preached to them again, they gave me letters of recommendation to the methodist ministers who resided along the course of my journey through the State. I could not but gratefully regard the kind dealings of my Heavenly Father towards me in my visits to this people; although my reception was so rude and repulsive at the first, yet my way was enlarged, my messages welcomed, and my subsequent treatment warmly cordial and affectionate: such are frequently the ways in which the Lord conducts His saints—

"Behind a frowning Providence,
He hides a smiling face." [79]

Having preached to them on the Thursday evening, my departure was arranged for the morrow; the friends having obtained my promise, that, with the Lord's permission, I would come and preach to them again on my return. On the morning, before I left, the superintendent minister of the Circuit came on a visit to Bath from Augusta; and hearing of my preaching there, treated it at first as many other ministers do, with great contempt, and reprobated the ministry of a female; but after hearing somewhat more of the matter, his sentiments became changed, he was introduced to me, and became one of my very kind friends.

It is true, that in the ordinary course of Church arrangement and order, the Apostle Paul laid it down as a rule, that females should not speak in the church, nor be suffered to teach; but the Scriptures make it evident that this rule was not intended to limit the extraordinary directions of the Holy Ghost, in reference to female Evangelists, or oracular sisters; nor to be rigidly observed in peculiar circumstances. St. Paul himself attests that Phœbe was a servant or deaconess of the Church at Cenchrea; and as such was employed by the Church to manage some of their affairs; and it was strange indeed, if she was required to receive the commissions of the Church in mute silence, and not allowed to utter a syllable before them. The apostle John wrote his second epistle to a Christian lady, as a matron of eminence and authority; exhorting her believing children by her, and bidding her to prove the doctrines of those who visited her in the capacity of Christian teachers: honourable mention is made of many other Christian females who promoted the cause of Jesus; and Paul wished every assistance to be given to those women who laboured with him in the Gospel. Tryphena laboured with Tryphosa in the Lord; mention is made of the services of many of the sisters of Nereus, of the mother of Rufus, many others are also very respectfully referred to by St. Paul, the prophet Joel predicted that God would pour His Spirit on His handmaids, and that they should prophecy as well as His servants; and this prophecy, Peter, on the day of Pentecost, asserted was fulfilled; and if so, the Christian dispensation has for its main feature the inspirations of the holy prophetic Spirit, descending on the handmaids as well as on the servants of God; and thus qualifying both for the conversion of men, and spread of the Gospel. Priscilla took upon herself the work of a teacher, when, in conjunction with her husband Aquila, she expounded to Apollos the way of God more perfectly; the four virgin daughters of Philip the Evangelist, were prophetesses or exhorters, probably assisting their father in his evangelic labours: being prophetesses or exhorters, the work in which they were employed was prophecy or exhortation; and those brethren certainly err, who fetter all and every ecclesiastical circumstance, and even the extraordinary inspirations of the Holy Spirit with the regulations given by the apostle to a church, the brethren of which extensively possessed the gift of utterance, and were therefore in no need of female speakers; and a Church, too, which owing to its disorders and excesses, required the most stringent rules for its proper regulation. The superintendent minister desired me to tarry some days in Augusta; furnished me with letters of introduction to the brethren there, and in the event of the preacher, who was appointed to preach on the following Lord's day in his stead; failing to come, he made the necessary arrangements, and directed me to supply his lack of service. I set off for Augusta in the steam boat at two o'clock, P.M., and arrived there at nine in the evening; and it being dark, I was unable to find the inn to which I had been directed; but the lord was with me to preserve me. Being alone so late at night, I felt uncomfortable, as a female and a stranger, and wandered about until I came to the principal hotel, into which I entered and received great kindness from the landlord. In the morning he went himself to Mr. Robinson, and informed him I was inquiring for him, whereupon that gentleman came to the hotel for me, conducted me to his house, and very kindly entertained me. From the moment I consented to tarry in Augusta, till the next Lord's day, I felt a very heavy cloud upon my soul, for I had received no direction from the Lord upon it, but had acted upon my own judgment. I went mourning by day, and passed two nights in sleepless sorrow. Mr. Robinson informed me that the committee of the society were about to meet in the evening, that the question of my preaching there must be submitted to them, and he would inform me of their decision, but the time passed by and I heard nothing thereof. On the Lord's day morning, after breakfast, as I was praying in private to my heavenly Father, and desiring to know why my soul was thus shut up in confusion and obscurity, the Lord was pleased to give me this answer, "Thus saith the Lord, the brethren are divided in their sentiments; nevertheless, though clouds and darkness be with thee, I will deliver thee; my presence shall go with thee, and I will give thee rest." I then went into the parlour, and said to Mrs. Robinson, "My dear madam, since my coming here, I have not enjoyed that rich endowment of the light of the Holy Spirit which I usually experience, nor could I imagine the reason thereof." I further stated, that my heavenly Father had showed me the reason, viz., that I have come amongst a people who are divided in their sentiments; and that the brethren are not perfectly joined together in the same mind, and in the same judgment. She then burst into a flood of tears, and said, "Well, if they will not receive those whom God is pleased to send, we cannot help it." When the time came for morning service, I accompanied Mr. and Mrs. Robinson to the chapel. The congregation assembled, but the minister, who was appointed to preach, did not come: after waiting some time for the preacher, and he not coming, Mr. R. came and requested me to take the pulpit; but having made no preparation whatever to conduct the public services, I declined, stating that I had no desire to intrude myself upon the attention of the congregation contrary to the feeling of the church; upon this, a gentleman present said he would not bind the rest of the brethren by his peculiar view; that he would go to another meeting, and leave them at liberty to act as they pleased. He then withdrew; and one of the brethren rose and assured me that all the brethren present were of one mind as to my preaching; and hoped that I would consider myself amongst my friends and not feel the least embarrassment.

I then repaired to the desk, and conducted the service, though with but little of my accustomed unction and freedom. In the afternoon, however, it pleased God to grant us a time of refreshing indeed. The chapel, which was large and commodious, was densely crowded; and, at the conclusion, one of the brethren arose and proclaimed that a meeting would be held there in the evening also; and in the evening, so great was the concourse, that crowds remained at the chapel doors unable to gain an entrance; and numbers were forced to retire disappointed of any accommodation. The presence of the Holy One was also manifested, and the glory of God filled the house. Although greatly fatigued with the exertions of this day, at five o'clock on the following morning, I took the stage for Bangor, and rode seventy miles that day over a remarkably uneven ground, sometimes ascending the sides of the mountains, and at other times jolting through the rocky valleys. After a very fatiguing journey we arrived at Bangor at four o'clock, P.M., and I was kindly received by Mr. Brown, a very respectable gentleman of colour, who stood in high repute among the people: this gentleman went and apprised the Methodist preacher of my arrival: who soon came to see me, and gave me invitations to the pulpit, the classes, and the family in which he resided. I attended their quarterly meeting, and also a love feast, with very great enjoyment and profit to my own soul: the meeting was attended with divine power of very perceptible density; the people spoke with great feeling, and fluent utterance; the Spirit of the Lord directed and inspired the meeting, and much good was effected on that occasion. My visit to Bangor was replete with reciprocal benefits to them and myself. I truly saw there the grace of God, and was glad; for the Lord sent the Spirit of His Son into the hearts of many, crying, Abba, Father! and sealed them with His Holy Spirit of promise. After remaining with them a few days, I took my leave of them and returned by the route by which I came. The day was very rainy; and the coach was closely shut up, that no inside passenger could be seen; nevertheless, I had not been in Augusta an hour, before Mr. Robinson came to the house where I was, to engage me to preach in the chapel that evening. I accordingly went and preached, during one of the most terrific thunder-storms I ever witnessed; the heavens gathered blackness; the God of glory thundered, He uttered His voice, and that a mighty voice, which divided the flames of fire: the awfulness of the evening gave an increased solemnity to the service; in the night a vessel was lost upon the coast; and all hands except two perished. In the morning I went by the stage coach to Bath; and two young men, the only survivors of the crew of the wrecked vessel were amongst the passengers. I was very kindly received by my dear friends in Bath; and, according to previous engagement, I preached in their Chapel in the evening; and a delightful visitation of the love of God was enjoyed by the congregation. I felt a most spiritual union with this people, which I believe will be renewed with increased delights in the world of bliss; the Lord had enabled me to endure with meekness and patience, the repulsive treatment I met with from them on my first introduction amongst them; and we afterwards became more closely united and endeared to each other, than we perhaps might have been, if my first reception had been more courteous; their subsequent behaviour was full of kindness and tender affection; we enjoyed many happy hours in each other's company, and the time of my departure was painfully affecting. I then returned to Portland, after an absence of about three months; and after an abode there of some few weeks, I journeyed to another part of the Lord's heritage, going from one town to another, the Lord having opened many doors to me, and given me access to every denomination of Christians, my labours greatly abounded. My earthen vessel was continually exhausted, and as continually replenished; my bodily frame was often wearied in the service of my Saviour, Proprietor and Lord; and many an hospitable home was opened by his providential care, to furnish me with refreshment and repose.

"Here I raise my Ebenezer,
Hither by thy help I've come,
And I hope, by thy good pleasure,
Safely to arrive at home." [80]

At one little town that I visited, it having been announced that I should preach in a large school room usually appropriated for that purpose; when I was proceeding thither, accompanied by some friends, at the time appointed, my mind suddenly became disquieted; and I said, 'what is the matter, for I feel that there is something not right'; the friends who were with me, however, made light of my inquiry; but it soon appeared that some dissolute and ruffianly persons had conspired together to come and break up the meeting; and they had so far intimidated the brethren who should have opened the doors, that they durst not go forward to prepare the place! One of the sisters then procured the key, and opened the room. A great concourse of people assembled; and I commenced the service in entire ignorance of the disturbance which was projected. In a short time afterwards the conspirators entered the room, their leader tarrying at the door; the power of the Lord was visibly present; and the rabble were overawed and restrained from [their] purpose. Their champion growing impatient, then made his appearance—an unusually stout and ferocious looking man: he came close up to me, making a demonstration as if he intended to seize or strike me, but this producing no impression upon me, he stood over me as if he would take my life; but God was with me, and I felt no fear. He then seated himself beside his companions, pulled their hair, and groaned aloud, in derision of the Methodists! Those groans rested upon my spirit; the thread of my discourse was suspended, and I was directed to rebuke and exhort him personally, telling him that those groans would soon be repeated in reality; and it was not improbable that he might be suddenly cut off from the land of the living, and required to give a woeful account of himself at the bar of God. I thus cleared my soul of his blood, and left him in the hands of God. On the next day, as I was walking in the town, this very man came and civilly accosted me, and invited me to call at his house, which I did, and prayed with him and his family, and departed. Proceeding further, I met with the gang of his confederates; who addressed me, and entreated my forgiveness for their misbehaviour on the previous evening; and while I assured them of my forgiveness, I exhorted them to seek forgiveness from God, whose majesty had been insulted by their disrespectful conduct toward His servants and the ordinance of His worship. I then left the town; and, in a few days afterwards, I learnt that their champion had died suddenly, from the rupture of a blood-vessel in the lungs! having gone from his house but fifteen minutes before in perfect health: this event made a deep impression on the minds of the people in that locality, and caused the fear of God to rest upon many. I then visited another part of that country, where an abundant field of labour was presented before me; and the Lord applied His word as a two-edged sword, to the conviction and awakening of many souls; but lest I should be too much elated with my ministerial prosperity, my course received a check by the oversetting of the chaise in which I was returning one evening from the house of God, by which my ankle was broken, and I was laid by for a time; but after a few months, my hurt was recovered, and I resumed my work in the vineyard of the Lord. I then returned to Portland, and thence proceeded to Boston, which I left for Rhode Island; where I passed some time amongst the Christian brethren. In the town of Providence there was a great shaking among the dry bones;[81] the Spirit of God entered into them, and many began to live. I proceeded from thence to New Bedford, where I was cordially received by the minister of the Freewill Baptist congregation. I preached there many times; and then went to the Island of Nantucket, intending, in a few days, to return to New York and see my daughter, from whom I had been absent more than two years, and whom I had a great desire to see: but God ordered it otherwise; for when about to sail for New York, the wind shifted, and was so contrary, that the vessel could not go out of the harbour, and I returned again on shore to the house of my friend; before the wind became favourable, I was attacked with a very severe fit of illness, by which I was confined for a long time: I therefore sent for my daughter to come to me; and, on her arrival, the interview was very affecting to us both. The physician gave no hopes of my recovery, but prayer was made on my behalf by day and night. Miss Sarah M. Coffin, a young lady in the vicinity, incessantly visited me, and prayed much and fervently for me. One evening, while praying by my bed-side, she used these words, which were written on my heart as with an iron pen, or the point of a diamond—"Lord, if consistent with thy will, spare our sister Elaw, and take my life in her stead; for she is useful to thy cause, and I am but a feeble worm, and but of little worth." Her affection for me was as great as that of Aquila and Priscilla for St. Paul, who would have laid down their own necks upon the block for him.[82] One day I was so ill, that my attendants were expecting my breath to cease. The medical attendant came in, and informed them, that he was about to fetch the principal physician on the island to see me. The friends were then sitting around me, and an elderly lady, a Baptist, came into the chamber, sat down, and looked at me awhile, and then said, "Mrs. Elaw, I am bidden to tell you, that you will get better; God has a great work for you yet to do, and I think you will travel some thousands of miles yet." On her departure, our second preacher came in, and such was the weakness of my faith in the word of Him who had said, "Thou shalt see London, and declare my name there," that I requested the minister to attend my funeral;

gave him a portion of Scripture to preach from, and the hymns I wished to be sung on the occasion. Having promised compliance, if the event so required, he kneeled down and prayed the Lord to grant that I might yet be raised up, to stand forth in the name of God and declare His truth. While he was praying, I felt the evidence of the Holy Spirit, witnessing, that his prayer was heard, and that God had granted the request of his lips. From that very hour I began to amend; and some time after, Miss Coffin came in and asked how I was, saying, that she had requested a lady with whom she was acquainted, a Quakeress, to make special prayer to the Lord for me; for said she, "We cannot have thee die." She further stated that the friendly Quakeress had waited upon God on my behalf, and had received this answer by the Holy Ghost: "She shall get better, and in this Island shall hereafter be her home." As far as my own mind was concerned, I had no anxiety either to live or die, knowing, that for me to live would be for Christ's service, but to die, my gain. I sometimes thought, I shall never see England: yet it was generally met by an internal whisper, "the mouth of the Lord hath spoken it." However after an illness of eight months' duration, my health was re-established, and I was again brought forth to the service of my heavenly master; and the kind friends would not consent for me to leave the island: my daughter also married and settled in it, thus verifying the prediction of the prophetess, that my home should hereafter be on this delightful spot.[83] The Lord thus established my goings here; and, as my strength increased, so also did my labours. I had a numerous class to lead, and much employment in the ministry also. There were two chapels in the occupation of the society;[84] in the one, situated in the upper part of the town, I statedly preached on the Lord's-day afternoon; and, in the evening, I assisted our beloved minister in the large chapel, where we enjoyed a little heaven below. Numerous souls were awakened and converted to God; and inquiry after the way of life and salvation was prevalent in every part of the town. The work of God was our entire pursuit; and we knew nothing among the people, but Jesus Christ, and Him crucified. I was constantly going from house to house, both early and late; and thus I spent two happy years in the pleasant island of Nantucket, the Lord blessing both my going out and my coming in.

I afterwards took my daughter with me, and went into the land of our nativity to visit our brethren and see how they did: we came to the city of Philadelphia, had a joyful meeting with our brethren, and abode in that city for a little space: while there, I engaged to go to a small town at some distance, whither I had been once before; but my arrangements for this journey were twice frustrated; and on returning from my second disappointment I called upon a friend in Philadelphia, and remarked, that it appeared to be contrary to the mind of God for me to go thither: while thus talking, there appeared a young man standing before me, and although conscious that it was a supernatural appearance, I involuntarily exclaimed, "what is this?" The suggestion then took possession of my mind, that if I yet persisted in going thither, the Lord would there convert this young man by my ministry as a token that He had sent me. In a third attempt, I was more successful; and when I appeared in the congregation, I looked for him; but saw no young man whose person and apparel I could identify as the man whom I had seen in my vision: however, on the last evening of my stay there, after I had preached, the same young man, habited in the very apparel I had beheld in the vision, came forward and shook hands with me; testifying, that the Lord had sent me to awaken his soul, and separate him from his sins unto the Lord. He corresponded with me several years afterward, and gave evidence that he was standing fast in the faith, and progressing in the knowledge of God, and I was informed that he continually made mention of me in his prayers in the public congregations as well as in private. Having tarried some time with my friends in those parts, we returned back to New York; and having promised to accompany the brethren there to a camp-meeting in the neighbourhood, the time for holding which had not arrived, I left my daughter there, and proceeded on to Albany, which is distant about three hundred miles: the Lord graciously preparing the way by His providential operations. I preached in many chapels throughout that region; and the Methodists opened an extra house purposely for me; a very large and commodious building, but greatly insufficient to contain the masses who flocked thither to hear the word of God: the presence of the Lord accompanied my ministry, and rendered it the power of God to the salvation of many. When it was first announced that a female would preach in that chapel, a gentleman in the vicinity had a strong desire to come and hear me, and proposed for his lady to accompany him; but she objected, that it was unbecoming in a woman to preach; and also, that God never commissioned women to preach: he however, very much urged her, and at length he overcame her objections by persuasions; and they came, and the word was effectually sown in her heart with quickening power from God, her former sentiments became completely reverted; for, as she had never before experienced the searching and converting power of the word under a sermon, she was ready to imagine that none beside myself on earth had received the commission of God to preach the gospel; when she got home, she read of Christ sending the women to inform the disciples and Peter, that he was risen from the dead; she then reprobated the folly of her former objections; for said she, I now perceive that the first preachers of the resurrection were women: thus the Scriptures become as a new volume, when the Lord opens and illuminates the eyes of our mind. The Scriptures ever develop new and surprising truths to the regenerate soul; and in proportion to our measure of grace, and of the Spirit of God, is the illumination which accompanies our perusal of the Scriptures: that soul is not in the enjoyment of spiritual life, who reads the Scriptures without some perception of their unparalled glories, the divine lustre of which is so peculiar that the expositions furnished by the wisdom of this world, and all the elucidations of human learning, fail of any imitation of its radiance: it is the high privilege of those who are begotten by the Word of truth to read the Scriptures, not as the word of man, but as they are indeed, the Word of God, a sacred volume, the production of the infinite God; the true key of this heavenly book is the Spirit of truth; under whose guidance and illumination we ascertain and enter into the mind of God; therein beholding as in a mirror, the glory of Jesus, we become increasingly assimilated to the same image, from one degree of glory to another, as by the Spirit of the Lord.

While I was in this district, I had intelligence of my only surviving brother, and took a further journey of three hundred miles to Utica, to see him; I found him there, married and comfortably settled in life.[85] I had not seen him since his departure from our parental roof; at which time I was a child of six years of age. It was an affectingly joyful meeting to us both; and my gratitude to the Lord was heightened by finding in him a fellow-traveller to the kingdom of heaven, and a member of the Baptist church in Utica. I there met with Mrs. Jones, a female preacher, who had come from England, where it appeared her ministry had been popular, though it was otherwise with her in America. Being myself a member of the parent stock, or the old Methodist Society, I possessed an advantage over many other labourers, in having access to many pulpits which they had not. The dear brethren in Utica freely opened their chapels to me; and we enjoyed many very blessed opportunities of edification to our souls. In one of their large chapels in which I preached, a number of young men conspired together, and came to hear me, with their hands filled with stones; intending, if I uttered any sentiments which they disapproved of, to pelt me therewith: my brother had driven me to the place in a carriage and pair; the chapel was amazingly crowded, the presence of the Lord overshadowed the assembly, and the worship suffered no interruption from the young gentlemen, who came, not to be instructed in the way of truth, but to sit in judgment on and try my discourse by the standard of their petty opinions. After service, my brother went to fetch the horses from some stables adjacent, these tyros were standing there;[86] and he overheard their conversation, discovered their wicked plot and heard them confess that they knew not what ailed them when they entered the chapel; but their arms seemed bound and held down, and were so paralized that they dropped the stones upon the floor, and that their emotions were such during the service as they had never felt before. Having spent a very happy week with my brother, I was compelled to hasten back to New York to fulfil my engagement with the brethren there. On going to the water side to take my passage in the two o'clock steamer, the captain informed me that he had no room for another passenger; though my complexion appeared to be the chief reason of his refusal. I was therefore in a strait, for the performance of my engagement with the brethren in New York depended on my going that day; however, I learnt that there was another steamer about to start at seven in the evening; and on my application, the captain thereof agreed to take me with him. I therefore thanked God and took courage. We had a very pleasant passage, and many of the persons on board belonged to the household of faith; and what with edifying conversation, and the relation of each other's experience, we enjoyed a little Bethel. On the deck in the morning, I noticed several of the gentlemen engaged in very earnest conversation, and perceived that their discourse had reference to me; I therefore withdrew into the cabin, and had been there but a few minutes when one of them came and requested me to preach them a sermon on board. I replied that I felt no desire to preach by the will of man, and to gratify a human curiosity; he then assured me that the gentlemen who concurred in this request, were persons of integrity, whose aim was not novelty and curiosity, but edification. I then objected that the captain might not approve of such an attempt; he said he would ask permission of the captain and withdrew. The captain's consent being obtained, the crew came, and seated themselves in the cabin to the number of sixty. I then read a hymn, prayed, delivered a short address, concluded the service and took my seat. In a short time, I again perceived them in close conversation, and apparently talking about me, and I therefore withdrew; the same gentleman presently called me back, and said, "these gentlemen are greatly gratified by your discourse, and desire your acceptance of your passage money"; upon which he presented me with a sum which more than covered the expense of my passage. I was therefore astonished at the fresh display of the kind providence of my indulgent God; for I was then much straitened in pecuniary matters, and was three hundred miles distant from New York; they then informed me that five of their number were ministers of the gospel, and I saw how remarkably God had overruled matters to prevent my passage in the earliest vessel, to introduce me to so many Christian friends, and arrange for me so convenient a supply of money for my necessities. I arrived in New York safely; and after fulfilling my engagements with the brethren proceeded home to Nantucket, where we found all things well, and the brethren rejoiced at and welcomed our return. We arrived at home on a Saturday, having been a week on our journey from New York, at a very critical point of time. In the evening after our arrival, our dear minister, Mr. Pierce, called to see us, and requested my assistance on the approaching Lord's day. I therefore resumed my former labours in the congregations. On Tuesday, December 10, 1834, my daughter was safely delivered of her first-born son, and the blessing of the Lord very apparently rested upon the family.[87] Soon after this, our Baptist brethren being destitute of a minister, and the coloured people of that denomination having a chapel on the island, requested me to preach stately to them; which, with the consent of Mr. Pierce, I did,[88] and the Lord wrought marvellously among them; the holy fire was greatly diffused throughout the town; many of the coloured people were turned to the Lord, and I had the pleasure of seeing them at the sea-side immersed into Christ, they putting on the Lord Jesus in the ordinance of believing baptism. Our methodist class-meetings also were powerfully attended with the presence and operations of the Holy Spirit; and indeed a wonderful revival of the work of the Lord ensued, which extended to every part of the town, and to every denomination of Christians. On the meeting of the conference, our dear minister, Mr. Pierce, was removed from the island, and the Rev. J. Lovejoy was stationed there in his stead.[89] He manifested himself a faithful minister of the cross of Jesus, and I enjoyed with him the same intimate friendship and unity of faith, of purpose and effort as with Mr. Pierce. My daughter was some time afterwards attacked by a very serious illness, which continued upon her for a long time without any prospect of amendment; but one day, our minister called to see her, and prayed most fervently with her, and during prayer, the Lord vouchsafed a surprising manifestation to her soul, and from that very hour both she and the infant began to recover.

Having laboured for some time at home with very great success, my mind again began to be impressed with the weight of more distant spheres of labour, and my impressions seemed directed to the States of New Hampshire and Vermont. About this time it happened that I was from home a few weeks on a visit; and as I was sitting in the house of God, I was caught up in spirit, away from and far above all sublunary things; and appeared to be standing on a very elevated place in the midst of tens of thousands, who were all seated around, clothed in white; my own complexion and raiment were also white, and I was employed in addressing this immense concourse: it was such a scene as had never before entered into my conceptions; and presently it disappeared, and I found myself again in the chapel. I pondered this wonderful vision over in my mind, and concluded that it was given to me as a token that the Lord had destined me for enlarged and more elevated spheres of effort; and the Christian friends to whom I related it, also thought it a prelude to my future ministerial work. After this, I returned home, and in a few weeks afterwards, the same vision, but much nearer and more vivid than before, was presented before me in the chapel, as I was sitting under a sermon; and after a short interval it was presented to me a third time in the class meeting; but more vividly still. I related these visions to Mr. Lovejoy's mother, who concurred in my interpretation of them; adding that she thought it was my duty to go out again on an itinerating ministry: some time after this, the sisters of our society presented me with a quantity of apparel, with some money, which they had secretly prepared and subscribed; bidding me to go in the name of the Lord, and call sinners to repentance. Thus again was that Scripture verified to me, "Seek ye the kingdom of God and His righteousness, and all these things shall be added unto you."

I left home again in July, 1835; and was absent fifteen months: the Lord graciously prepared the minds of the people everywhere for my ministry; and many received the word with gladness and singleness of heart. I was in Boston when Mr. George Thompson was lecturing there on the abominations of slavery;[90] great crowds were attracted to his lectures, and much light was diffused by his zealous exertions in the cause of emancipation. From Boston I went to Lynn to attend the Conference. I was there introduced to Bishop Heading, and spent an afternoon in his company.[91] He requested a sight of my testimonials and letters of recommendation, which I handed him; and he expressed his entire satisfaction with them, but inquired if it should be found that my ministry was calculated to excite contention, many persons being strongly averse to the ministry of females, whether I would be willing to relinquish it. To which, I replied, that no ambition of mine, but the special appointment of God, had put me into the ministry; and, therefore, I had no option in the matter; and as to such Christians as take up ignorant and prejudiced objections against my labours; men whose whims are law, who walk after the imagination of their own hearts, and to whom the cause of God is a toy; I could not for a moment study their gratification at the sacrifice of duty. It is an easy matter to adopt a string of notions on religion, and make a great ado about them; but the weight of religious obligation, and the principle of conscientious obedience to God are quite another matter. I enjoyed the good bishop's company, and heard him with pleasure avow that he should be sorry in any way to discourage me.

From Lynn I itinerated from city to city, and from village to village, preaching the gospel of the kingdom in the fear of the Lord; and great was the number of those who believed and were baptised.

On my visit to Flushing, I preached from Isaiah xxxviii. 1, "Set thine house in order; for thou shalt die and not live." Under that sermon many persons were awakened, and among the number was one poor woman who cried to the Lord for mercy, and applied for admission into the church; but her application was rejected, because she was then cohabiting with a man by whom she had borne five children, yet had neglected to comply with the matrimonial form required by the law of the state. Whether her position was that of mere concubinage or marriage de facto; and whether the brethren were in their decision equally justified by Scripture as by the law of the state and the sense of society, are points which may admit of much discussion: the marriage customs and laws set forth by God in the

Scriptures, are so widely opposite from those of civilized nations in modern times, that when such cases arise, and the sacred and secular authorities clash upon them, it is not easy to determine what course ought to be pursued by a Christian communion. Happily, however, these parties immediately complied with the requirement of the American marriage law, the usage of society, and the dictum of the church; upon which they were admitted into the Methodist connexion, lived happily in the Lord, and became respected as good members of society.

On leaving Flushing, I took a long and circuitous route, and after an absence of fifteen months, returned home with great peace of mind.

I remained at home this time for the space of three years, with the exception of an occasional short journey, and visit of a few weeks; and throughout this period, my mind was often burdened with the weight of a voyage to England. I often argued the matter before the Lord in prayer, pleading my ignorance, my sex, my colour and my inability to minister the gospel in a country so polished and enlightened, so furnished with Bibles, so blessed with ministers, so studded with temples; but the Lord said, "say not, I cannot speak; for thou shalt go to all to whom I send thee, and what I command thee, thou shalt speak."

In 1837, when on a visit to some religious friends, one morning, I saw a remarkable vision; I appeared to be in a strange place, and conversing with a stranger, when three enormous balls of fire came perpendicularly over my head, and each of them exploded and burst at the same moment: I instantly appeared to fall to the ground; but was caught up by an unseen hand, and placed upon an animal, which darted with me through the regions of the air, with the velocity of lightning, and deposited me inside the window of an upper chamber. I there heard the voice of the Almighty, saying, "I have a message for her to go with upon the high seas, and she will go." This occurrence took place just three years prior to my departure from America.

In 1839, the Lord was pleased to send me again into the Southern states; and as I travelled from city to city, I felt the impression that the time was near when I must leave the land of my nativity for a foreign shore. In the town of Providence, Rhode Island, I preached on a Thursday evening in a large Room, for Mr. Bedell. On the following Lord's-day, I attended the Wesleyan Chapel, where I heard Mr. Bedell in the morning, and, by his invitation, occupied his pulpit in the afternoon, on which occasion the chapel proved much too small for the crowds which assembled: after the service, some leading gentlemen from another denomination came to Mr. Bedell, and offered him the use of their chapel, which was much larger than his, for the evening service. It was thankfully accepted, and I preached there in the evening, to an immense audience. Mr. Bedell and his lady were both of them natives of England; at that time he was stationed in the

Providence circuit. I had not been in their company a quarter of an hour when both of them avowed their concurrent impression, that I was destined by the Lord to minister the gospel in a foreign land: such an observation appeared to me very remarkable. From Providence I visited New York, Philadelphia and Baltimore; and wherever I went, the inquiry was continually made, if I was not about shortly to embark for England, accompanied by observations that my ministry was ultimately destined for a different arena than was furnished by America. I went on to the city of Washington, and our meetings there were greatly distinguished by the presence and operations of the Holy Spirit. Lady Hunter, of whom mention is made in my former visit to that city thirteen years before, presented me with a contribution in aid of this purpose; and I could not but remark, how the Lord everywhere moved the minds of my friends to make it a topic of conversation; thereby keeping it always before me, and increasing the stimulus of my mind towards it; and without any solicitation of mine, they presented me their cheerful contributions; yea, both white and coloured brethren, voluntarily came forward with their free-will offerings, to enable me to undertake the voyage, and bade me go and preach to strangers in a strange land, in the name of the Lord. Many were the proofs besides those related in this work, that the Lord gave me of His purpose that I should come to England; and being now many hundreds of miles distant from my daughter, and feeling that the Lord's time had arrived, I wrote to apprise her thereof, and shortly after returned homewards as far as New York, where I attended the anniversary of the abolition society:[92] many of the speakers on that occasion came over to England to attend the great anti-slavery meeting in Exeter Hall.[93] I then returned home; and was very affectionately received by my dear daughter; and made all possible dispatch in preparations for my departure.

The parting moment was painful in the extreme; for my daughter, and her two dear little boys, were entwined in the strongest affections of my heart; but I durst not disobey Him who had said unto me, as he had said unto Abraham, "Get thee out from thy country, and from thy kindred, and from thy father's house, unto a land that I will show thee."[94] On the 10th of June 1840, I rose from the bed on which I had laid for the last time; the recollection of that bitter morning even now suffuses my eyes with tears, and interrupts the delineations of my pen: the morning was calm, our minds resigned and peaceful, and we took, and held each others hand, in silence; which was at length broken by my daughter, who said, "Mother, we part now, but I think we shall yet meet again; the will of the Lord be done, and God be with thee." At nine o'clock, A.M., I bade farewell to those dear ties, and started for New York, where I tarried until the 1st July; and then I took the steam-boat to go to the ship Philadelphia, Captain Morgan, which vessel was lying in quarantine. Soon after our arrival on board, she got under weigh, and set sail for the port of London. My feelings on leaving the land of my nativity, and all that was dear to me on earth, were acutely indescribable; but God commanded, and I obeyed; bidding farewell to my country, and, committing my dear friends to the grace of God. The wind was fair, the passengers agreeable, and we were soon carried beyond the view of land. On the following morning, I awoke and presented my thanksgivings to my heavenly Father for His preserving care of me throughout the night. I then went upon deck, and surveyed the broad canopy above, and the rolling ocean beneath, gently moving wave after wave, as we glided over its tremulous surface. I observed the birds of the air flying over our heads, and wondered, at such a distance from land, that they were able to take such excursions without resting. I beheld the finny tribes pouring forth by thousands. I was now floating on the great and wide sea, wherein are things creeping innumerable, both small and great beasts. There go the ships! there is that great leviathan whom thou hast made to play therein. These wait all upon thee, that thou mayest give them their meat in due season. Oh Lord, how manifold are thy works! in wisdom hast thou made them all! the earth is full of thy riches. Psalm civ. 24, 27.

On the 23rd day of July, we were cheered with the sight of land; and on the 24th, we came to anchor off Falmouth, where most of the cabin passengers left us. On the evening of the 25th, we came safely into the London Docks: this was on a Saturday; and on the morning of the Lord's-day, I first set my foot on British ground. As I proceeded along Ratcliff Highway, I was much surprised to see the shops open, and many kinds of business in the course of transaction, women crying fruits for sale, and the people intent on traffic and marketing. I was indeed astonished, that in the metropolis of the most Christian country in the world, such a want of respect should be indicated towards the day which Jesus signalised by His resurrection, and His apostles practically set apart for the commemoration of His eucharistic sacrament, and the ordinances of His religion. Whether the literal and exact requirements of the fourth commandment be, in the case of Christians, transferred from the Jewish Sabbath to the "Lord's-day," is a point upon which all the disciples of Christ are not agreed; but if Christians are not bound to observe an absolute quietude and rest thereon, they certainly are bound to pay it that respect which is due to the day on which our redemption was assured by the Lord's resurrection—a day which was made sacred by the practice of His apostles, and by their inspired authority, called the "Lord's-day." Having taken apartments in Wellclose-square [appendix B, fig. 8], in the evening I attended at the Countess of Huntingdon's chapel, in Pell-street,[95] and heard a discourse which afforded some encouragement to the heart of a female stranger in a foreign land. Some days elapsed ere I met with any of the Methodist family; but, going on the Wednesday evening again to Pell-street chapel, as I was passing a window, I caught sight of a lady, whose appearance powerfully arrested my attention; and it appeared that the feeling of surprise and interest was mutual. I turned back, and spoke to her, and inquired if she was acquainted with any section of the Methodist body? She said that her daughter should on the following evening conduct me to the Wesleyan chapel of St. George, which she did accordingly; and I found that several class meetings were held on that evening; on that occasion, I met with Mr. A——[,] who introduced me to Mr. C——[,]one of the local preachers; and I was admitted into the class led by him, and enjoyed a very sweet time of refreshing from the presence of the Lord. I became acquainted also with Mrs. T.——[,]a true sister in the Lord, who has since fallen asleep in Jesus: and was introduced to a gentleman who interested himself greatly on my behalf very considerably enlarged the circle of my acquaintance, and even ushered me before the committees of the peace and anti-slavery societies.[96] I found my situation rather awkward in reference to the latter body. I was first received by a deputation of three gentlemen, and afterwards admitted before the board. It was really an august assembly; their dignity appeared so redundant, that they scarcely knew what to do with it all. Had I attended there on a matter of life and death, I think I could scarcely have been more closely inter-rogated or more rigidly examined; from the reception I met with, my impression was, that they imagined I wanted some pecuniary or other help from them; for they treated me as the proud do the needy. In this, however, they were mistaken. Among many other questions, they demanded to be informed, whether I had any new doctrine to advance, that the English Christians are not in possession of? To which I replied, no; but I was sent to preach Christ, and Him crucified: unto the Jews a stumbling-block, and unto the Greeks foolishness:[97] they also wished to be informed, how it came about that God should send me? to which I replied, that I could not tell; but I knew that God required me to come hither, and that I came in obedience to His sovereign will; but that the Almighty's design therein was best known to Himself; but behold! said I, "I am here." Pride and arrogancy are among the master sins of rational beings; an high look, a stately bearing, and a proud heart, are abominations in the sight of God, and insure a woeful reverse in a future life. Infidels will indulge in pomposity and arrogance; but Christians are and must be humble and lowly. As a servant of Jesus, I am required to bear testimony in his name, who was meek and lowly, against the lofty looks of man, and the assump-tions of such lordly authority and self-importance. Ere this work meets the eye of the public, I shall have sojourned in England five years: and I am justified in saying, that my God hath made my ministry a blessing to hundreds of persons; and many who were living in sin and darkness before they saw my coloured face, have risen up to praise the Lord, for having sent me to preach His Gospel on the shores of Britain; numbers who had been reared to maturity, and were resident in localities plentifully furnished with places of worship and ministers of the gospel, and had scarcely heard a sermon in their lives, were attracted to hear the coloured female preacher, were inclosed in the gospel net, and are now walking in the commandments and ordinances of the Lord. I have travelled in several parts of England, and I thank God He has given me some spiritual children in every place wherein I have laboured.

Soon after my arrival, I met with a gentleman, who advised my immediate return to my own country; adding that if he had been in America before my departure and had known my intention, he would have advised me better: I replied, that I had no will of my own in the matter; but my heavenly Father commanded, and I durst not confer with flesh and blood, but obeyed and came: but like other men destitute of faith in God, he did not comprehend this kind of argument; and persisted in his worldly reasonings, saying that people did not give away their gold here, and I had much better return. It is to be deplored that there are so many Christians of this person's cast: who are of the world; speak in accordance with its principles and sentiments, and walk according to its course. Instead of having little faith, they discover none at all: ignorant of the Scriptures and of the power of God, the love of the Father is not in them. Having parted with this Laodicean gentleman, I called upon Mrs. H., in Princes-square: and my mind being somewhat damped, I sat a few minutes in silence, which Mrs. H. broke by an affectionate inquiry into my circumstances; at the same time, presenting me with a handsome donation; telling me not to be discouraged, for the Lord, would open my way and sustain me: my mind was cheered and my faith strengthened by this opportune proof of the power of God to furnish succours and raise up friends for His people even in a land of strangers.

In a few days after, Mrs. T. introduced me to some of the Bible Christians, or Bryanites, as they are called; who are, I believe, a secession from the Wesleyan Methodists; our reception from them was very cool; but one of the brethren was about to preach in the street; and he invited me to preach in his stead. Accordingly at the time appointed, we repaired to the street and commenced the meeting; a very great crowd assembled, and I preached to them; but the meeting was broken up by two policemen, who came and tapped me on the shoulder, and desired me to desist; they demanded what authority I had for preaching? A gentleman present said, "she has her authority in her hand," that is, "the Word of God:" we then departed.

On the following Lord's-day morning, I attended with Mrs. T., at Salem chapel; and, in the afternoon, I preached in Stepney-fields, to a very numerous auditory. A very heavy thunder shower fell during the service, yet very few persons retired in consequence of it. When the service was terminated, a gentleman and lady came, and inquired of me where I resided? and desired me to call and visit them; which, in the course of a few days, I did, and was very affectionately received: the lady, Mrs. T. then invited me to spend a day with them, to which I consented, and enjoyed a heavenly day in their company. She then engaged me to spend a week with them; I did so, and a delightful week it was. The house was a little Bethel to us, and in the stated morning and evening worship of the family, the Lord manifested Himself in very rich displays of grace. Before my week expired, Mrs. T. sent to my apartments for my trunk, and bade me account her house my home during my sojourn in England. Their second daughter, who has since fallen asleep in Jesus, a most interesting and excellent young lady, was then greatly afflicted with a disease of the heart: our communion in the Spirit was exceedingly choice and precious; I richly enjoyed and highly prized her society.

I visited a number of small chapels in this vast metropolis, and endeavoured to advance my heavenly Father's cause by attending many religious tea meetings; some of which I found very edifying and profitable to the soul. I also partook of a breakfast with a number of ministers and friends at Mr. B. T—rs., by his special invitation;[98] and after this, I was sent for to Ramsgate, and travelled through the county of Kent, preaching the word in many of the towns and villages as I passed through them. When in Canterbury, my mind was much struck with the mutations of time upon the works of man. I beheld there some stately edifices which were venerable with age; I ascended the eminence of the Dane John, from which I had a full view of the town; the spot where some of the martyrs of Jesus sealed the truth with their blood, was pointed out to me; and as I gazed upon the memorable place, I thought of those faithful servants of God with much sympathy and yearning of heart.

Having received an invitation from some of the Primitive Methodists in Yorkshire, to go down and labour among them, I went thither by railway, and reached Pontefract about eight o'clock on the evening of the 30th of December, 1840; the distance was great, being about 170 miles; and I was very much fatigued with the journey. The hireling will make the best bargain he can; but they who bear the commissions of Jesus will find no sinecures involved in them, but frequently hard labour and harder fare. On my arrival, I was very kindly received by Mrs. Clift; and after a good night's repose, I was on the next morning much invigorated. On the following day, December 31, Mr. Colson the superintendent minister, and Mr. Crompton his assistant, called to see me, and explained the objects they had in view in sending for me.[99] In the evening we attended a tea meeting of the Sunday School; on which occasion the children sang some beautiful anthems, and repeated some pieces with much correctness; the meeting was afterwards addressed by some of the brethren, and also by myself. At the conclusion of the meeting, we observed a watch night, as is customary with the Methodist societies, which was attended with much of the presence of God, the gracious manifestation of His Spirit, and with spiritual benefit to the souls of many. The weather was very inclement and rigorous; and an abundance of labour was presented before me, which I entered into with much delight and vigour, though with considerable weariness and distress to the body.

> "My shrinking flesh complains,
> And murmurs to contend so long;
> My mind superior is to pains:
> When I am weak, then am I strong."

On the 3rd of January, 1841, I went to Brotherton, and preached in the chapel belonging to the brethren; it was completely crowded, and the Lord was in the midst of us to bless His people with the manifestations of His grace and love. After service, I returned the same evening to Pontefract, very much exhausted with fatigue. On the following day Mr. T—— came to conduct me to Thorp, where I preach in the evening, from "Enter ye at the strait gate," Matt. vii. 13, with considerable energy of spirit; but, throughout my labours in England, I have found a far less favourable soil for the seed of the kingdom in the British mind than in the American.[100] Human nature must be in every country radically the same; God is the same; yet the word preached is generally attended in America with far more powerful and converting results than in Britain. The population of the United States have not been so extensively vitiated by the infidelity and sedition of the press; and being more thinly spread over an immense territorial space, there is less of contamination than in the more condensed masses of English society; and they perhaps possess more honest simplicity of character, and less of the self-sufficiency of a licentious intellectuality and worldly wisdom. It is not for me, however, to account for the cause; the fact is but too apparent. I had many seals to my ministry in Yorkshire,[101] notwithstanding the general barrenness of the mental soil; and found, in many of its towns, and especially in Leeds, a very loving, lively and benevolent Christian people; not only in the Methodist, but in other denominations also; and amongst the society of Friends. I attended one of the meetings of the Friends there, and whilst sitting among them, was moved by the Spirit to address them, and the dear friends received the message which came through the medium of their coloured sister with patience and delight.

I went to Leeds on the 4th of February; a place rendered memorable to the Methodist societies by the labours of Mrs. Fletcher, whose ministry the Lord so signally blest with the communications of His Spirit: the first place I preached at in

Leeds was a chapel in Leylands, which had been in the occupation of the late Anne Carr, who had recently departed this life in the faith of Jesus; the place was then in the occupation of her companion in labours, Miss Martha Williams,[102] and the Lord graciously gave me some seals to my ministry in that chapel. From thence, I went, on the 7th, to Mr. R——ds, and laboured with the Primitive Methodists on Quarry Hill. I attended several missionary meetings in their connexion, which were held in various circuits; taking up my abode chiefly at Miss P——s, and Mr. A——s; under the hospitable roof of the latter friend, I spent many weeks, in peace and happiness, blessed with abundance of blessings spiritual and temporal. I also preached in Stanningley, for the primitive brethren; and for the Wesleyans, in their chapel; on which occasion, a very remarkable solemnity pervaded the assembly; and the Lord was pleased to direct my utterance, and give it such a pointedness, as made it apparent that it was a message from Himself. While I abode in that town, I lodged at Mr. G. W——s, with whose lady I went, by invitation, to breakfast with the minister, Mr. H. who was stationed there; we enjoyed a sweet and refreshing season in the family devotions of the morning; and I felt a strong attachment in the Spirit to Mrs. H——, who, though young in life, was blessed with the possession of deep piety or devotion; and a very sweet unction of the Holy Ghost abode on her spirit. From Stanningley I departed to Pontefract; and, in a few days afterwards, received a letter from a brother at the former place, informing me that one of the brethren there, had died suddenly, on the day of my departure; but they sorrowed, at the loss of a dear brother on whose behalf they possessed a well grounded hope. Among others of the towns I visited in Yorkshire, was Bradford. I also preached an anniversary sermon at Shelf; being, while I sojourned there, the guest of Mr. B——y.[103] On my return to Leeds, I met with a gentleman from Hull, who came to conduct me to that place. I accordingly went thither; and abode a few days, preaching in different parts of the town. On one evening there were ten persons who professed to find peace with God through our Lord Jesus Christ. On another occasion a female who had left her first love, and lost the vitality as well as the name of spiritual life, was recovered from her lapsed condition and obtained peace to her soul. On my departure I engaged to come to them again, and preach to them on the opening of their new chapel; and this poor woman had desired to open her mind to me, and relate what great things God had done for her by my ministry; but ere that day came, her spirit had taken flight from this region of sin and grief; but she left a message for me on her death-bed, to assure me that she died in the faith of Christ, confiding in the God of her salvation.

From Hull I returned to Leeds; and, during my temporary abode there, the church sustained a loss in the sudden death of our dear brother, William Dawson, who had been a zealous champion in the work of the Lord.[104] Several thousands of persons were congregated together on the day of his interment, to witness the procession, and manifest their respect to the memory of our departed brother. The corpse was brought out into the open air, and one of the ministers offered prayer to God; after which, Mr. Garland delivered an address, the local preachers and leaders then formed in order of procession, six abreast in the front of the hearse, and the cavalcade solemnly proceeded to the place of interment, which was several miles distant from Leeds; the whole distance being thronged by multitudes who anxiously witnessed the scene. From Leeds I took a tour of that part of the country, travelling from town to town, and village to village, preaching the gospel of the kingdom, and testifying to thousands of persons, repentance towards God, and faith in our Lord Jesus Christ. At the appointed time, I fulfilled my engagement at Hull, leaving on the 3rd of July; and on the day following, I preached at Brewery Fields, and had the pleasure to witness the conversion of four souls from darkness to light: at Keithly, I met with a gentleman and his wife, who were from Liverpool on a visit, and who gave me a very pressing invitation to come over to Liverpool and see them, which I promised to do. I preached on an anniversary occasion at Leylands, when seven souls entered into the liberty of the gospel. On the 23rd, I went to Wirksworth, accompanied by sister W——ms, and we were kindly received by Mr. S. E. and the friends there; I preached on the afternoon and evening of the day following in the chapel; when four persons received very manifest spiritual benefit. I also preached in the Wesleyan chapel in that town, and much enjoyed the interviews with its minister with which I was privileged.

Having written to the family in Liverpool who had so pressingly invited me to visit them, to apprise them of my coming, on the 2nd of August, I took leave of sister W. and the kind friends at Wirksworth, and travelled thither by way of Manchester, and arrived in Liverpool about six o'clock in the evening. On going to the residence of the parties who had invited me, I found that the lady and her daughter were absent from home; and the gentleman's memory was so reluctant, that he very distantly recognised me. I was greatly fatigued with my journey, and somewhat disappointed after such a journey, to find my reception so different from the invitation. I soon took my leave of one whom I found not at all careful to entertain strangers, or practice the Christian duty of hospitality, and went in search of lodgings, which I had great difficulty in procuring: but after wandering from place to place, and making many fruitless applications, I at length succeeded. It was of the Lord's goodness that I was at that inauspicious time possessed of sufficient money for my exigencies. My visit to this town was replete with discouragements. I attended several meetings of the association, who were holding their annual conference there at that time. I also made inquiries for the Wesleyans, and attended at Brunswick Chapel; and afterwards called upon the Rev. Mr. H.,

who received me with kindness, and referred me to Mr. D.[,] the Wesleyan superintendent minister at that station. On my visit to Mr. D., he left directly on my
introduction, to attend a funeral; but Mrs. D. entered into conversation with
me, and assuming the theologian, reprobated female preaching as unscriptural;
adding, that Mr. D. was greatly opposed to it, and always put it down if possible:
she further said, that Paul ordained that a woman should not be suffered to speak
in the church: but to sit in silence, and ask information of her husband at home. I
was, however, too blind to discern, that for a female to warn sinners to flee from
the wrath to come; to preach Christ to them, invite them to come to Him, and
exhort them to be saved, was equally disorderly and improper with the inter-
ruptions of a church in its meetings and services, by the inquisitive questions of
the females present; nor could I possibly understand how my ministry, which is
directed to bring sinners to repentance, and employed in humble and affectionate attempts to stir up the pure minds of the saints, by way of remembrance and
exhortation, involved any dictation or assumption of authority over the male sex.
The apostle directed that a woman, when praying or prophecying, should have her
head covered; from which it may be inferred, that the praying and prophecying
of a woman is allowable; but Mrs. D. was differently minded, and thought that a
preaching female ought to depart from the Methodist body, and unite with the
Quakers; but the Lord, who raised up Deborah to be a prophetess, and to judge
His people, and inspired Hulda to deliver the counsels of God, sent me forth not
as a Quakeress but as a Methodist, and chiefly employed me to labour amongst
the Methodists.[105] I mentioned to her, some of the methods, by which the Lord
made known to me His will, that I should go and preach the gospel; and these she
met, by supposing, that it was possible I might have been misled. By this time,
Mr. D. returned, and his Christian charity seemed put to some little expense on
finding that I had not decamped; I presented him my testimonials and certificates;
as he returned them, he said, "But do you not know that we do not allow women
to preach; and that there is nothing in the Scriptures that will allow of it at all?"
Addressing me with much assumed authority and severity. "We do not allow,"
sounded very uncouthly in my ears in a matter in which the commission of the
Almighty is assumed. I again related some of the manifestations made to me by
the Holy Ghost in reference to this matter; to which he replied, that he could not
see how God could, consistently with Himself, give me such directions. Doubtless
he said the truth; for the line of worldly wisdom, self-sufficient reason and opin-
ionated faith, can never gauge the operations of the Spirit of God; and always
either rejects them at once, or meets them with, "How can these things be?" He
then complimented me by adducing some instances, in which female preachers
had misconducted themselves; and wound up his vituperations by saying, that

the success of my labours in the ministry proved nothing in my favour; for that God would ever bless His word by whomsoever preached. Perhaps, had I taken upon myself to have investigated this gentleman's call to the ministry, I might have written Tekel upon it, for his spiritual condition falls far short of the standard I have received: but Paul says, "Who art thou that judgeth another man's servant; to his own master he standeth or falleth," and, "Why dost thou judge thy brother." [106] I then departed from this iron-hearted abode, somewhat distressed and wounded in spirit and at a loss what step I should take next.

But thanks be unto God; He knoweth how to deliver the godly out of temptations, and will not suffer us to be tempted above what we are able to bear. On the following morning I awoke, with these words passing through my mind,

> "Angels are now hovering round us;
> Unperceived, they mix the throng;
> Wondering at the love which crowned us;
> Glad to join the holy song.
>   Hallelujah!
> Love and praise to Christ belong."

I then felt the assurance of the Holy Spirit that the dark cloud which had so thickly and heavily pressed upon me was breaking; and a way soon after opened for me to visit Manchester, which in a few days after I did; and took lodgings on Chetham-hill, of Mrs. H—— who conducted me to Mr. R——'s, a local preacher, at whose house I was invited to spend the day: in the evening the class met there, and I assisted to lead it; the people were in a healthy, spiritual condition; and we enjoyed a sweet fellowship of the Spirit and communion with each other. On the 28th, I preached in Stanly Street; and on the 31st, in the association chapel in Stork Street, to a numerous audience. In a few days afterwards, I was sent for to visit a lady who was in great distress of mind. On entering the apartment where she was sitting, I shall never forget the expression of despair which sat on her countenance: she informed me that on the previous Lord's day, she came in the afternoon from motives of curiosity to hear me, and that the discourse had cut her to the heart, and portrayed her character as one self-destroyed by suicidal sin: the Bible was lying by her side; I took it up, opened at, and read from Isaiah lxi. 1–3, "The Spirit of the Lord God is upon me, because the Lord hath anointed me to preach good tidings unto the meek; he hath sent me to bind up the broken hearted, to proclaim liberty to the captives, and the opening of the prison unto them that are bound: to proclaim the acceptable year of the Lord, and the day of vengeance of our God; to comfort all that mourn; to appoint unto them that mourn in Zion; to give unto them beauty for ashes, the oil of joy for mourning, the garments of praise for the spirit of heaviness, &c." She then broke out in rapturous exclamations, praising God for sending me as a messenger of salvation to her; declaring herself filled with joy, and wondering at the change which had taken place within her soul; she confessed her unworthiness to receive such unexampled mercy and grace; having gone to hear me as she acknowledged, without any thought of good, but of mere curiosity; and she glorified God in me. This dear lady was one of many of the earliest seals to my ministry in Manchester. On one occasion, I accompanied my friend, Mrs. H——, to visit a family of her acquaintance; they made no pretensions whatever to religion; but our visit proved a blessing indeed to them: several of their neighbours were present; and among them, a private in the police force and his wife; and, as I inquired of their prospect, relative to a future state of existence, his wife informed me that he had been a religious man, but had fallen from grace; and with much earnestness intreated me to discourse with him in particular. I did so; and the Lord gave me a message to him, which went to his heart; he burst into tears; lamented that his calling was of such a description, that the class of persons to whom he belonged were regarded as the offscouring of the human race, and that few cared for their souls; adding, that the hardships of their situation were peculiarly distressing; and expressed great gratitude to God and acknowledgments to me for the sympathy I had evinced for him. We then bowed down before the Lord in fervent prayer, and all present were greatly moved, and deeply affected. A great door and effectual was opened to me of the Lord, in Manchester; and many there became the crown of my rejoicing in Christ Jesus. I again became fully occupied in the service of my heavenly Master, going from chapel to chapel, and from town to town.

I preached one day at the house of Mr. W——, under the bank, from Luke xiii. 7. "Cut it down; why cumbereth it the ground." Many persons were deeply affected under that sermon; and among them, one poor man who came in a few days afterwards to Mrs. W——, and asked permission to meet in the class, stating that he had been wholly deprived of sleep ever since he heard that sermon. On the class-night, I preached a short discourse, which was followed by a prayer-meeting, and this man and four others experienced the pardoning love of God.

On the 15th of September I went by appointment to preach at the house of Mr. L. under the Bank; and just before the meeting commenced, the powers of darkness suddenly assailed my spirit, and so burdened and obscured me, that in a short time I had no light or spirit within me; and I commenced the service with a weight upon my mind as if all the people were hanging upon me. A hungry people exhausts a spiritual ministry, a carnal people paralyses it, an unbelieving people drags it down, a rebellious and resisting people grieves it, an erroneous people inflames it—the cause of my darkness, however, was not in the people; nor was I able to ascertain the reason, which has hitherto been hidden from me. In my first prayer the cloud was dispelled, and I proceeded with my work in the light of the Lord; but as I returned home to my lodging, the darkness returned upon my soul. In the morning the Lord smiled upon my soul again: and I arose with a light and cheerful heart, rejoicing in God with joy unspeakable and full of glory.

On the 23rd of October, I preached in the afternoon and evening to numerous audiences at Hayfield, with much freedom; and the people were very attentive and much edified.

On the 27th, Mr. Ellery, the superintendent of the Tonnon Street circuit, with his wife, called and took me home with them; I preached for him in the evening; and seven persons were under that sermon brought into the liberty of the children of God. On the 1st of November, I attended a Wesleyan Missionary meeting at Chetham; and enjoyed it as a time of refreshing from the Lord. On the 7th, I preached morning and afternoon at Tonnon Street Chapel; and preached a charity sermon in the evening, in Berry Street Chapel Salford. While in Manchester, I took an opportunity of going with several of the brethren and sisters to visit the deaf, dumb, and blind school,[107] where we witnessed the substitutes for tongues, ears and eyes in successful operation. Truly marvellous is the immense variety of resources, which the bountiful God of nature has placed within the reach of, and at the service of man.

On the 27th, I went to Glossop to preach three anniversary sermons; on my arrival in the town, Mr. H. came to the coach to meet me, conducted me to his house, and very kindly entertained me: the anniversary was a delightful day; and numbers found it good to be in attendance. I preached again on the following evening, and the place was excessively crowded: on the day after, I returned to Manchester. On the 5th of December I went to Stockport to preach some charity sermons; and the crowd was so great, that it was with great difficulty I reached the pulpit; many hundreds of persons were forced to retire who could not gain admittance. I preached again on the 8th, and spent a very happy week there in visiting the brethren and sisters, and returned again to Manchester. On the 10th, I went to Hollingsworth; on the Lord's day morning I led the class, and preached in the afternoon and evening in the chapel. On the Monday a great many of the friends brought their provisions together and spent the afternoon in singing, prayer and spiritual conversation: in the evening they all repaired to the chapel, and I preached again to a great congregation. Two gentlemen were present who were utter strangers to all the friends; and, as they placed themselves just before me, laughing and tapping each other, their design was apparently not the edification of their souls. I preached on that evening from Proverbs iii. 5, 6,[108] and, under the sermons, their laughter was checked, and they hung down their heads and strove to conceal their dejection. After service the congregation was detained some time by a very heavy shower of rain; and I sang one of the American hymns; many shed a profusion of tears: and these gentlemen seemed rivetted to the spot, and were the last to retire from the chapel. On the next day, I was about to return to Manchester; and on my way to the coach office, I called at Mr. H——'s, to bid him and his family farewell, when Mrs. H. exclaimed, "Oh! are you going? I am very much disappointed; for I wished you and some other friends to spend the afternoon with us, and I have been making preparations for it; and I was in hopes it would do me good: for I feel that I am a poor and a lost sinner; I am very much burdened"; her tears and sobs suppressed her further utterance; and I needed no further persuasive to stay that day at their house; and on that evening, she obtained peace with God through faith in our Lord Jesus Christ; and on the next Lord's day, she came forth and gave evidence of having become a new creature in Christ Jesus. On the 11th, I returned to Manchester, and removed my lodgings to St James' street; in the evening, I attended a tea meeting in Beetle-street, at which Mr. F. presided. On the 25th I went to Staleybridge, where I received a message from the friends at Hollingsworth, desiring me to attend a tea meeting there that evening. I accordingly went thither, and found Mrs. H. still rejoicing in the love of God: we had a very comfortable tea meeting. On the Lord's day I preached in the afternoon and evening at Staleybridge; and also on the Monday evening. On the 31th. Mrs. F——d. of Salford, the lady of the superintendent sent for me to come and spend the day with them; which I did, and it being the last of the year, at nine o'clock in the evening we went to the chapel to commence the watch meeting: several of us were speakers on the occasion, and it was a season of much solemnity and godly comfort. Thus we witnessed the expiration of the year, with thanksgivings for the divine kindness which had been vouchsafed to us therein; and hailed the new year with prayer for and earnests of sustaining grace and prospective mercies. I tarried in Manchester about nine months; visiting and preaching in very many towns and villages in its vicinity and within ten or twenty miles around it; the Lord being with me to direct and sustain my willing exertions in His holy cause. I preached about two hundred times during my continuance here; and ultimately by His direction, took my leave of the dear friends to see them no more in the flesh, till the trumpet of God shall sound the muster of the blood-bought congregation to the throne of Jesus.

On the 13th of June, 1843, I travelled by railway to Huddersfield; met with a very kind reception from Mr. S. Routledge; and, in the afternoon, Mrs. R. accompanied me on a visit to Mr. Keys, a class leader in the Wesleyan connexion.[109] I attended, and led his class in the evening, and enjoyed a happy season with the people. Several of Mr. R.'s work-people were members of his class; and they went and informed Mrs. R. that they had enjoyed a most blessed opportunity with me; the information sunk with great weight into her mind, for she was at the time in great concern about the salvation of her soul, and very much distressed on account of her sins. On my return to her house, she said to me, "I have earnestly endeavoured to find rest for my soul; but there is no rest for me, Mrs. Elaw." We then kneeled down before the Lord in prayer for her, and He removed her burden and manifested His comforts to her spirit through faith in Christ Jesus. On the 17th, I went to Shelf, and visited my kind friends, Mr. and Mrs. B. I assisted in the anniversary sermons of the Primitive Methodists, visited a number of the friends, led several of their classes, and preached also in the Wesleyan chapel, where we enjoyed a very rich manifestation of the presence of God, and a delightful opportunity to our souls. I staid, here a fortnight, passing the time very pleasantly in the family of Mr. B. I also visited frequently at Mr. G——y[']s; his wife is a very godly woman, whose adorning is not of the outward person, but of the hidden man of the heart, in that which is not corruptible; a meek and quiet spirit, which is in the sight of God of great price. This lady is one of the genuine daughters of Sarah; chaste in conversation, subdued in temper and reverent to her husband.[110] Oh, that many flighty, petulant, high-minded and insubordinate wives, who profess the religion of Jesus, would pay more attention to the duties of Christian wives, and like this pious lady, adorn the doctrine of God their Saviour. Little Miss G, a child of ten years of age, had already savingly experienced that the Lord is gracious, and rejoiced in the God of her salvation, she manifested as grave and steady a deportment, as might have been expected from the years of a Christian matron.

I returned to Huddersfield on the 11th of July, where I remained a few weeks; it is delightfully situated; being entirely surrounded with majestic hills, with several streams of water running through it, which conduces much to the prosperity of its manufacturing enterprise. There are in this town four places of worship belonging to the Episcopalians; two very large Wesleyan chapels, and two others occupied by the Primitive Methodists. The houses are neat, and chiefly built of stone; there are several bridges watering places and baths. It has a large market; and appears to be situated in a fruitful soil, abounding with fruit trees; the gardens are extensive and many of them tastefully laid out; and the approaches to it are by railway and good high roads. On the 29th, I again visited Hull, when I preached morning and evening to immense congregations; and afterwards we held a prayer-meeting; and the Lord blessed the word that day; many were comforted, and many others inquired "what must we do to be saved."

On the 2nd of August, I embarked on board a steamer for London: there were a great many passengers on board; several of whom were from very widely distant parts of the earth. Some of the passengers requested me to preach to them, and the captain having given permission, we ascended the poop, and there held our meeting, which many persons seemed much interested. One gentleman afterwards came and inquired my name, saying that he was about to write to his wife, and wished to give her an account of a meeting so interesting and so novel to the crew of a steam-ship. I arrived in London about six o'clock in the evening very much fatigued. On going to my friend's, Mr. T., I found Mrs. T. was absent from home. I lodged that night at Mrs. F——'s; and the day following, I went to my former lodgings in Princes-square. My mind was somewhat cast down by these matters; for, notwithstanding the extensive exercises my faith has experienced, I am often too much a mere creature of circumstances.

On the 7th I went to Great Queen-street chapel to hear Bishop Soul from America, and was very much fatigued with the length of the walk.[111] My mind was at this time very cloudy and dark; and I formed the resolution to call upon and have an interview with the Bishop; but as I began to get myself ready for the visit, I was seized with a fearful tremour and loss of strength. I sunk down upon a chair, and pondered within myself the reason of this visitation, and it occurred to me, that my design of going to the Bishop was taken without the permission of God being first obtained. I therefore abandoned this project, and the cloud on my spirit soon disappeared, and my peace was restored. Shortly afterwards, Mr. D——y came and engaged me to preach in Crosby Row chapel, Borough; Mr. G. engaged me to preach in his chapel, I also made an engagement to preach for Mr. P. and another to preach for Mr. O. in Whites-row chapel. I also preached in Timothy chapel, Ratcliff Highway, for Mr. B. and for many other ministers and congregations in other chapels, after fulfilling a host of engagements: and a variety of labour, I [received] an invitation from the north of England; and on the 27th of November I went on board a vessel for Berwick-upon-Tweed. We had a very boisterous passage; and, in the night, a gale of wind laid the vessel completely on her side. The passengers all concluded that we should soon be overwhelmed in a watery grave; but the Lord held our lives in His preserving care, and the vessel was got upright again. At eleven o'clock on the night of the 30th, we came to anchor in the port of Berwick. I went ashore, the same night, to Mr. J. R——'s, the superintendent, who very kindly received me; and thence retired to Mr. G——s. Many persons were converted to God under my ministry in this town; among the number of whom, was Miss A. G.; she had been to chapel with me, and, on our return, several of the preachers accompanied us; before we parted, we kneeled down in prayer together, and the Lord then and there gave her the knowledge of salvation by the remission of sins. The town of Berwick is one of great antiquity; the people pointed out the remains of an old castle, which is said to have priority over the Christian era; also, the ruins of an old abbey of remote antiquity. The streets of Berwick, I was informed, have been drenched with human blood. There are several places of worship in the town belonging to different denominations; and the pasture fields in the vicinity are very beautiful and green. There is also an elegant pier, which is a convenient promenade for the townspeople, and an extensive fishery. From this place, I went over to Holy Island, and preached to the fishermen, and enjoyed some very blessed meetings among them. This is a place of great antiquity, and was formerly inhabited by a great number of monks. On my return to Berwick, Mr. R. conducted me to Newcastle-upon-Tyne. I went from thence to Shields on the 25th of December, and reached there late in the evening; but my Heavenly Father had been there before me, and prepared the way. A comfortable home was provided, and generous open hearts to receive the stranger at Mrs. T——[']s. When I arrived at her house, I was not aware that it had been arranged for me to lodge there. I therefore sat waiting to go I knew not whither. Mrs. T. bade me take off my out-doors apparel, at which I inquired if I was to stay there? and she replied, "Yes, this, is your house as long as you stay in these parts; and we shall receive our reward in heaven." She then related how her mind had been exercised, until she came to the resolution to receive me under her roof. The Lord grant to this dear lady an hundred-fold more in this present time, and in the world to come, everlasting life. My labours here commenced on the 25th, in the new chapel. Mr. R. of Berwick, preached in the morning and evening, and myself in the afternoon: it was an auspicious commencement. On Monday, I attended a tea-meeting, which proved a very interesting time; and many excellent addresses were delivered by the speakers. After this, I went and preached at Newcastle, and returned again to South Shields. The sphere of effort was enlarged before me, and in labours I became more abundant. In heat and cold, through wet and dry weather, by night and day, I laboured in that part of God's vineyard, preaching the gospel of Christ incessantly, wherever opportunity was afforded me. One of the seals to my ministry here, was a descendant of Abraham, according to the flesh—a Jew outwardly, who, believing in the Lord with the heart unto righteousness, became a Jew inwardly also.

The success of my ministry, in Shields, was very gratifying; but here as in many other places, I endured a considerable share of persecution from the opponents of female preaching; some opposing my ministry of mere caprice, and others from mistaken convictions. Satan never fails to find a pretext by which to inspire his agents with opposition against that ministry which is of God. While in this neighbourhood, I was sent for to visit a young man confined to his bed with mortal disease: though favoured with Christian parents, it appeared that when in health, he had indulged in sentiments very inimical to revealed religion: subdued however by a sickness which exhausted his spirits and secluded him from the accustomed gaieties of life, he became susceptible of more serious impressions and of juster views. On my first visit to him, he was not only very weak in body, but very dark as to his perceptions of spiritual things. As I read the Scriptures, conversed with and opened to him the way of salvation, he was led to a discernment of the great atonement for sin in the cross of Jesus, and cried to the Lord for mercy: the Lord heard our united prayers, and spoke peace to his soul. He took refuge in the propitiation set forth by the Most High, became justified by faith, and believing, found peace with God through our Lord Jesus Christ. His surviving days were employed in the praises of Him who had called him out of darkness into His marvellous light; and he rejoiced in hope of the glory of God: the love of God was richly shed abroad in his heart by the Holy Ghost; and after languishing a few weeks more in the flesh, he found the rest which he sought; departing to be with Jesus, which is far better than a protracted abode among the ills of mortality.

On the 28th of January, 1843, I preached again at Newcastle, on the opening of a chapel that had been long closed: but was now taken by the Ebenezer society for the cause of the Lord: the meetings were well attended; and I had the pleasure of knowing that some persons were converted to God therein. I generally found Newcastle a very barren and rocky soil to work upon; for the wickedness of the people is very great; and the cry of it, like the cry of Sodom, must ere long reach unto heaven;[112] but nevertheless God hath a chosen remnant even there, whom He delights to bless; and I might enumerate many names here dear to me, whom I love for the truth's sake which dwelleth in them.

On the 8th of September, I went to Rainton Hall; and preached on the following Lord's day to a numerous congregation in Middle Rainton; the place was filled with the glory of the Lord, and the people with the Holy Ghost; the next day we had a delightful tea meeting.[113] On the 12th, I visited Colliery-road; passed the day at Mrs. L——[']s, took breakfast at Mr. R——[']s, and returned to preach at Rainton. Just before I went into the meeting, I was called in to see a sick woman, who related to me a remarkable vision which she had seen. On the 14th; I preached at Pittenton to a very large audience; and the meeting was attended with much power and spiritual assurance; after the service the friends presented me with a small sum of money for which I was thankful to my Heavenly Father. On the 15th, I went to New Lampton, and was cordially received by Mr J. H——n: on the 15th, I preached to a large assembly, and on the next Lord's day I preached again to a dense mass of people, and held a prayer meeting after preaching. On retiring from that meeting, I was filled with the love of God too full to conceal my emotion, and I seemed to hear a concert of angelic voices singing the hymns of God in the air over my head.

On the 19th, I went to Lumley, and preached in the new connexion chapel to a large and listening audience. It was a very solemn season; there being a very fatal distemper raging in the town at the time, which had prostrated many persons in death, and rendered their surviving relatives and friends so many bereaved mourners: the next day I returned to New Lampton, greatly exhausted by much travelling and preaching. On the 23rd, I went to Hettingly hole, and visited a young woman then dying, whose death occurred a few hours after. On the 24th, I preached in the Seceders Chapel to an immense throng of people; the vapours which arose from so compacted a concourse, as it condensed, ran down the walls in streams of water; and I caught a severe cold on this occasion. On the 27th, I preached there again to another multitude: the day following I spent the afternoon at Mr. W——s, whose daughter, a widow, was dying: we bowed the knee in prayer to God for her; and I received the assurance that our petitions were granted: she spoke not, but when I arose, she took my hand, and looked at me with an affectionately languishing smile. On the 30th, I went to Colliery row, being in very bad health. I preached three sermons there, and likewise held a love feast; and taking a last farewell of my dear friends, I returned on the 4th of October to New Lampton, and on the 5th, preached at Newbottle, in the Wesleyan chapel; the friends connected with which expressed themselves greatly edified, invited me to preach there again on the following Lord's day, and gave me a ticket for their tea meeting of Monday. One of the brethren engaged early to inform me by note on what part of the Lord's-day I should occupy their pulpit; however, I received no note from him, and therefore I went not. On the Monday, having a ticket for their tea meeting; I went with several of my friends; but could not obtain admittance; for the interval from Saturday was too great for their memories: they had all forgotten me; nor was there one who was able to recognise the preacher who had so delighted them the previous week, they had probably received a philippic from some petty Authority against female preachers, which had blotted me out altogether from their thought and feeling. On my return in the evening, I was attacked with a very severe fit of illness, which confined me to my bed for five months; but my Heavenly Father was graciously pleased to make my consolations abound throughout this period of affliction; that dear lady Elizabeth Gardiner, was unremitting in her kind attentions to me, and with great benevolence administered to my necessities. Mr. A. gave proof of the constancy of his kindness, and sustained the burden of my sickness without prospect or desire of remuneration; the kind friends loved not in word only, but in deed and in truth: my medical attendant also was very assiduous and kind.

I have felt much gratitude to the Lord for enkindling so great a friendship for me in the bosoms of many persons in England; many of my English acquaintance possess a large share of my affections; and an imperishable image in my memory; but I know by experience the heart of a stranger; many and deep and raging have been the billows of affliction which have rolled over my soul since I crossed the Atlantic Ocean. My reader may perceive that I have not been an idle spectator in my Heavenly Master's cause. During my sojourn in England, I have preached considerably more than a thousand sermons. I have expended all my means in travels of no little extent and duration; devoted my time, employed the energies of my spirit, spent my strength and exhausted my constitution in the cause of Jesus; and received of pecuniary supplies and temporal remunerations in comparison with my time and labours a mere pittance, altogether inadequate to shield me from a thousand privations, hardships, target-fires, vexatious anxieties and deep afflictions, to which my previous life was an utter stranger.

After an absence of six months, on my recovery, I returned to my kind friends in Shields, and the next day went to fulfil an engagement I had entered into when I was last there. As I proceeded to the place, I did not expect to return again alive, my exhaustion and debility was so extreme; but the Lord sustained me; and my strength was equal to my day. I preached four sermons in the space of three days, and returned more convalescent than I went. In a few months' time, I became fully occupied again in the work of the Lord, and continued my labours in Shields, Newcastle and Sunderland until the month of July, 1844, when I bade my kind friends a final farewell, to see them no more until we meet in the kingdom of God. My last address to the dear friends in Shields was attended with a great sensation among the people, and was a very affecting season. On the 31st of July I left Shields, embarking at seven o'clock that evening on board a steam vessel for London. On my arrival in the port of London, I was met at the water side by my very kind friends, Mr. and Mrs. B.T. My soul truly rejoiced to meet my dear brethren and sisters in Christ of this metropolis once more in this vale of tears; and the Lord soon made my way clear on this my third visit to this great city. I have enjoyed much of the divine life in my soul since I have been here; my first residence was in Solomon's terrace, Back Road, St. George in the East; but I was obliged to leave it on account of the intemperate habits of one of its inmates. Drunkenness is an awful vice, and though debasing to both sexes, seems yet more unbecoming in a woman; it is a prolific parent of crime, being the origin of a thousand other evils. The Most High has strikingly reprobated this sin, by attaching to it the capital punishment of banishment from the kingdom of heaven.[114] About the commencement of the present year, 1845, I removed to the residence of Mr. T. Dudley, 19, Charter-house-lane, where I enjoy a comfortable home.[115] I soon after visited Jewin-street chapel; and have cause for thanksgivings to God for directing me to that place of worship.[116] My first visit to this chapel was on the watch night of the evening of December 31, 1844: I also attended at another meeting, commonly known among the Wesleyans as a covenant meeting, the object of which is a renewed dedication of our entire selves to the kingdom, service and glory of Christ. In a few evenings afterwards I joined Mr. Self's class; he is an able and experienced leader; I much enjoy and highly prize his judicious Christian counsel as a class leader: and feel a great attachment to each member of the class; I think the friends are growing in grace, in the knowledge of the truth, and increasing with the increase of the life of God. I esteem class meetings as a most wise and benevolent provision for the spiritual necessities of the saints; they appear somewhat to resemble the ancient church meetings of the primitive Christians which were instituted by the apostles; and might easily be vested with yet closer approximation to them, and increased powers of edification: such meetings greatly tend to preserve the purity and transparency of the renewed heart; there the weary soul is invigorated, the doubting mind confirmed, the dismayed heart encouraged: the tempted are instructed, the heedless are admonished, and the lukewarm stimulated; the class-meeting is the place where the saints compare notes; and behold in each other's experience their own lineaments and image.

Let me exhort my dear Christian friends of every name and denomination, by no means to omit any possible attendance on the means of grace, which are intended for their growth in the divine life and image; that they may not only hold fast where to they have attained, but become filled with the life and power, and display the perfection of the Christian religion; being the children of the resurrection, the sons of God, and receive an abundant entrance into the everlasting kingdom of our Lord and Saviour Jesus Christ. Slumbering virgins, the Bridegroom cometh![117] Rouse timely to the midnight cry. I exhort all Christians, believing that there is but one church of Jesus Christ in this wilderness; and I trust she will soon come forth as the morning, leaning on her beloved, fair as the moon, clear as the sun, and terrible as a bannered army. May all who are of the household of faith stand fast in the liberty wherewith Christ has made them free. Dear brethren, the time is short, it is ominous, and it is perilous: be steadfast, unmoveable, always abounding in the work of the Lord. Be not carried about with every wind of doctrine; at the same time, reject not, nor fight against any statement of the Scriptures of truth, but with all confidence, aptitude and simplicity, as little children, receive and adopt all their inspired instructions. Mark, I beseech you, the signs of the times; they are awfully portentous: Christ's words are every where fulfilling, "Because iniquity shall abound the love of many shall wax cold. Perilous times are verging upon us: He has asked the question, when the Son of man cometh will He find faith on the earth?"[118] Alas, of outward profession there is abundance; but of true faith, a melancholy dearth. May we be prepared to answer this question for ourselves, by keeping our faith in continual exercise.

I have now furnished my readers with an outline of my religious experience, ministerial labours and travels, together with some of the attendant results, both on the continent of America and in England: these humble memoirs will doubtless continue to be read long after I shall have ceased from my earthly labours and existence. I submit them, dear Christian reader, to thy attentive consideration, and commend this little volume and each of its readers to the blessing of the adorable God, the Father, Son and Holy Spirit. Amen.

Finis.

W. & R. Woodcock, Printers, 20½, Warwick-lane, & Brunswick-st. Hackney-rd.

Appendix A

Rebecca Elaw Pierce Crawford

In the years after her mother left for England, Rebecca's life changed dramatically. She had a third son, David, in 1846, and her husband died sometime before 1849.[1] Left to raise her three boys alone, Rebecca earned a stellar reputation in the community as a good mother, working widow, and, later, minister's wife. As a testament to her Christian motherhood, the May 5, 1849, *Nantucket Inquirer* published an article entitled "A Case of Integrity" that chronicled the good Samaritan actions of her twelve-year-old son, Thomas, who later died of consumption at twenty-one.[2] The article reports that a businessman who regularly visited the island lost his "pocketbook containing 44 dollars and some papers," and young Thomas found and promptly returned the property. The writer used the incident to make the case for anti-racism, noting that "the honest widow received a satisfactory remuneration in money, in addition to the approval of a good conscience. It is gratifying to be able to record each instance of correct conduct in a race who have too often been looked upon with contempt."

Although their father had died, the Pierce boys would have had many male role models among their extended New Guinea family. One man, Rev. James Crawford, was a close neighbor in both proximity and relationship, as he and Rebecca later married. The Crawfords, a well-known Nantucket family, lived just a few doors away from the Pierces. James Crawford, who escaped enslavement in Virginia, moved from Rhode Island to Nantucket in 1848 with his wife, Ann, and daughter, Julia Ann. Ann Williams Crawford was originally from South Carolina and sister to Julia Williams Garnet and Diana Williams. In 1857 James Crawford and his brother-in-law, Henry Highland Garnet, worked together to raise money in Nantucket and England to purchase Diana and her daughter, Cornelia Read, who had been kidnapped and sold into slavery.[3] Crawford, passing as a white man, made two separate trips to Charleston, South Carolina, where Diana was sold, and to Wilmington, North Carolina, where her daughter, Cornelia, was sold. Crawford successfully brought them both to the Crawford homestead in Nantucket where he had established himself as a popular barber and preacher.

Most of the Nantucket community had contributed to the purchase fund, and they came together to mourn the death of Ann and, again, two years later, when her sister Diana, Crawford's second wife, died. It's not surprising that he and Rebecca, his widowed neighbor, would have grown close over the years, given her reputation as a stalwart Christian and community caregiver. James and Rebecca married in 1868 and enjoyed many years as a leading family in Nantucket. Always a valuable citizen, now a minister's wife, Rebecca Crawford lived the rest of her life as a good friend and leader in the community. Rebecca and James died in 1883 and 1888, respectively, and both are buried in the Crawford family plot in the African Burial Ground.

Appendix B

Images and Archival Materials

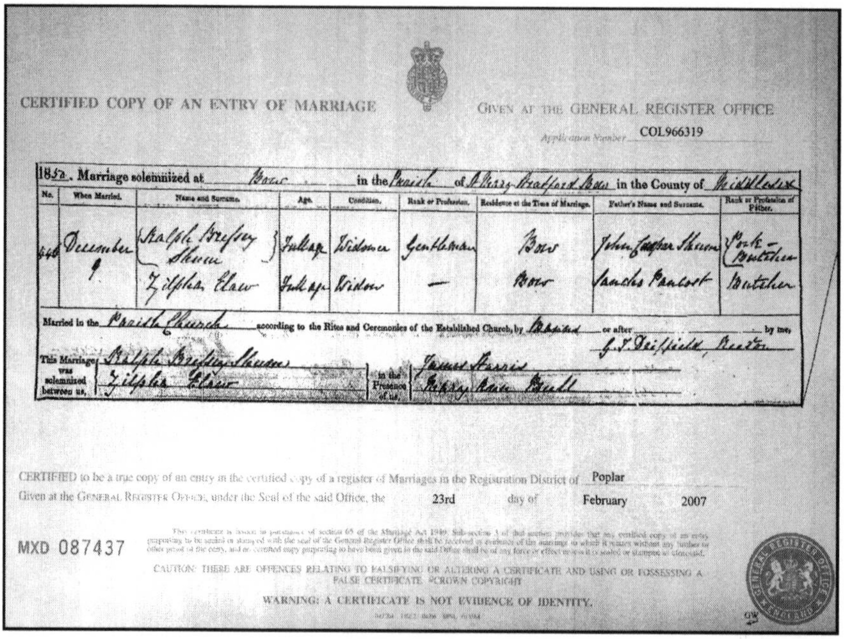

CERTIFIED COPY OF AN ENTRY OF MARRIAGE

GIVEN AT THE GENERAL REGISTER OFFICE

Application Number COL966319

1852. Marriage solemnized at Bow in the Parish of St Mary Stratford Bow in the County of Middlesex

No.	When Married.	Name and Surname.	Age.	Condition.	Rank or Profession.	Residence at the Time of Marriage.	Father's Name and Surname.	Rank or Profession of Father.
446	December 9	Ralph Bressey Shum	Full age	Widower	Gentleman	Bow	John Jasper Shum	Pork-butcher
		Zilpha Elaw	Full age	Widow	—	Bow	Sanchs Pancost	Butcher

Married in the Parish Church according to the Rites and Ceremonies of the Established Church, by Banns or after ______ by me, G. T. Driffield, Rector

This Marriage was solemnized between us, Ralph Bressey Shum, Zilpha Elaw

in the Presence of us, James Harris, Mary Ann Bull

CERTIFIED to be a true copy of an entry in the certified copy of a register of Marriages in the Registration District of Poplar

Given at the GENERAL REGISTER OFFICE, under the Seal of the said Office, the 23rd day of February 2007

MXD 087437

This certificate is issued in pursuance of section 65 of the Marriage Act 1949. Sub-section 3 of that section provides that any certified copy of an entry purporting to be sealed or stamped with the seal of the General Register Office shall be received as evidence of the marriage to which it relates without any further or other proof of the entry, and no certified copy purporting to have been given in the said Office shall be of any force or effect unless it is sealed or stamped as aforesaid.

CAUTION: THERE ARE OFFENCES RELATING TO FALSIFYING OR ALTERING A CERTIFICATE AND USING OR POSSESSING A FALSE CERTIFICATE. ©CROWN COPYRIGHT

WARNING: A CERTIFICATE IS NOT EVIDENCE OF IDENTITY.

Fig. 1. Marriage certificate for Ralph Shum and Zilpha Elaw. (General Register Office, England)

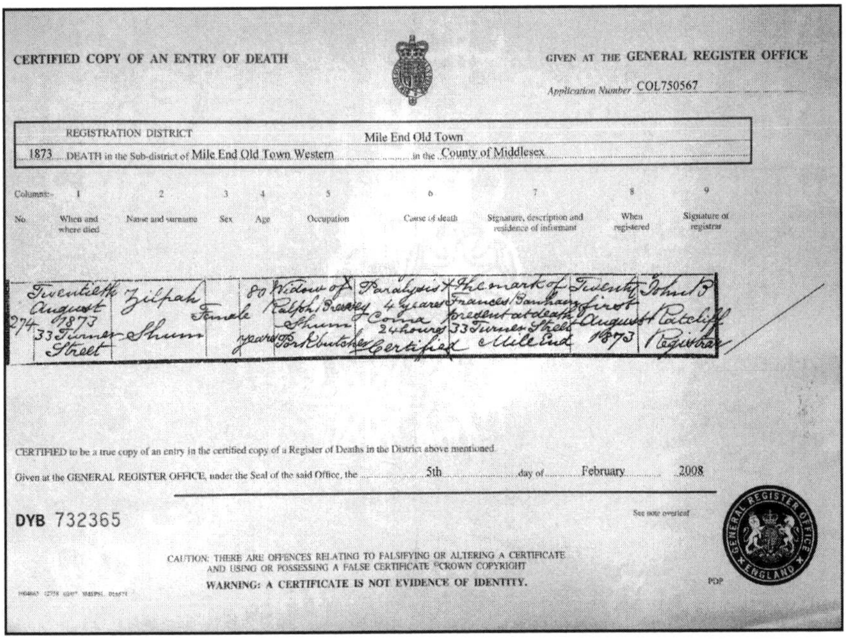

CERTIFIED COPY OF AN ENTRY OF DEATH

GIVEN AT THE GENERAL REGISTER OFFICE

Application Number COL750567

REGISTRATION DISTRICT Mile End Old Town

1873 DEATH in the Sub-district of Mile End Old Town Western in the County of Middlesex

Columns:-	1	2	3	4	5	6	7	8	9
No.	When and where died	Name and surname	Sex	Age	Occupation	Cause of death	Signature, description and residence of informant	When registered	Signature of registrar
274	Twentieth August 1873 33 Turner Street	Zilpah Shum	Female	80 years	Widow of Ralph Brewey Shum Pork butcher	Paralysis 4 years Coma 24 hours Certified	The mark of Frances Banham present at death 33 Turner Street Mile End	Twenty first August 1873	John B Ratcliff Registrar

CERTIFIED to be a true copy of an entry in the certified copy of a Register of Deaths in the District above mentioned.

Given at the GENERAL REGISTER OFFICE, under the Seal of the said Office, the 5th day of February 2008

DYB 732365

See note overleaf

CAUTION: THERE ARE OFFENCES RELATING TO FALSIFYING OR ALTERING A CERTIFICATE AND USING OR POSSESSING A FALSE CERTIFICATE ©CROWN COPYRIGHT

WARNING: A CERTIFICATE IS NOT EVIDENCE OF IDENTITY.

GENERAL REGISTER OFFICE ENGLAND

Fig. 2. Elaw's death certificate. (General Register Office, England)

Obituary: "London Shum,—On Wednesday, the 20th ult., at her residence, Norfolk Street, Commercial Road, E., in the 81st year of her age, Mrs. Zilpah Shum, formerly of Nantucket, North America. For many years a class leader and a most consistent member of the Wesleyan Society in the St. George's Circuit." *Methodist Recorder and General Christian Times*, September 12, 1873, p. 527.

Fig. 3. Saint Mary's Chapel, Bow Road, c. 1830. Elaw and Ralph Bressey Shum married here December 9, 1850. (London Metropolitan Archives–City of London)

Figs. 4 and 5. Saint Mary's, commonly known as Bow Church, in the Tower Hamlets community. (© John Salmon cc-by-sa/2.0)

For the Inquirer and Mirror.

• IN MEMORY.

The death of Mrs. Rebecca Elaw Crawford, wife of Rev. James E. Crawford, of this town, is an irreparable loss to her husband and to her two surviving sons. For half a century she has lived in our community, and ever bore the name of one most estimable in her daily life, and truly faithful to all her domestic duties. She was a christian woman in the highest and the truest sense, and a devoted member of the Methodist Church. She was born in Buck's County, Pennsylvania, on the 22d of Feb., 1812, and was brought up in Burlington, New Jersey. She afterwards came to Nantucket, and married Mr. Thomas Pierce, in 1833. Left a widow for a number of years, no sacrifice was too great for her in behalf of her two sons who now mourn the loss of a dear mother. On the 22d of Nov., 1868, she married Rev. James E. Crawford. Mrs. Crawford was the daughter of Zilpha Elaw, well known as a Methodist preacher. Mrs. Elaw went to London on a Christian mission, where a chapel was built for her. She died in London, leaving a remarkable record as a religious teacher. All that sympathy and due respect can afford are now tendered to the bereaved husband and surviving relatives of Mrs. Crawford. One by one the aged people of our town are departing; but there is consolation for the sorrowing in the following tender lines :

"Death hath left no breach
In love and sympathy, in hope and trust;
No outward sound, or sign, our ears can reach,
But there's an inward, spiritual speech
That greets us still, tho' mortal tongues be dust."

* *

Fig. 6. *The Inquirer and Mirror* obituary for Rebecca Elaw Crawford.

Fig. 7. Tower Hamlets Cemetery Park and Nature Reserve. Elaw was buried in a public grave of Tower Hamlets Cemetery, and it is not possible to locate her exact gravesite. Founded in 1841, the cemetery was populated mostly by Londoners living in the East End, Elaw's neighborhood. Public graves, intended for those who could not afford private plots, were not numbered or mapped. Each public gravesite buried several unrelated people in one unmarked plot. By the twentieth century, the burial grounds held more than 350,000 people. After decades of overcrowding and neglect, the cemetery was closed in 1966 and is now a nature preserve. (Author's photo)

Fig. 8. Elaw's first London home. Elaw's boarding room at 32 Wellclose Square was just left of the Old Court House, number 33 on the corner (Wellclose, like many London squares, is numbered sequentially, not by odds and evens). By the time she arrived in 1840, industrialization and the square's proximity to docks had transformed the square. Populated with lodginghouses, pubs, shops, and several sugar refineries, the square was burdened by pollution and poverty. According to a Wesleyan missionary, "Houses of ill-fame are swarming," and "the neighbourhood teems with lazy, idle, drunken lustful men, and degraded, brutalised hell-branded women, some alas! girls in their early teens" (qtd. in "The Lost Squares of Stepney," *Spitalfields Life*, December 30, 2012). (London Metropolitan Archives–City of London)

Fig. 9. Danish-Norwegian Church (renamed the British and Foreign Sailor Church in 1845) in Wellclose Square. In the seventeenth and eighteenth centuries, Wellclose square, which featured a handsome courthouse, the Danish embassy, and the baroque-style Danish-Norwegian Church, boasted fine mansions and well-turned homes. The watercolor executed in 1845 seems to depict a nostalgic portrait of the Square, featuring the "Mariner's Church," the common name for the Danish-Norwegian chapel frequented by seamen. (London Metropolitan Archives–City of London)

Figs. 10 and 11. Elaw's final home in East End London, 33 Turner Street, Stepney Fields. (Author's photos)

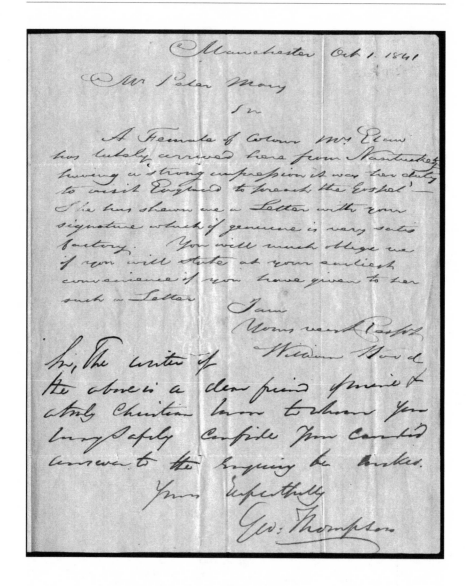

Figs. 12 and 13. Letters from William Wood, Peter Macy, and George Thompson regarding Elaw's letters of introduction. (Special Collections Research Center, Syracuse University Libraries)

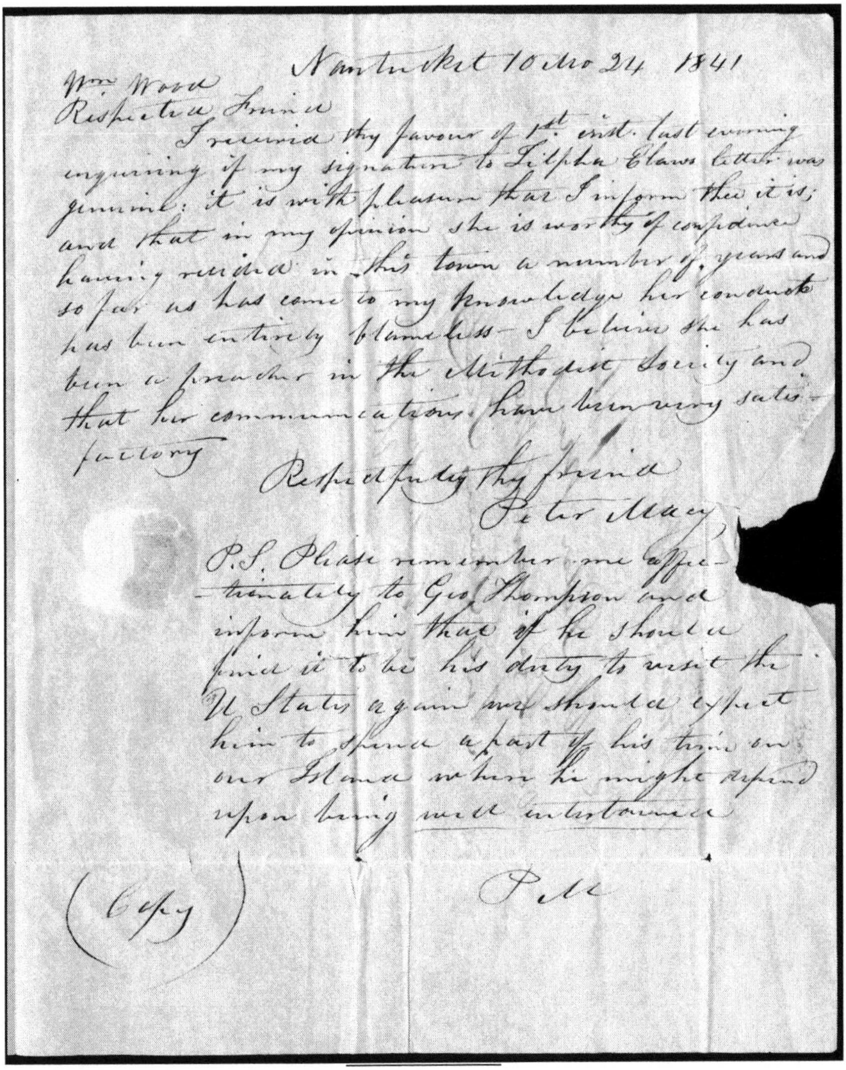

Wm Wood

Nantucket 10 Mo 24 1841

Respected Friend

I received thy favour of 9th inst. last evening enquiring if my signature to Zilpha Elaws letter was genuine; it is with pleasure that I inform thee it is; and that in my opinion she is worthy of confidence having resided in this town a number of years and so far as has come to my knowledge her conduct has been entirely blameless — I believe she has been a preacher in the Methodist Society and that her communications have been very satisfactory

Respectfully thy friend

Peter Macy

P.S. Please remember me affectionately to Geo Thompson and inform him that if he should find it to be his duty to visit the U States again we should expect him to spend a part of his time on our Island where he might depend upon being well entertained

P M

(Copy)

Fig. 14. Jewin Street Wesleyan Chapel, London. Elaw records that she preached here. (London Metropolitan Archives–City of London)

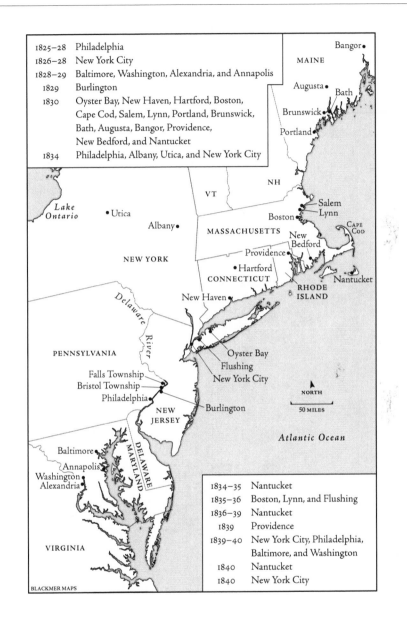

1825–28	Philadelphia
1826–28	New York City
1828–29	Baltimore, Washington, Alexandria, and Annapolis
1829	Burlington
1830	Oyster Bay, New Haven, Hartford, Boston, Cape Cod, Salem, Lynn, Portland, Brunswick, Bath, Augusta, Bangor, Providence, New Bedford, and Nantucket
1834	Philadelphia, Albany, Utica, and New York City

1834–35	Nantucket
1835–36	Boston, Lynn, and Flushing
1836–39	Nantucket
1839	Providence
1839–40	New York City, Philadelphia, Baltimore, and Washington
1840	Nantucket
1840	New York City

Fig. 15. Zilpha Elaw's travels in the United States, 1825–40. (Kate Blackmer Maps)

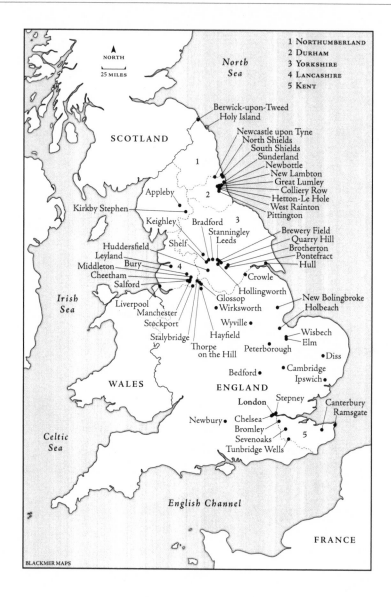

Fig. 16. Zilpha Elaw's travels in England, 1840–65. (Kate Blackmer Maps)

Timeline

By no means exhaustive, this table is intended to provide a broad context for Elaw's ministry and life writing.

	Zilpha Elaw's Life	Women's Ministries	U.S. Black Protestantism in Context
c. 1790–93	Birth of Zilpha Panco.		Lemuel Haynes, first Black ordained minister in the United States (1785), is the only known Black pastor to white congregations.
1792			Absalom Jones founds African Episcopal Church of Saint Thomas, the first Black Episcopal church in America.
1793			The Fugitive Slave Act is passed, allowing enslavers to reclaim fugitives in free states.
1794		Manumitted by her Presbyterian enslaver, Old Elizabeth begins attending Methodist meetings around 1796.	Richard Allen purchases a lot in Philadelphia and invites Bishop Francis Asbury to dedicate it as a worship center named Bethel Church.
1799			The Methodist Episcopal Church General Conference officially grants ordination to African Americans. Bishop Asbury ordains Richard Allen, the first Black deacon.

CONTINUES ▷

	Zilpha Elaw's Life	Women's Ministries	U.S. Black Protestantism in Context
1801			The Cane Ridge Revival, a week-long camp meeting in Kentucky, inaugurates the Second Great Awakening in the United States.
c. 1802	Mother dies in childbirth with twenty-second child. Indentured to Pearson and Rebecca Mitchell.		Napoleon orders reinstatement of slavery on Saint-Domingue (Haiti).
c. 1803–4	Father dies.		In 1804 the Republic of Haiti is established as a result of a revolutionary war between Haitians and France, their enslavers.
1805–6		Dorothy Ripley is the first woman to preach in the U.S. House of Representatives Chamber.	Joy Street African Baptist Church organizes in Boston. The church was in the African Meeting House, which also served as the school for Black children.
1807		The Primitive Methodist Church in Britain first allows female ministers. Jarena Lee first hears the voice of God commission her to preach the Gospel.	John Gloucester, formerly enslaved, organizes the first African American Presbyterian Church in Philadelphia. British Parliament abolishes the slave trade.
1808	Admitted into the Methodist Episcopal Society by Rev. J. Polhemos and baptized by Rev. Joseph Lybrand.	At the age of forty-six, Old Elizabeth begins preaching. African American women of Newport, Rhode Island, form the African Benevolent Society.	Abolition of the slave trade in the United States.

CONTINUES ▷

	Zilpha Elaw's Life	Women's Ministries	U.S. Black Protestantism in Context
1808–10		Fanny Newell marries a preacher and begins exhorting alongside her husband in Maine and Vermont.	The Abyssinian Baptist Church of Harlem is founded; seamen from the Ethiopian Empire (Abyssinia) help lead a protest against segregated church seating.
1810	Marries Joseph Elaw.	The Christian Connection Church first ordains women.	
1811	Zilpha and Joseph Elaw relocate to Burlington, New Jersey, to a house near a chapel.		
1812	Daughter, Rebecca Elaw, is born.		By 1812 one in every thirty-six Americans is a member of the Methodist church.
1813–14		Abigail Roberts is first inspired to preach by Nancy Gove Cram, a preacher of the Free Will Baptist Church.	In Wilmington, Delaware, the Union Church of Africans becomes the first Black church in the United States organized and led independently of a white-majority church.
1815		Clarissa Danforth is ordained in New England; she is the first woman ordained by the Free Will Baptist denomination. Danforth was converted by and often preached with Charles Bowers, a Black Free Will Baptist preacher. The first petition to license women ministers in the African Methodist Episcopal Church General Conference is defeated.	Presbyterian minister George Bourne loses his pastor position. His ordination is revoked after he advocated for the immediate emancipation of enslaved people.

CONTINUES ▷

	Zilpha Elaw's Life	Women's Ministries	U.S. Black Protestantism in Context
c. 1816–18	Sister, Hannah, dies in Philadelphia, Pennsylvania.		The African Methodist Episcopal church denomination is formed as a response to racism in the Methodist Episcopal church. Richard Allen is chosen as bishop.
			The American Colonization Society is formed.
1818	First records attending a camp meeting.		Morris Brown, founder of the African Church (Emanuel AME) in Charleston, South Carolina, is jailed for illegal gathering for worship without white supervision.
1819	Receives vision that she will live to see another camp meeting.	During an African Methodist Episcopal worship service, Jarena Lee preaches her first sermon. Shortly afterward she begins her traveling ministry.	Methodist Episcopal church responds to John Stewart's successful ministry among Native Americans and forms the Methodist Missionary Society.
1820		Deborah Peirce publishes *A Scriptural Vindication of Female Preaching, Prophesying, or Exhortation.*	
		Sara Hedges begins a twelve-year Methodist ministry before joining the Christian Connection.	

CONTINUES ▷

	Zilpha Elaw's Life	Women's Ministries	U.S. Black Protestantism in Context
1822		Harriet Livermore begins preaching in Christian Connection and Free Will Baptist congregations in New Hampshire.	James Varick becomes the first bishop of the newly organized African Methodist Episcopal Zion Church. Charleston's AME church is burned down shortly after one of its preachers, Denmark Vesey, is convicted and hanged for allegedly plotting an insurrection against slavery.
1823	Joseph Elaw dies from tuberculosis (January 27).		Black AME members in Charleston, South Carolina, continue meeting secretly until after the Civil War.
c. 1823–25	Opens school for Black children in Burlington, New Jersey, which closes after two years. Friends Society contributes books and money for the school.	Harriet Livermore publishes her first book, Scriptural Evidence in Favor of Female Testimony.	
c. 1825–27	Places her daughter in the care of a relative before going to Philadelphia, Pennsylvania.		Four people die in Philadelphia's Mother Bethel Church after red pepper was poured into the stove during a service, causing a stampede to escape the smoke.
1827		Harriet Livermore preaches in front of Congress. Salome Lincoln Mowry delivers her first sermon at a religious meeting, beginning her preaching career around Massachusetts.	Samuel Cornish and John Russworm publish *Freedom's Journal*, the first Black newspaper. Slavery abolished in New York.

CONTINUES ▷

	Zilpha Elaw's Life	Women's Ministries	U.S. Black Protestantism in Context
c. 1828–29	Preaches in New York. Returns home for a few weeks before traveling to the South in April.		The Oblate Sisters of Providence is founded in Baltimore, Maryland. It is the first Roman Catholic congregation founded by women of African descent.
c. 1830	Travels throughout the East Coast preaching and attending camp meetings (winter). In August Rebecca Elaw marries and settles in Nantucket with her mother and husband.	In a church trial in New York, the Methodist leadership excommunicated Sally Thompson when she refused to stop holding meetings. Christian Connection preacher Hannah Cogswell spends more than three years preaching in New Hampshire. Wealthy Monroe begins preaching in western New York; she eventually moves to Michigan.	The Methodist Protestant church is organized to protest the Methodist Episcopal church governance. The first National Convention of Free People of Color held at Mother Betherl AME in Philadelphia, Pennsylvania.
1831	Preaches in Nantucket churches for the next few years.	Rebecca Miller begins fourteen-year preaching career with the Christian Connection.	Nat Turner, Methodist preacher, is hanged and skinned for planning the Southampton Insurrection that killed more than fifty white people.
1832		Nancy Towle, an itinerant preacher from 1821–32, publishes her memoirs.	Sam Sharpe, Jamaican Baptist preacher, is hanged for planning passive resistance to slavery that resulted in the Christmas 1831 rebellion.
1834	Rebecca Elaw gives birth to a son (December 10).	Rebecca Cox Jackson begins itinerant preaching after leaving the AME church, her husband, and her children.	All Black churches are banned in Charleston, South Carolina.

CONTINUES ▷

	Zilpha Elaw's Life	Women's Ministries	U.S. Black Protestantism in Context
1835–36	Preaches in Boston, Lynn, and Flushing, Massachusetts, for fifteen months before returning home to Nantucket.	Jarena Lee publishes *Religious Experience and Journal of Mrs. Jarena Lee*, one of the first extended life accounts of a Black woman in America.	Angelina Grimke publishes *Appeal to the Christian Women of the South*, which urges Southern Christian women to denounce slavery.
1840	Leaves her daughter and two grandsons in Nantucket for New York City (June 6). Takes a steamboat to Philadelphia, from where she sets sail to London (July 1). Docks in London (July 25).	Julia A. J. Foote starts preaching for the AMEZ Church.	
1841	Preaches throughout the Manchester District (August–December).	Wealthy Monroe, Abigail Stone, and Elizabeth Stiles become members of the Eastern Michigan Christian Conference.	
1843	Preaches in Yorkshire County (June–July). Preaches throughout the towns of Rainton, Pittenton, New Lampton, Colliery Row, and others (September–October). Preaches in the Sunderland District (November–December).		Sojourner Truth converts to Methodism and carries out her calling as a social activist for Black folks and women. Abolitionists split from the Methodist Episcopal church over slavery and church governance, creating the Wesleyan Methodist Church Connection.
1844	Preaches in Shields (April–July).		

CONTINUES ▷

	Zilpha Elaw's Life	Women's Ministries	U.S. Black Protestantism in Context
1845	Settles in London to write her memoirs.		The Methodist Episcopal church divides into Northern and Southern denominations over the issue of American slavery. The Southern Baptist Convention is founded as a result of a split between Northern and Southern Baptists over slavery (May 8–12).
1846	Self-publishes *Memoirs of the Life, Religious Experience, Ministerial Travels and Labours of Mrs. Zilpha Elaw.*		
1847		Rebecca Cox Jackson joins the Shaker community in Watervliet, New York.	
1849		Jarena Lee self-publishes an expanded edition of her autobiography.	Harriet Tubman escapes her Maryland enslaver for refuge in Philadelphia, Pennsylvania.
1850	Marries Ralph Bressey Shum in London.		The U.S. Congress passes a new Fugitive Slave Act as part of the Compromise of 1850.
1853		Antoinette Brown Blackwell becomes the first woman in the United States to be ordained in a major Protestant church (Congregationalist). Old Elizabeth retires from itinerant preaching at the age of eighty-seven.	Western Colored Baptist Convention organized in Alton, Missouri.

CONTINUES ▷

	Zilpha Elaw's Life	Women's Ministries	U.S. Black Protestantism in Context
1859	Preaches in Cambridge County and throughout the Lincolnshire District.	Rebecca Cox Jackson and Rebecca Perot establish a Shaker community for women in Philadelphia.	
1861		Mary A. Will becomes the first U.S. woman ordained in the Wesleyan Methodist Connection.	The start of the Civil War brings one of many church splits and southern Presbyterians form the Presbyterian Church in the Confederate States of America.
1863–65	Last known newspaper account of Elaw's preaching in August 1864.	Olympia Brown is the first woman ordained by the Universalist denomination. Catherine Booth leaves the Methodist Connexion to found the Christian Mission (renamed the Salvation Army) with her husband, William Booth. Elizabeth, ninety-seven years old, publishes *Memoir of Old Elizabeth, A Coloured Woman.*	Civil War ends; the AME Church of Charleston, South Carolina, is formally reorganized and renamed the Emanuel AME Church.
1870	Paralyzed and living with caregiver.		Southern Black Methodists form the Colored Methodist Episcopal church.
1873	Dies in her London home (August 20).		

NOTES

INTRODUCTION

1. Quakers associated with the Friends General Conference worship together without pulpits or leaders. Their worship meeting is a practice of expectant waiting in order to hear the "still small voice" of God (1 Kings 19:12). They take literally the command to "be still and know that I am God" (Psalm 46:10) and only speak if they hear a message that must be shared with the community. The Quakers' assertion that God is in everyone leads them to avoid creeds, abhor violence, and recognize human equality under God. Indeed, they were the first Protestant denomination to encourage women preachers, to educate boys and girls together, regardless of race, and to protest enslavement.

    John Wesley (1703–91) founded Methodism while he was a fellow at Oxford. As an Anglican priest, Wesley's theology placed scripture at its core but also stressed that spiritual experience was an equally legitimate source of doctrine. Rejecting the Calvinist ideas of predestined and limited access to Christian salvation, Wesley embraced an Arminian theology that God's grace was available to anyone who chose it. Methodism, as Wesley intended it, focuses on an individual's free will to overcome the original and inherent depravity of humans. Methodism is about method—how does one reach salvation and, ideally, Christian perfection? Wesley provided specific rules and maps for moving through life as a Methodist, and the structure privileges spiritual journey as its doctrine and its polity. The Methodist Societies, or the Connexion, as Wesley termed it, were faith communities of people willing to live every day as a quest for Christian perfectionism known as sanctification. The Methodist Connexion depended on a system of districts with several ministry circuits (societies and stations); churches divided into classes (small group meetings for support and accountability); and, most importantly, itinerant preachers who moved among the circuits (to bring God's message to all people and provide theological cohesion between the circuits). Thus, physical and spiritual movement were interdependent and central to the mission. As David Hempton puts it, "Methodism was a missionary organization that thrived on mobility and expanded in association with the rise of markets and the growth of empire" (7).

2. I use the term "celebrity" here, not in the sense that Elaw was always celebrated, but rather in the sense that she drew large crowds, had many followers, and regularly attracted media attention. Much of her fame could be attributed to the controversy and curiosity as much as to her well-documented preaching talent. I concur with Ryan Hanley's important assessment of British Black writing in the 1700s that for the majority of Black authors, their fame happened "in proportion to the extent that their work reflected the interests of the abolitionist movement. In modern historical and critical studies, as well as in popular culture, this remains the case" (24).

3. In North America only the Quakers recognized women preachers, and no denomination ordained women. In England, there were no ordained women ministers, but

John Wesley's mother, Susanna, is widely credited for influencing her son's theology. As he and his brother, Charles, began shaping Methodism, Wesley opposed women's preaching, although he never strictly forbade it. As early as the 1760s, Wesley began to allow that a few extraordinary women may have been called to preach and cautiously supported women's labors as lay preachers and exhorters. His relationship to women lay preachers was always tentative and complex, and his 1791 death precipitated waning support for female leadership in English Methodism. In 1803 Wesleyan Methodists banned women preachers, in part because Francis Asbury, Wesley's appointed superintendent of the American colonies, was not amenable to women's leadership. He thought families to be a distraction from serving God and given the rigors of traveling in rural areas, Asbury privileged celibacy, whiteness, maleness, and mobility. Likewise, Baptists, the second-largest denomination, were reneging on previous agreements for more female authority in their churches. By the nineteenth century, many Protestant denominations had reverted to women keeping silent in many aspects of worship (Westerkamp 115–17).

4. By the 1830s, the pseudoscience of phrenology, founded by German physiologist Franz Joseph Gall, was widely used to justify the enslavement of Africans and genocide of Native Americans. Gall believed that the shape and size of skulls provided information about the brain and intellectual capacity. Unsurprisingly, his hypothesis and research concluded that nonwhite humans were inferior.

5. Evangelicalism is based on the conviction that sin is endemic to man's nature but stresses the value of individual work toward salvation. Evangelists believe that it is the responsibility of the church to go out into the world and spread the gospel. The movement "began in the eighteenth century and influential works such as Henry Venn's *Compleat Duty of Man* (1763) and William Wilberforce's *Practical View of the Prevailing Religious System of Professional Christians* (1797) continued to be read well into the nineteenth century" (Jay 2). There were a variety of evangelical denominations, but "the Methodist and Baptist communions, [were] the two most important Evangelical bodies. . . . Between 1815 and 1860, the forces of Evangelical Protestantism organized in unprecedented fashion in a massive campaign to bring Christ and culture into greater proximity" (Sernett 27). Methodism, which began as an established movement within the Anglican church, eventually separated from the church, and Wesley's movement became its own church. The explosive growth of Methodism was worrisome to many English clergy. For example, when West Cornwall became a Methodist stronghold, one vicar complained that "we have lost the people. . . . The religion of the mass is become Wesleyan Methodism." Yet another vicar felt his country was "wholly given up to dissent and perversity" as there was "Methodism in every house" (qtd. in Rule 48–49). The expansion across the Atlantic was even more impressive. In *Women and Religion in Early America, 1600–1850,* Marilyn J. Westerkamp documents that American Methodism grew from 65,000 to more than 500,000 members between 1800 and 1830. "In 1850, with more than one million members, the Methodist churches reflected the largest evangelical network" in the United States (111).

6. The First Great Awakening, England's Evangelical Revival, was a Christian revivalist movement that flourished roughly from the 1730s through the 1780s. At the start of the eighteenth century, Britain had reached an all-time low of actively religious citizens. The membership in Christian churches, in particular, had been in steady decline since the Napoleonic Wars and reflected a growing disillusionment with the Enlightenment. Several new religious societies formed to foster a renewed investment in Christian piety and became denominations after separating from the Church

of England. Many of the new denominations were evangelical, and it didn't take long before the Protestant evangelical movement crossed the Atlantic, making a significant impact on the culture of Britain and its American colonies. For more on the Evangelical Revival and its transatlantic growth, see Richard Carwardine's *Trans-Atlantic Revivalism*; D. Bruce Hindmarsh's *The Evangelical Conversion Narrative* and *The Spirit of Early Evangelicalism*; Mark Noll's *American Evangelical Christianity*; and Seth Perry's *Bible Culture and Authority in the Early United States*.

7. "Spiritual autobiography" is a broad term that encompasses letters, diaries, journals, and books made public through publication or by sharing orally what someone has written about their religious conversion (either from nonbelief to religion or from one level or category of faith to another), spiritual reflection, the practice of converting others, or some combination of such. For example, Methodist classes and district and conference meetings often included the recital of letters or journal entries recently received. Clergy provided the bulk of these missives, but laity also wrote, shared, and published. Although there were denominational, theological, and social distinctions, the overall format of the genre was strikingly similar. Overall, there was great public demand for spiritual narratives, and publishers were eager to meet it.

8. While few Americans could afford oceanic travel in the 1700s, the next century witnessed the United States' first measurable number of citizens with the means and desire to travel abroad simply for recreation. The nineteenth century introduced the first American leisure class. For more on nineteenth-century travel and travel writing, see Nigel Leask's *Curiosity and the Aesthetics of Travel Writing*; William Stowe's *Going Abroad*; and Carl Thompson's *Travel Writing*.

9. After Joseph Benson succeeded Wesley's editorship in 1804, the contributions of women to the *Methodist Magazine* (renamed from *Arminian Magazine* in 1798) dramatically changed its publishing practices concerning women. The magazine did not publish any female autobiographies after 1804, and other forms of women's writing, such as letters and hymns, were practically eliminated by 1821. See Margaret Jones's "From 'The State of My Soul' to 'Exalted Piety.'" In fact, D. Bruce Hindmarsh records that "at least one woman preacher's autobiography . . . was explicitly rejected 'lest it be a precedent to young females in the Connexion.' Obituary notices of other women preachers passed over this aspect of their ministry in silence" (238). To this point, see Elaw's obituary in appendix B, fig. 2. Also, see Catherine Brekus's *Strangers and Pilgrims* for a discussion of a similar decline in the United States.

10. George Whitefield, another founder of Methodism, maintained a more Calvinist belief that individual salvation is predestined by God. This caused a split from the Wesley brothers, who believed in Arminianism, the individual's ability to atone for sin and achieve sanctification.

11. Wesley requested brief narratives from the lay preachers and often published them in his *Arminian Magazine* with the intention of establishing standards, providing models, and publicly documenting the success of the revival. Most were serialized in the magazine, but some were published separately as books and abridged for the magazine. Wesley insisted on publishing the autobiographies and portraits of *living* preachers—a practice that was at first quite controversial. However, inclusion in the magazine was an honor and mark of distinction by the end of the eighteenth century. Hindmarsh notes that "the *Arminian Magazine* was still the chief vehicle for the publication of the preachers' lives, but clearly the lay preachers of the Evangelical Revival formed a group who were exceptionally articulate about their religious experience" (234). During Wesley's editorship, no women were included in preacher autobiographies, with the exception of Sarah Mallet, an example of women's

preaching as extraordinary exceptions. Mallet was known to preach only in "altered states of consciousness" through "fits and trances" (237). Wesley did, however, admire and highlight many women's spiritual experiences by printing their letters to him (Hindmarsh 232–34).

12. Eighteenth- and nineteenth-century publications included a variety of newspapers and weekly magazines, such as *The Weekly History* (1741), *The Glasgow Weekly History* (1741), and *The Christian Monthly History* (1743). The London Religious Tract Society (1799) engendered the American Bible Society (1816), American Sunday School Union (1824), and American Tract Society (1825). In addition to these interdenominational ventures, the Methodists, Baptists, and other denominations added their own publishing arms to the religious market. In the United States, the success of the Methodist Book Concern encouraged other denominations to establish their own presses. It took more than fifty years for secular presses to match the distribution of the evangelical books, pamphlets, magazines, and hymnals. By the nineteenth century, no matter the faith (Jewish, Muslim, Catholic, or Protestant, etc.), worship communities that did not strategically utilize the press quickly floundered. For an engaging discussion of evangelical print culture, see Candy Gunther Brown's *The Word in the World*.

13. I do not suggest a false dichotomy between selfhood and spirituality. Rather, I make a distinction between material desires and divine quests.

14. Christian salvation is to be delivered, or saved, from the consequences of human sin. In *Holy Boldness*, Susie Stanley explains that Wesleyan Methodists believed one could achieve Christian perfection through sanctification, the removal of original sin inherited from Adam and Eve. While this could happen through spiritual practice and development, American Methodists, in particular, believed that sanctification could be granted instantaneously by God (2).

15. Although women did participate in the tradition of writing spiritual conversion narratives, to preach and to travel alone were considered exceptional and not necessarily acceptable ventures, nor were such activities fully sanctioned by Methodist or Baptist denominations. Thus, published pre-1900 evangelical narratives were authored mostly by men, predominately white, even though many women kept (and shared) journals, diaries, and sometimes full spiritual autobiographies that were never published. As Catherine Brekus notes, preaching women were largely and purposefully forgotten by those who were documenting their own religious and social movements. As talented preachers, their religious conservatism offended early feminists, but their insistence on preaching was too radical for religious conservatives (*Strangers* 7).

16. Citing the "egregious discrimination" suffered by Rebecca Jackson, Elaw, Jarena Lee and Old Elizabeth, Joycelyn K. Moody asserts that while "the nascent African American Protestant church accepted Black holy women as exhorters and heartily endorsed them as 'mothers[,]' . . . women preachers were condemned, even execrated, by both men and women, whites and blacks" (44). In fact, in addition to the many physical threats against Black women preachers, Jackson was threatened with excommunication for evangelism, the AME Book Concern forbade the publication of Lee's second autobiography, and the AME Church Conferences of the 1840s and 1850s consistently voted against the ordination of women preachers (Moody 44–45).

17. The Primitive Methodists were founded in 1807 by Hugh Bourne and William Clowes after they were inspired by American Methodist preacher, Lorenzo Dow's camp meetings. The society, a people's movement consisting primarily of farm, mill, and factory workers in rural areas, believed that it was returning to the origins of

John Wesley's doctrine. While staying true to the district circuit system formulated by Wesley, Primitive Methodists adopted the American-style open-air revivals that privileged enthusiastic worship earning them the derogatory nickname "ranters." Like Wesley, they did not forbid women preaching. Unlike Wesley, they actively supported women's ministries. By 1838, two years before Elaw's arrival, the conference meeting reports 67,666 society members. The Primitive Methodists joined the 1932 Wesleyan and United Methodist unification.

The Bryanites were a small but fast-growing Methodist sect named after William O'Bryan (né Bryant), a Wesleyan preacher in Devon. After their split from the Wesleyans in 1815, the Bryanites (also known as the Bible Christians) spread throughout North Cornwall even after O'Bryan left the Methodist denomination in 1832. The Bible Christians were closely aligned with Wesleyan Methodism but did not discourage women preachers. O'Bryan's wife, Catherine, was one of the many female preachers they employed. Both the Primitive Methodists and the Bryanites struggled in urban areas. Neither were able to secure a large membership nor establish many churches in Greater London, but in most other English counties they were at least as popular and sometimes more widespread and established than the Wesleyans. By 1907, when the Bible Christians were incorporated into the United Methodist Church, they had very few women preachers.

Catherine Brekus documents that over two hundred women were preaching in Great Britain by the 1840s (*Strangers* 133). The high number of women preachers and the British ban on enslavement likely contributed to Elaw's attraction to England. She may have envisioned it as a welcoming space for her efforts given the available avenues for a Black woman to preach without fear of bondage.

18. A shilling was worth one-twentieth of a sterling pound and is equivalent to the spending power of approximately five pounds in 2020.

19. Today, Douglass's *Narrative of the Life of Frederick Douglass* (1845) and Jacobs's *Incidents in the Life of a Slave Girl* (1861) are globally anthologized and taught in high school and college classrooms. In 1845 Jacobs worked as a nanny and traveled to England with her employer, Nathaniel Parker Willis, after the death of his wife. In the same year, Douglass fled to England, where he lived and lectured as a fugitive from enslavement. He returned to the United States in 1847 after a few Englishwomen purchased his freedom. He fled to England again in 1859 to escape the racial violence that ensued after John Brown's uprising at Harper's Ferry. Neither Douglass nor Jacobs expressed high opinions of the Protestant revivalism they experienced in the South. Jacobs wrote that when she "attended a Methodist class meeting [she] went with a burdened spirit, and happened to sit next a poor, bereaved mother. . . . The class leader was the town constable—a man who bought and sold slaves, who whipped his brethren and sisters of the church at the public whipping post, in jail or out of jail. He was ready to perform that Christian office anywhere for fifty cents" (59).

20. When Elaw traveled to the South, the obvious racial danger was conjoined with male preachers' uneasiness about the numbers and accomplishments of women as church members, organizers, and talented interpreters of scripture and doctrine. The uncomfortable truth was that Methodist and Baptist growth and stability depended almost entirely on the tireless work of women members. As Christine Heyrman eloquently explains in *Southern Cross*, male evangelicals "bristled when the sisters came forth too often or too forcefully. Preachers admired women who could move audiences, but felt unnerved when they outshone the brethren. . . . Early Baptist and Methodist preachers knew that they depended on women a great deal, but perhaps wished that they needed them a good deal less" (177). While these men were limited

in the ways that they could monitor and, if necessary, silence white women, they had no such limitations when it came to Black women. Elaw could have, at any moment, become the scapegoat and victim of male rage over the perceived impudence of white women.

21. After Jackson fired most of his cabinet in response to the "Petticoat Affair," the media often publicized the growing cadre of supporters who became unofficial advisors, termed his "kitchen cabinet."

22. Elaw references Anne McCarty Lee (1798–1840), married to Major Henry Lee IV (1787–1837), whom Elaw incorrectly refers to as a general. At the time that Elaw reports staying with "Lady Lee," President Andrew Jackson, grieving the recent loss of his beloved wife, Rachel, was enduring heavy critique and ridicule for his protection of Rachel's close friend, Lady Anne Lee. Her husband, Henry, the son of General "Light Horse Harry" Lee and half-brother to General Robert E. Lee, had been dogged by a very public adultery and financial scandal involving Anne's younger sister and her estate (of which Henry was guardian) which earned him the nickname "Dark Horse." In the midst of this scandal, Anne, who had become addicted to opioids after the death of her infant daughter, spent time rehabilitating at the Fountain of Health (a resort reported to have healing waters) in Nashville, Tennessee. There she was befriended and encouraged in her recovery by Rachel Jackson, and the Jacksons are credited with reuniting the estranged couple. Thus, the friendship between the Lees and the Jacksons was cemented, and they were with Rachel during her final illness and with Jackson at her funeral. During the time that Elaw reports she visited their home, the Lees had recently traveled to Washington with Andrew Jackson for his inauguration (Lee wrote the inaugural speech) and were awaiting Henry's appointment to consul in Algiers. Jackson, acting out of loyalty for his friend and political worker, had secretly assigned the dangerous post to Lee after years of unsuccessful attempts to get him a government position. Indeed, less than a year after moving to Algiers, the Senate discovered the appointment and voted to recall him. The Lees emigrated to Paris.

Commodore John Rodgers (1772–1838) was perhaps the most revered officer of the early American Navy. He served under the first six U.S. presidents. At the time that Rodgers presumably offered Elaw a permanent post in Washington, DC, he was president of the Board of Naval Commissioners. As such, he and his wife, Minerva Dennison Rodgers (1784–1877), were at the center of the Washington political elite. They were a founding family of the naval community built at Greenleaf Point (a peninsula where the Anacostia and Potomac Rivers meet).

23. Rachel Jackson's first husband, Jason Robards, accused her of bigamy in his divorce filings, and this became great fodder during Andrew Jackson's presidential campaign. Many charged that Rachel knew she was not yet divorced when she began dating and married Jackson. She and Andrew Jackson always maintained her innocence, citing the unclear and muddled nature of divorce proceedings at the time.

24. Rachel and Andrew Jackson built and continually expanded their antebellum mansion, the Hermitage, from 1804 to 1821. After a fire, it was rebuilt in 1834. The plantation also expanded from five to more than one hundred enslaved Blacks by the time of Jackson's 1845 death.

25. The British and Foreign Anti-Slavery Society (BFASS) was founded in 1839 as a successor to the Agency Committee of the Society for the Mitigation and Gradual Abolition of Slavery Throughout the British Dominions (1823). After the British Emancipation Act of 1833, the newly named BFASS worked for abolition in other countries and organized the 1840 World Anti-Slavery Convention in Freemason's

Hall, London. The BFASS was reorganized in 1990 as Anti-Slavery International, a human rights organization, charity, and lobby group. Elaw also mentions the Society for the Promotion of Permanent and Universal Peace. From their inception, these London-based organizations have historically shared some membership. The society was founded in 1816 to publish and distribute antiwar publications. Consisting mostly of Quaker pacifists, the group also had a heavy concentration of Protestant evangelicals such as Methodists and Baptists. Given their motto that "the cause of peace is the cause of God" their interest in Elaw is not surprising (Conway 274).

26. See Blockett's "Disrupting Print" for a more in-depth analysis of Elaw's letter to John Tredgold, secretary of the BFASS.

27. Modern scholars were introduced to Elaw's narrative in William Andrews's *Sisters of the Spirit*. In his introduction, Andrews cites 1830–1865 as crisis years during which publishing the narratives of enslaved fugitives was part of a national fight for civil rights. Recognizing that Black spiritual autobiographies were their precursors, Andrews's foundational work demonstrates how the spiritual narratives laid the necessary groundwork for such rhetorical battles to be fought.

28. An 1889 posthumous edition, *Elizabeth, a Colored Minister of the Gospel Born in Slavery*, was issued by the Tract Association of Friends, a Quaker publishing house. It includes an addendum that details Elizabeth's long, painful illness and death at almost 101 years old along with some discussion of her "out-speaking way [that] sometimes gave offence" (13).

29. Fifty years after the First Great Awakening, a second, more expansive Protestant revival swept several nations including the United States, England, Scotland, and Germany.

30. By the 1820s and 1830s, Black Americans had tired of the institutionalized racism within their denominations and formed many independent Black churches, primarily Methodist and Baptist. In 1792 Absalom Jones founded the African Episcopal Church of Saint Thomas in Philadelphia. In the MEC, Philadelphia's Bethel was the first African Methodist Episcopal Church dedicated in 1794, and Black New Yorkers built the AME Zion Church in 1800. As the AMEC proliferated in the mid-Atlantic and New England, Richard Allen, founder of Bethel AME, organized the AMEC denomination in 1816. Many predominately white denominations were experiencing considerable internal discord as they attempted to determine, articulate, and manage their official stance on human bondage in America. For example, the MEC debates over enslavement resulted in a denominational split creating the MEC South, a confederate church, in 1844. After emancipation, Black Methodists in Jackson, Tennessee, formed the Colored Methodist Episcopal Church in 1870, later renamed Christian Methodist Episcopal.

31. Elaw is mentioned in many published book chapters and articles about nineteenth-century preaching women, but the discussion is most often just a few sentences and rarely a full chapter.

32. Elaw's narrative gives the name Pierson Mitchel, but census records and several entries in the Quaker records for the Falls and Middletown Meetings spell the name as Pearson Mitchell.

33. Every Methodist Society is divided into classes. The classes, originally formed in 1742 as a method to collect money for the needs of the congregation, evolved into small worship groups whose primary function was to provide support and accountability for its members. Concerned that too many of his followers were not following his "General Rules" of Methodist living (do no harm, do good, and follow all the ordinances of God), John Wesley determined that these small, local classes of about twelve members were

ideal structures for maintaining these principles. Wesley resolved that the new duties of the class leader would evolve from simple collections to weekly check-ins with each member "to inquire how their souls prosper; to advise, reprove, comfort, or exhort, as occasion may require." In this way, the weekly class meetings became the most expedient method for "watching over one another in love" and thus a requirement for membership in a Methodist society (*A Plain Account* 253). The societies, which may or may not have had a physical church depending on their numbers and finances, constituted the larger Methodist Districts. Each circuit is comprised of several districts.

34. Referred to as "the travelling preacher, Rev. J. Polhemus" (page 13).

35. Methodist societies closely monitored the behavior of its members and frequently sanctioned, placed on probation, or disowned members who did not conduct themselves according to the guidelines provided by Wesley (guidelines that were interpreted and revised by district and superintendent ministers).

36. Historically, a fuller cleaned wool as one step of the cloth manufacturing process. After industrialization, the word became a general term for textile worker. Elaw may also have been referencing the biblical term which meant to clean or whiten cloth.

37. Many evangelical narratives describe attendance at camp meetings, and Elaw explains the uniquely American version of this Second Great Awakening phenomena to her English audience. The large outdoor revivals were modeled after the "communion seasons" of the Presbyterian Church of Scotland, later transmitted to the United States through the Great Revival in Kentucky. Known for the highly emotional and exuberant displays of worship, the meetings were renounced by most denominations, including the Presbyterians. However, the Methodist preferences for simplicity of venue, exuberant conviction, yet strict rules of behavior seemed to be a good fit for maintaining respectable decorum at spirited revivals. Officially, the camps in the Northeast were interracial, but in practice the tents and activities were segregated by race and gender (meetings in the South were completely separate). However, the large and sometimes turbulent nature of the meetings allowed for much intermingling, intended and unintended, of class and sometimes race. For more information on evangelical camp meetings, see Steven D. Cooley's "Manna and the Manual," Russell E. Richey's *Early American Methodism*, and Elisabeth Jay's *The Evangelical and Oxford Movements*.

38. Spiritual exhorters typically were not theologians but practitioners who persuaded and modeled how best to serve God. Since the role was not to teach but to enact scripture, exhorting was not considered text-based preaching—teaching from and interpreting scripture.

39. The 1790 census (conducted August 2) indicates that Elaw was not yet born. It lists her father, Sanco Panco, with a household of three, presumably himself, his wife, and Elaw's older brother, Joseph. The 1841 UK Census lists her age as forty-five, the 1871 UK Census lists her age as seventy-six, and her death certificate lists her birth year c. 1793. However, her narrative indicates that she was still indentured to the Mitchells when she joined the Methodist Society in 1808. That would suggest that she was not yet eighteen, placing her birth year between 1790 and 1792.

40. Isaac Sharpless, *Quakerism and Political Essays*, qtd. in Gloria Davis Goode's "From Bucks County, Pennsylvania to Nantucket, Massachusetts." It was important to record the manumissions to prevent freed Blacks from being imprisoned and sold again.

41. A committee appointed by the Quarterly Meeting of Bucks for the purpose of visitations met at the Middletown Meeting House in March 1776 after a weighty conference on slavery and committed to eradicating enslavement in Quaker homes

(Watring and Wright). See also James Moon, *An Account of Negroes Set Free Kept by James Moon of Woodburn, Son of Roger Moon Who Came from England, 1776–1782.*

42. The Fugitive Slave Act of 1793 was strengthened in 1850.

43. See *Bucks County Historical Society, Vol. 1,* "Early History of Bristol," pp. 515–36.

44. The 1790 census lists the two Panco families just a few entries below the Mitchell family, indicating that they were neighbors. Given the scarcity of records documenting their family, it is possible that the elder Pancos were enslaved and manumitted. One reference to Elaw's parents suggests that either her mother or father may have been Native American.

    Many poor children were indentured at the initiative of either the State or their parents in an effort to improve or stabilize their living situation. Some were orphaned, abandoned, abused, or otherwise vulnerable. Others were children whose parents sought a better economic future for their child; the indenture was often contracted to include education or a skilled apprenticeship. Some were informal arrangements, but many were formal, registered contracts. The legal contracts were specific and provided for the length of time; type and amount of education and training, if any; levels of basic needs and care (food, shelter, clothing); required labor and behavior of the child; regulatory terms by a civil authority; and a payment to be rendered at end of service, all of which was signed and recorded as a governing contract. Indentures typically ended at age twenty-one for men and between sixteen and eighteen for women, although it could be a decade or two longer for people of color. For women, sometimes a contract stipulated freedom at a certain age or marriage, whichever came first. As men were more likely than women to acquire positions in manual labor or at sea, more girls than boys were indentured. This system that Ruth Herndon and John Murray term "pauper apprentices" was widely used with varying success from the colonization of North America to the Civil War. The terms "apprentice" and "servant" were sometimes used interchangeably but often each term was reserved for very specific contracts depending on situation and location, particularly in many of the southern states where local courts were not inclined to have contracts labeling whites as servants. The treatment of the children ranged from loving familial affection to severe abuse (Herndon and Murray 1–10). The indenture relationship was more often than not a messy mix of master/servant/parent/child dynamic. Race and gender, of course, significantly affected the degree to which children were placed in service, and "girls of color benefited the least from the system, exiting indenture with the least literacy training and fewest work skills" (Herndon and Murray 16).

    In Elaw's case, being placed with Quaker neighbors who probably had a prior relationship with her parents may have worked in her favor. Her indenture seems to have been on the familial end of the spectrum given that she was well educated, and, years after her service ended, her "dear master" sent money when she was ill (page 32–33). See also Monique Bourque's discussion of the informal and unique variety of indentures in Southeast Pennsylvania. On the gendered nature of Black indentured servitude, see Erica Armstrong Dunbar, *A Fragile Freedom*, 27–28.

45. Encompassing South Jersey, southeastern Pennsylvania, and parts of Delaware and Maryland, the region was home to large numbers of free Blacks during the Revolutionary era. In 1780 Pennsylvania became the first state to abolish slavery, and by the mid-eighteenth century large-scale manumissions had occurred in most of Pennsylvania and New Jersey. In addition, many Blacks, whether born with free status, manumitted, or fugitives, benefited from the political and religious influence emanating from Philadelphia, the region's epicenter.

46. Joseph was presumably named after Rebecca's deceased father.

47. The African Baptist Church was reorganized as the York Street Colored Baptist Society and later as the Pleasant Street Baptist Church.

48. This may also have affected Elaw's travel plans. There is no evidence yet that Elaw did return to the United States; however, the timing coincides with the birth of her third grandchild, David Pierce, perhaps the reason for her intended return. The Great Fire of Nantucket, which happened during the publication year of her book, also may have influenced Elaw's travel plans. On July 13, 1846, the fire, fueled by storage containers of whale oil along the wharf, destroyed about one-third of the town, including most of the downtown area, leaving more than eight hundred people homeless.

49. Dudley's residence, 19 Charterhouse Lane, was in a commercial district and had a multi-use history. It is listed in the 1843 *London Post Office Directory* for copperplate printing and the 1853 *Shopkeeper's Guide* as a Berlin Wool Repository (distributors of popular embroidery patterns made from copperplate engravings of famous art). Dudley likely took over the printing business from the 1843 shop owner, Joseph Bishop.

50. The vehement argument between the two Wesleyans mimics the struggle of public perception that plagued Methodism since its inception. Denigrated for their vigorous and sometimes physical experience of receiving the Holy Spirit, Methodists were often branded as unseemly and irreligious. Methodist historian David Hempton vividly describes the charge of enthusiasm as "false belief in the inspiration of the Holy Spirit, an irrational attribution of everyday occurrences to divine intervention, a spurious belief in 'dreams, visions, fancies, reveries and revelations,' a predisposition to hypocrisy and laziness (since the road to heaven was paved with false imaginings), an illusory attachment to ridiculous doctrines such as Christian perfection, and a capricious view of the world that led often to insanity" (34).

51. In 1876 the *Wesleyan-Methodist Connexional Record and Year Book* reported that "the *Watchman Newspaper and Wesleyan Advertiser* has been in existence upwards of forty years, and though altogether unofficial in character, has been recognized for its commencement as a weekly journal of Methodist information" (99).

52. Interracial marriage in Britain is documented as far back as the sixteenth century and includes all manner of ethnic mixing among every class of society, from the almshouse poor to the royal family. In his 1778 book, *A Year's Journey*, Phillip Thickness complained that in "every country town, nay, in almost every village are to be seen a little race of mulattoes, mischievous as monkeys, and infinitely more dangerous" (qtd. in the introduction of Chamion Caballero's "Interraciality in Early Twentieth Century Britain"). By the nineteenth century, interracial marriage was a familiar occurrence, especially in the urban port cities of England. Although never encouraged and often marginalized, interracial couples could and did marry freely and raise families. For white women in particular, there was strong disapprobation and attempts at legal warnings, such as the threat of losing citizenship. However, the British were reluctant to introduce anti-miscegenation laws given their heavy reliance on colonial enterprises.

53. "The Story of the Schumm Family by M.S.W."

54. The will notes his residence as "25 K Norfolk St. Turner St." The 1861 census lists Z. Shum and servant at 25 K Turner St., but by the 1871 census her address is 33 Turner St. (See appendix B, figs. 10–11.)

55. *The Bury and Norwich Post* and *Suffolk Herald* reported an attempted rape in Bradfield. The victim was assaulted after going with her parents to "hear Mrs. Shum preach." Presumably, this unrelated information was added to the police report to

indicate the piety, and therefore innocence, of the young lady who was alone with her assailant.

56. Extensive wedding travel, often to visit distant family members, was deeply entrenched in British culture. See Helena Mitchie's "Looking at Victorian Honeymoons" for rich discussion of honeymoons and the privileged class in the 1850s.

57. *Census Returns of England and Wales, 1871.*

58. While the *Primitive Methodist Magazine* did acknowledge and sometimes spotlight women preachers, it was not uncommon for the Wesleyan publications (especially in Greater London) to downplay if not completely erase any historical memory of women in leadership positions.

59. As the entries in the Primitive Methodist journals indicate, race was an excluding factor. Few, if any, denominations were eager to employ a Black woman.

60. Starting with only 65 churches throughout the 13 colonies in 1776, the Methodist Society had established more than 13,000 churches during the Second Great Awakening. By 1850 more than a third of American congregations, 2.6 million, were Methodist (Finke and Stark 57).

Memoirs

1. Elaw mimics the second letter of Paul to the Corinthians, in which Paul writes of his gratitude and joyfulness despite the many hardships he has endured as an apostle to Christ. ("Grace *be* to you and peace from God our Father, and *from* the Lord Jesus Christ," 2 Corinthians 1:2.)

2. Elaw quotes Song of Solomon 1:5 ("I am black, but comely, O ye daughters of Jerusalem, as the tents of Kedar, as the curtains of Solomon"). However, in her version, she chooses to couple the descriptors "blackness" and "comeliness," using "with" instead of using "but" to juxtapose "black" and "comely" as intended in the original quote.

3. Elaw references Paul's report that sacrifice and generosity is rewarded and that he was given a trial, or thorn, as a weakness from which to find power. ("How that in a great trial of affliction the abundance of their joy and their deep poverty abounded unto the riches of their liberality," 2 Corinthians 8:2; "And he said unto me, 'My grace is sufficient for thee: for my strength is made perfect in weakness. Most gladly therefore will I rather glory in my infirmities, that the power of Christ may rest upon me,' " 2 Corinthians 12:9.)

4. "But they that will be rich fall into temptation and a snare, and into many foolish and hurtful lusts, which drown men in destruction and perdition. For the love of money is the root of all evil: which while some coveted after, they have erred from the faith, and pierced themselves through with many sorrows," 1 Timothy 6:9–10.

5. "Now therefore ye are no more strangers and foreigners, but fellow citizens with the saints, and of the household of God; And are built upon the foundation of the apostles and prophets, Jesus Christ himself being the chief corner stone," Ephesians 2:19–20.

6. Elaw was born c. 1793 in the borough of Bristol, Bucks County, Pennsylvania, about twenty-three miles northeast of Philadelphia.

7. Elaw refers to the Friends branch of Quakerism who hold silent worship meetings without a pastor or liturgy.

8. The 1800 U.S. Census records twelve white household members, with seven children and five members over the age of twenty-five. The 1810 Census records a family of nine, including four adults over forty-five. In addition, there were two free Blacks in the Mitchell household.

9. "Have I any pleasure at all that the wicked should die? saith the Lord GOD: and not that he should return from his ways, and live?" Ezekiel 18:23.

10. Gabriel, an archangel in the Christian and Judaism traditions, was a messenger angel who often announced important births (John the Baptist and Jesus). Gabriel was also the trumpeter of the last judgment in Revelation.

11. According to Elaw's timeline, this was probably 1807–9, which coincides with the reinvigoration of Methodism in the region. However, Bristol history notes that the region's first Methodist sermon was delivered by British army preacher Captain Webb in 1771. By the late 1770s, Francis Asbury and four other missionaries were working tirelessly to develop American Methodism—a mission requested by Webb and other Methodists who had come to the mid-Atlantic colonies decades earlier.

12. "Ask, and it shall be given you; seek, and ye shall find; knock, and it shall be opened unto you," Matthew 7:7.

13. Unless otherwise noted, all of the indented lyrics in the narrative are from early Methodist hymnals written by John and/or Charles Wesley and some are anonymously authored from older hymnals, such as the *Primitive Christians Hymnal*.

14. Acts 8 relates the Ethiopian eunuch's conversion. Philip the evangelist meets an African eunuch reading the Book of Isaiah. Philip shares the Gospel of Jesus and then, at the request of the African, baptizes him. Philip is taken away by the Holy Spirit and the eunuch "went on his way rejoicing." Some scholars speculate that the Ethiopian eunuch story suggests that Christians are to be open to minorities (racial and sexual). Elaw is clearly identifying herself as an African Christian in the same way that the Ethiope was willing and open to a conversion experience. She may also be making a commentary about her own literacy since the biblical Ethiopian was highly literate and educated as a person of importance in his government. (See Byron, McNeill, Rogers, Snowden, and Witherington.)

15. Elaw alludes to Colossians 1:12: "Giving thanks unto the Father, which hath made us meet to be partakers of the inheritance of the saints in light," grateful that she is now able to live in the light of Christ.

16. According to *A Century of Methodism in Germantown*, in 1808 Thomas Dunn and James Polhemus were the assigned ministers for the Bristol Circuit, which had approximately three hundred members that year. By the time Reverend Polhemus returned five years later, the Bristol Circuit recorded 536 members.

17. In the early years of the society, Methodists endured intense ridicule of their strict rules for living, their uneducated preachers, and their literal translation of spreading the gospel far and wide. The lay preachers, nicknamed "circuit riders," were often caricatured in newspapers riding broken-down horses or donkeys holding a Bible and yelling scripture. One depiction featured a farm family hiding in the house hoping the preacher would pass by their farmstead. These itinerant preachers, often working in rural and frontier regions, were indefatigable. Even on bitterly cold days that kept most people indoors, "their faithfulness in filling their appointments" inspired the "proverbial saying, 'There is nothing out today but crows and Methodist preachers' " (Gewehr 103).

18. "Mine heritage is unto me as a speckled bird, the birds round about are against her; come ye, assemble all the beasts of the field, come to devour," Jeremiah 12:9.

Alluding to this verse from Jeremiah, Methodists often referred to themselves as the speckled birds—spectacles to a hostile audience—among other Christians.

19. Methodists had strict rules for individual conduct, including no drinking, dancing, or swearing. Induction of a class member included a probationary period (typically six months) to observe that the person behaved appropriately and did not break any rules of the General Conference.

20. Lybrand was admitted into the ministry and appointed to the Philadelphia Conference in 1811. This would date Elaw's baptism no earlier than 1811.

21. Elaw refers to the continuing tensions between Britain and America and the resulting sanctions that led to the War of 1812. Starting with the Embargo Act of 1807 against Britain and France during the Napoleonic Wars (revoked by President Thomas Jefferson in 1809 due to inefficacy and unpopularity), the United States government continued to try to find ways to punish other nations without restricting its own trade such as the Non-Intercourse Act of 1810. All of this legislation had the unintended consequence of forcing more textile industry in New England as the population suffered from lack of access to British imports.

22. Immediately after her sanctification, Elaw is surprised to find herself in a leadership role as worshippers began to ask for her prayers. She likens herself to the New Testament leader, Phoebe. In Romans 16:1–2, Paul the Apostle identifies Phoebe as his sister in Christ and a deacon (an invaluable servant, caretaker, and teacher of the church). He entrusts Phoebe to undertake the journey to deliver his epistle to the Romans and requests that the Romans honor her with any assistance she may need. Elaw later references some, but not all, of the prophesying women of the Bible including Trypheana and Tryphosa (Romans 16:12) and Priscilla (Acts 18). Additional examples include Phillip the Evangelist's four daughters, who all prophesied (Acts 29:9), and Luke 2:36–38 lists Anna and an eighty-four-year-old widow as prophetesses who blessed the birth of Jesus Christ. In Acts 2, the description of the Holy Spirit at the Pentecost, Peter, quoting the Prophet Joel, tells the crowd that God declared, "I will pour out of my Spirit upon all flesh: and your sons and your daughters shall prophesy," Acts 2:17.

23. Enoch, son of Cain and father of Methuselah, lived 365 years and walked faithfully with God until "he was not; for God took him," Genesis 5:24.

24. Boudinot, a devout Presbyterian, was born in Philadelphia, and his father was a friend of Ben Franklin. Richard Stockton, signer of the Declaration of Independence, was his brother-in-law. He served as President of the Congress of the Confederation until 1783 and was later elected to the U.S. House of Representatives for New Jersey. Boudinot was also an elected member of the American Antiquarian Society and Founder of the American Bible Society. He was a well-known advocate for the civil rights of African and Native Americans.

25. "Welcome Cross," a hymn by popular eighteenth-century poet and hymnodist William Cowper.

26. Elaw's reference to modern Gaul (France) appeals directly to her British audience with her strong critique of deism, which questioned the legitimacy of the Bible as a source of Godly authority and rejected organized religion. At the time of Elaw's publication, British audiences by and large were concerned about the liberal thinking engendered by French philosophers of Enlightenment. Fearing the same kind of radicalism that spawned the French Revolution, Britain was much more suspicious of deism than were other Western countries and, in fact, prosecuted publishers who attempted to print and distribute the pamphlet. Interestingly, Boudinot, the influential New Jersey statesman whose home she visited, authored *The Age of Revelation or*

the Age of Reason Shown to Be an Age of Infidelity (Philadelphia 1801) as a pamphlet for his widowed daughter to refute Thomas Paine's *Age of Reason*.

27. The Fishers of Philadelphia were part of a large and affluent Quaker family, descendants of John Fisher who came to Pennsylvania in 1682 with William Penn. Hannah, Elaw's sister, may have been referencing Thomas and Sarah Fisher's home, Wakefield, near the Germantown neighborhood of Philadelphia.

28. "For then will I turn to the people a pure language, that they may all call upon the name of the LORD, to serve him with one consent," Zephaniah 3:9. The first occurrence of glossolalia—speaking in tongues—occurs in Acts 2:1–4, on the day of the Pentecost. It is considered to be the miracle that helped to form the Christian church as we know it today. For some denominations, speaking in tongues was a requirement to accept Jesus Christ as a savior, while others discouraged or forbade it.

29. "Forasmuch then as the children are partakers of flesh and blood, he also himself likewise took part of the same; that through death he might destroy him that had the power of death, that is, the devil," Hebrew 2:14.

30. "Not that we are sufficient of ourselves to think any thing as of ourselves; but our sufficiency *is* of God," 2 Corinthians 3:5.

31. "And Moses said, Thus saith the LORD, About midnight will I go out into the midst of Egypt: And all the firstborn in the land of Egypt shall die, from the firstborn of Pharaoh that sitteth upon his throne, even unto the firstborn of the maidservant that *is* behind the mill; and all the firstborn of beasts. And there shall be a great cry throughout all the land of Egypt, such as there was none like it, nor shall be like it any more. But against any of the children of Israel shall not a dog move his tongue, against man or beast: that ye may know how that the LORD doth put a difference between the Egyptians and Israel," Exodus 11:4–7. With this comparison to Moses, Elaw situates her own exceptionalism.

32. According to the *Minutes of the Annual Conferences of the Methodist Episcopal Church for the Years 1773–1839*, Volume 1, this was most likely John Potts who was admitted into the connection as a deacon in 1796 and an elder in 1798. By 1814 he was assigned to the East Jersey district (part of the Philadelphia Conference) and in Burlington by 1820.

33. The important distinction between exhortation and preaching is that exhorters were to speak about religious experience (often after a sermon) and only licensed preachers were authorized to "take," or read, biblical text and then teach it. The hierarchy of a Methodist ministry career typically moved from class leader to exhorter, local minister, and then, if qualified, to itinerant preacher. Marriage or failing health would often move itinerant preachers back to being local ministers.

34. Elaw refers to Joseph's brothers who abducted and sold him because he dreamed that he was to be their spiritual leader (Genesis 37:1–11) and to Paul, who recorded that everyone abandoned him when he faced heresy charges in the Roman court (2 Timothy 4:16).

35. Bare feet are commonly considered a sign of humility in Christianity.

36. Consumption was the common term for an infectious bacterial disease that we now call pulmonary tuberculosis.

37. Hymn by Samuel Medley (1738–99).

38. Herndon and Murray call these contracts "pauper apprenticeships." They were often official indentured relationships that impacted the care and work of destitute or orphaned children such as Harriet Wilson (*Our Nig*), Lee, and Elaw.

39. The Bethel AME Church Carpenter Street School in Woodbury, built in 1840, was the first school in New Jersey specifically for educating African Americans. Since

public education was not funded in New Jersey until 1844, schools were founded and supported primarily by religious and philanthropic institutions. As Elaw notes, there was little available for the education of African American children unless private citizens opened schools, sometimes with support from a benefactor or group.

40. "Princes shall come out of Egypt; Ethiopia shall soon stretch out her hands unto God," Psalm 68:31.

41. British common term for available cash or funds in hand.

42. "And they called the name of that place Bochim: and they sacrificed there unto the Lord," Judges 2:5.

43. Elaw references Luke 10:4 and 22:35, in which apostles of Jesus are sent "as lambs among wolves" and told to "carry neither purse, nor scrip." Later, they are reminded that when they did so, they were successful and wanted for nothing. The purse was similar to a money belt and a scrip was a small satchel or travel bag. In *Memoir of Old Elizabeth*, the author also references "purse, nor scrip" to describe the unavoidable poverty of itinerant preaching as a Black woman. Not all but most white women preachers had some level of economic support from husbands, family wealth, or denominational salary.

44. Elaw is most likely referring to the Baltimore Annual Conference of the African Methodist Episcopal denomination led by Richard Allen in the 1820s.

45. Elaw describes her ministry in a slave state as a Christian message to unknowing or unbelieving audiences who will be judged by her missive yet will not be able to deny the truth that she reveals as a messenger of God. She references Paul's instructional letter to the Corinths (1 Corinthians 14:25) in which he privileges language of love (prophecy) over ecstatic utterances (praying in tongues), which he felt only edifies the individual rather than the church. "If therefore the whole church be come together into one place, and all speak with tongues, and there come in *those that are* unlearned, or unbelievers, will they not say that ye are mad? But if all prophesy, and there come in one that believeth not, or *one* unlearned, he is convinced of all, he is judged of all: And thus are the secrets of his heart made manifest; and so falling down on *his* face he will worship God, and report that God is in you of a truth," 1 Corinthians 14:23–25. She ends with another allusion to prophecy when John writes that Jesus prophesied to the Samaritan woman who later testified to her people: "Come, see a man, which told me all things that ever I did: is not this the Christ?" John 4:29.

46. As William Andrews documents in *Sisters of the Spirit*, the Janney family of Pennsylvania were devoted members of the Society of Friends who relocated to Alexandria in the mid-eighteenth century. Abijah's son, Samuel, a published biographer, autobiographer, essayist and poet, was also a well-known antislavery activist.

47. "A word fitly spoken *is like* apples of gold in pictures of silver," Proverbs 25:11.

48. At least eight yellow fever outbreaks were reported in Virginia between 1801 and 1855. According to an English visitor, the fever "which raged there virulently" contributed to destroying trade in the city (Rambler 278).

49. In 1792, after his self-funded mission trip to Calcutta, India, William Carey, a Particular Baptist preacher (also referred to as Reformed or Calvinistic Baptists), published a paper on the importance of Christian missionary work. Soon after, at least three British missionary societies were founded of varying denominations. By the 1820s, when Elaw was asked about a mission trip, both Britain and American denominations had organized mission trips focusing mostly on the African continent. American mission societies included Black American groups such as the African Baptist Missionary Society. The mission work and, in some cases, settlements

in sub-Saharan Africa were an effort to Christianize and "civilize" people in Camer-oon, the Congo, Guinea, Liberia, Sierra Leone, and South Africa. The work often focused on establishing schools and churches to educate the "heathen" children and effect the religious conversion of their parents. Africa continued to be the focus of British- and U.S.-based missionary societies throughout the nineteenth century. See William Carey's *An Enquiry into the Obligations of Christians*; Emily Conroy-Krutz's *Christian Imperialism*; and Eunjin Park's *"White" Americans in "Black" Africa*.

50. Elaw references Anne McCarty Lee (1798–1840), married to Major Henry "Dark-horse" Lee IV (1787–1837), whom Elaw incorrectly refers to as "General." At the time that Elaw reports staying with "Lady Lee," President Andrew Jackson, grieving the recent loss of his beloved wife, Rachel, was enduring heavy critique and ridicule for his friendly protection of Rachel's close friend, Lady Anne Lee. Her husband, Henry, the son of General "Light Horse Harry" Lee and half-brother to General Robert E. Lee, had been dogged by a very public adultery and financial scandal. While mourning the death of his and Anne's two-year-old daughter, Henry impregnated Elizabeth, Anne's teenage sister. Elizabeth later delivered a stillborn baby. Henry, guardian of Elizabeth's estate, was relieved of guardianship and generally shunned, earning the nickname "Dark Horse." In the midst of this scandal, Anne, who had become addicted to opioids after the death of her infant daughter, spent time rehabilitating at the Fountain of Health (a resort reported to have healing waters) in Nashville, Tennessee. There she was befriended and encouraged in her recovery by Rachel Jackson, and the Jacksons are credited with reuniting the estranged couple. Thus, the friendship between the Lees and the Jacksons was cemented, and they were with Rachel during her final illness and with Jackson at her funeral. During the time that Elaw reports she visited their home, the Lees had recently traveled to Washington with Andrew Jackson for his inauguration (Lee wrote Jackson's inaugural speech) and were awaiting Henry Lee's appointment to Consul in Algiers. Jackson, acting out of loyalty for his friend and political worker, had secretly assigned the dangerous post to Lee after years of unsuccessful attempts to get him a government position. Indeed, less than a year after moving to Algiers, the Senate discovered the appointment and voted to recall him. The Lees then emigrated to Paris.

51. Commodore John Rodgers (1772–1838) was perhaps the most revered officer of the early U.S. Navy. He served under the first six U.S. presidents. At the time Rodgers presumably offered Elaw a permanent post in D.C., he was president of the Board of Naval Commissioners. As such, he and his wife, Minerva Dennison Rodgers (1784–1877), were at the center of the Washington political elite. They were a founding family of the naval community built at Greenleaf Point (a peninsula where the Anacostia and Potomac Rivers meet).

52. Elaw refers to Paul's appeal to Philemon (Philemon 1:1–16) after Onesimus, Philemon's slave, has not been in Philemon's service but rather has worked with Paul while he was imprisoned. Paul reasons that Philemon should now receive Onesimus not as his slave but as his brother in Christ and partner in faith.

53. As she reflects on the institution of slavery, Elaw refers to the laws of the second table—the commandments etched on the second stone tablet presented to Moses by God. The first four commandments outline a Christian's duty to God, and the second table, commandments 5–10, concern humanity—Christian obligations to the self and others.

54. In his last letter to Timothy, Paul is close to death, encouraging Timothy to preach, and giving him final instructions. He cautions him not to privilege earthly things

over his love of God like Demas, who "hath forsaken me, having loved this present world, and is departed unto Thessalonica," 2 Timothy 4:10.

55. Elaw refers to Psalm 89: "I will sing of his love forever." Noting that although this is not the mountain of Moses, she alludes to verse 4 of the psalm: "the north and the south thou hast created them: Tabor and Hermon shall rejoice in thy name."

56. Elaw compares her feelings to Paul's affection and concern for his new converts: "My little children, of whom I travail in birth again until Christ be formed in you," Galatians 4:19.

57. "And the angel said unto them, Fear not: for, behold, I bring you good tidings of great joy, which shall be to all people," Luke 2:10. Elaw preached to enslavers and their captives from this text, which is an interesting message, in particular, for enslaved people.

58. "When I was a child, I spake as a child, I understood as a child, I thought as a child: but when I became a man, I put away childish things," 1 Corinthians 13:11.

59. By the end of the nineteenth century, Oyster Bay, New York, was a busy stopping point for connecting trains to Boston, Philadelphia, Baltimore, and Washington, D.C. It was a popular summer resort area and boasted a four-thousand-seat "camp-meeting" tabernacle. As early as 1814, the Methodist Society of Huntingdon held many camp meetings in Oyster Bay (eight miles west of Huntingdon), and in 1833 Oyster Bay formed its own Methodist Society. According to Claire Bellerjeau, the independent historian who found an unpublished poem by Jupiter Hammon, the federal census for 1790 and 1810 documents that African Americans represented 16 percent of the 4,100 residents of Oyster Bay population (Lane n.p.). The region seemed to be a popular destination for outdoor revivals. In his 1833 travel book, *Three Years in North America*, British lawyer James Stuart describes attending an 1830 Methodist camp meeting in nearby Mosquito Cove. He reports that "some time after . . . I happened to go part of the way in the steam-boat with a great party of men of colour and their families, who were proceeding to a camp-meeting, under the charge of their own clergymen, who were men of colour" (428–29).

60. "For we wrestle not against flesh and blood, but against principalities, against powers, against the rulers of the darkness of this world, against spiritual wickedness in high places," Ephesians 6:12. "And having spoiled principalities and powers, he made a shew of them openly, triumphing over them in it," Colossians 2:15. "Wherein in time past ye walked according to the course of this world, according to the prince of the power of the air, the spirit that now worketh in the children of disobedience," Ephesians 2:2. "In whom the god of this world hath blinded the minds of them which believe not, lest the light of the glorious gospel of Christ, who is the image of God, should shine unto them," 2 Corinthians 4:4.

61. The book of Nehemiah relates his mission to rebuild the wall of Jerusalem in spite of opposition from some of the most influential men of the city. The governor of Samaria, Sanballat the Horonite, ridiculed Nehemiah and then led an army to attack the workers.

62. Elaw references 2 Samuel 6:6–7 and Uzzah's irreverent act of disregarding God's clear instructions not to touch the ark. While transporting the ark to David on an oxcart, Uzzah reaches out to steady the rocking ark. He is swiftly struck dead by God as a consequence for touching it but also for presuming that the ark, a symbol of God's covenant, needed his protection.

63. "Some indeed preach Christ even of envy and strife; and some also of good will. The one preach Christ of contention, not sincerely, supposing to add affliction to my bonds. But the other of love, knowing that I am set for the defence of the gospel," Philippians 1:15–17.

64. John Newland Maffitt, an Irish immigrant, began preaching in the New England Methodist Circuit by 1822 and, like Elaw, soon had a ministry extending from Maine to Virginia. Maffitt became infamous for his dramatic and unconventional style of preaching. He was an active antislavery supporter. However, like so many other abolitionists, he did not fully believe in the case for Black civil rights in America. A few months before arriving in Hartford, Connecticut, he delivered a Fourth of July sermon, "A Plea for Africa," for the American Colonization Society advocating the emancipation and gradual removal of enslaved people to West Africa.

65. Many Hebraic and biblical scholars understand *urim* and *thummin* to mean "dark" and "light," "curse" and "blessing," while others use the traditional translation "lights" and "perfections." Elaw appears to be using another accepted translation of *thummin* as "innocent" as in a judgment of guilty (cursed) or not guilty (innocent). *Urim* and *thummin* appear several times in the Old Testament as items (often placed in a breastplate) used to divine the will of God. Some believe the items to be two stones or sticks. Some rabbis believed they were two stones inscribed with Hebraic letters.

66. "For the word of God is quick, and powerful, and sharper than any two edged sword, piercing even to the dividing asunder of soul and spirit, and of the joints and marrow, and is a discerner of the thoughts and intents of the heart," Hebrews 4:12.

67. "The next day John seeth Jesus coming unto him, and saith, Behold the Lamb of God, which taketh away the sin of the world," John 1:29.

68. "For I determined not to know any thing among you, save Jesus Christ, and him crucified," 1 Corinthians 2:2.

69. "Know ye not that ye are the temple of God, and that the Spirit of God dwelleth in you?" 1 Corinthians 3:16; "Put on the whole armour of God, that ye may be able to stand against the wiles of the devil," Ephesians 6:11.

70. "He maketh me to lie down in green pastures: he leadeth me beside the still waters," Psalms 23:2. "Now unto him that is able to keep you from falling, and to present you faultless before the presence of his glory with exceeding joy," Jude 24.

71. According to the book of Joshua, after the death of Moses, Joshua was commissioned to lead the twelve tribes of Israel to Canaan, the land promised to them by God.

72. *The Historical Sketch of Salem, 1626–1879* reports that a "*Mission Chapel*, for the use of the colored people, was erected in 1828." Originally known as Union Bethel, the church reorganized in 1839 as the Wesleyan Methodist Church. This 1879 history does not, however, mention the work of the church founder, John Remond, father of Sarah and Charles, both famous antislavery orators. Remond and his wife, Nancy, were successful Black entrepreneurs and tireless civil rights activists in Salem. Remond was a principal advocate for building the church. An 1827 advertisement in the *Salem Gazette* solicits "any person desirous of digging and completing the Cellar . . . will please apply to John Remond, William Willams, Prince Farmer, Building Committee" (3). The significance of Elaw delivering the inaugural sermon would indicate some relationship with the Remond family given that she spent an entire winter in Salem.

73. "Now I beseech you, brethren, mark them which cause divisions and offences contrary to the doctrine which ye have learned; and avoid them," Romans 16:17; "For ye are yet carnal: for whereas there is among you envying, and strife, and divisions, are ye not carnal, and walk as men?" 1 Corinthians 3:3.

74. Abyssinian Congregational Church, incorporated in 1828, was the geographic center of Portland's Black community, located in one of its poorest neighborhoods near the docks. The church later joined with another Congregational church and the building also housed a school for approximately fifty Black students (Connolly 360). Most of

the membership were impoverished seamen and widows, and the congregation was largely illiterate. Nonetheless, like most Black churches of the period, Abyssinian was central to the daily lives of its community, serving as the home for sewing circles, youth and adult education, and antislavery meetings. In addition to hosting famous speakers including Frederick Douglass and William Lloyd Garrison, Abyssinian was a significant contributor to the Colored Conventions, a national political organizing movement for Black Americans that lasted until well after the Civil War (Boch et al. 9–10). See Foreman, Casey, and Patterson for comprehensive analysis of the Colored Conventions.

75. "And when they were come up out of the water, the Spirit of the Lord caught away Philip, that the eunuch saw him no more: and he went on his way rejoicing," Acts 8:39.

76. Elaw refers to Bowdoin College in 1830. Their class of 1826 included John Brown Russwurm, among the first group of African American college graduates in the nation. In 1827, Russwurm and Samuel Cornish published the first African American newspaper, *Freedom's Journal*.

77. *Nabal*, also a Hebrew word for "foolish" or "senseless," is described as churlish and vindictive in his affairs, generally a mean-spirited person (1 Samuel 25:3).

78. God's blessings are for those who obey. Being in the perfect will of God brings peace and righteousness that flows from within and never goes dry.

79. "God Moves in a Mysterious Way" (1774), a hymn written by William Cowper.

80. The hymn "Come Thou Fount of Every Blessing" was written by Robert Robinson, an English dissenter, in 1757, shortly after he converted to Methodism. Robinson converted to Baptist soon after.

81. Elaw alludes to Ezekiel in the Valley of Dry Bones, where he was commanded to prophesy: "and as I prophesied, there was a noise, and behold a shaking, and the bones came together, bone to his bone. . . . So I prophesied as he commanded me, and the breath came into them, and they lived, and stood up upon their feet, an exceeding great army," Ezekiel 37:7–10.

82. In Paul's letter to the church in Rome, he writes: "I commend unto you Phebe our sister, which is a servant of the church which is at Cenchrea: That ye receive her in the Lord, as becometh saints, and that ye assist her in whatsoever business she hath need of you: for she hath been a succourer of many, and of myself also. Greet Priscilla and Aquila my helpers in Christ Jesus: Who have for my life laid down their own necks: unto whom not only I give thanks, but also all the churches of the Gentiles," Romans 16:1–4.

83. Rebecca Elaw married Thomas Pierce (b. c. 1810), a Nantucket mariner, in January 1833. The 1840 U.S. Census lists Thomas Pierce as head of family and "Persons Employed in Navigation of the Ocean." The "Free Colored Persons" category lists one female age 24–35, one female 36–55, and two males under 10. Presumably Rebecca, her mother, and her two sons were living in the home, and Thomas was away at sea at the time. Thomas and Rebecca had three sons: Joseph (1834–92), Thomas (1837–58), and David (1846–1911). Thomas Jr. died of consumption at twenty-one years old. Thomas Sr. died sometime between late 1844 and 1849. Rebecca remarried James Crawford, the town barber and beloved community preacher, in November 1868. Rebecca died of "intermittent fever" on October 21, 1883 in Nantucket, Massachusetts (1840 U.S. Census).

84. Nantucket had two MEC chapels. Elaw was a member of the Centre Street Church. Rebecca Elaw and Thomas Pierce, Sr. are listed as members of Fair Street Church.

85. Her brother, Joseph Panco, is listed in the 1830 U.S. Census as head of household in

Utica New York, Oneida County. The Pancos lived in proximity to six other Black families, totaling 42 people of color listed among the 156 people registered on the same census page. No other page of the Utica census lists this many Black families; in fact, most pages list only a single or no Black families. Several pages list free Black individuals living in white households (most likely as laborers or servants). The Pancos are listed as a free colored family of five with one male and one female age 10–23, two males 36–54, and one female 36–54.

86. In general, this term was used to indicate inexperience combined with arrogance. For instance, the August 24, 1834, edition of *Railway, Locomotives and Cars* includes a note, "my report was not considered by him worthy of note; indeed I was treated as a tyros; one whose remarks and observations were not worthy listening to" (538).

87. Rebecca Pierce gave birth to Joseph E. Pierce (d. January 1892).

88. Elaw references Rev. Thomas Pierce (no known relation to Rebecca's husband), minister of record for the Centre Street Methodist Episcopal Church of Nantucket, 1832–33. The Black Baptist Nantucketers who left the white Summer Street Baptist Church formed the York Street Colored Baptist Society in 1831. They later became the Pleasant Street Baptist Church ministered by Rev. James Crawford, Rebecca Elaw Pierce's second husband. See Myron Dudley's pamphlet *Churches and Pastors of Nantucket, Mass., from the First Settlement to the Present Time, 1659–1902*.

89. Dudley's genealogical paper, "Two Centuries of Churches and Pastors in Nantucket, Mass.," lists John Lovejoy as minister from 1834 to 1835 and again in 1848 (10).

90. George Thompson (1804–78), an English Wesleyan preacher, worked with William Lloyd Garrison on antislavery fund-raising during Garrison's 1833 trip to England. Thompson later toured the United States as an agent of the British and Foreign Anti-Slavery Society from October 1834 to November 1835. During his tour, Thompson condemned the American churches, especially the Methodists ministers, for their stalwart defense of and participation in slavery, North and South. On October 21, 1835, a mob of thousands attempted to tar and feather Thompson, who was scheduled to speak at a meeting of the Boston Female Anti-Slavery Society. That mob instead seized Garrison, put a rope around his neck, and dragged him through the streets. Thompson, who made a lasting impression on many in the MEC, was denounced as a foreign agitator and may be best known for his 1851 lecture at Boston's Faneuil Hall. In London, Thompson was a major organizer of the 1840 World's Anti-Slavery Convention and was likely involved in the BFASS committee that invited and offended Elaw in 1841.

Thompson is mentioned in a letter from William Wood requesting that Peter Macy of Nantucket verify his signature on Elaw's letter of recommendation (see appendix B, fig. 12). In his response to Wood, Macy refers to Thompson's 1835 "Fast Day" lecture at a Methodist Meeting house in Boston. The letter author is most likely the William Wood of Salford, baptized in the Gravel Lane Wesleyan Methodist Chapel in 1798. By 1834 he was a lawyer and the corresponding secretary for the Manchester First Circuit in the Wesleyan Methodist Conference. Peter Macy was a descendant of Thomas Macy, reported to be the first white settler of Nantucket. The Macys were known for their anti-racist sentiments. Peter, an active abolitionist, addressed the Anti-Slavery Convention at Nantucket where Frederick Douglass gave his first speech and was hired as a lecturer. He was also a leader in the 1840s fight to integrate the public schools in Massachusetts, a fight that began on Nantucket.

91. Elijah Hedding (1780–1852) was pastor of the Lynn MEC from 1813 to 1814 and 1818 to 1819. Elected Bishop in 1824, he lived in Lynn until 1837, when he left during the antislavery and anti-masonry agitations. Although he was a staunch

defender of expanding the MEC through revivals and lay preachers, Hedding and other bishops such as Joshua Soule felt that abolitionists were radical agitators with no place in church business. While Hedding stated publicly and in print that he condemned the slave trade and the "system of slavery," he stopped short of condemning slavery as a deal-breaker for being a member of or leader in the Methodist Church.

92. Founded in Philadelphia by William Lloyd Garrison and Arthur Tappan, the American Anti-Slavery Society (1833–70) held annual May meetings in New York. Well-known members included Frederick Douglass, Henry Highland Garnet, James Forten, Sarah Parker Remond, Charles Lenox Remond, Robert Purvis, Lucretia Mott, Lewis Tappan, Wendell Phillips, Lydia Maria Child, Elizabeth Cady Stanton, and Susan B. Anthony. The society had several splits over the years due to differences in approaches to abolitionism, the first being Garrison's more radical, non-religious dissension.

93. The British and Foreign Anti-Slavery Society organized the 1840 World Anti-Slavery Convention in Exeter Hall, London, June 12–23. The activist attendees included formerly enslaved speakers, ministers, scholars, politicians, journalists, educators, and others. The public proceedings attracted more than a thousand daily spectators.

94. In Genesis 12:1–3, God commands an elderly Abraham to move his family to Canaan and promises "I will make you into a great nation, and I will bless you; I will make your name great, so that you will be a blessing. I will bless those who bless you and curse those who curse you; and all the families of the earth will be blessed through you."

95. Selina Hastings, Countess of Huntingdon (1707–91), was perhaps the most influential female figure of eighteenth-century English Methodism during the Protestant revival movement known as the First Great Awakening. After hearing George Whitefield and the Wesley brothers preach (at the urging of her sisters-in-law, both fervent Methodists), Selina was converted, much to the chagrin of her husband, the Earl of Huntingdon. He immediately called for an Anglican bishop to bring her to her senses, and it was rumored that Selina almost converted the bishop. When she was widowed after twenty years of marriage, Selina devoted herself (and her fortune) to converting others. Known as the Countess of Huntingdon Connexion, several Methodist districts served by an extensive network of new traveling preachers were funded by the countess, who sold much of her jewelry and property to purchase land and chapels for the Methodist mission. The countess and several of her royal women converts also traveled the country to convert other royals and advise the lay preachers of the Connexion, including the Wesley brothers and Whitefield. One such preacher, David Taylor, is credited with converting thirteen-year-old Francis Asbury, who was sent to America at age twenty-six to establish the Methodist Episcopal Church in 1771 and became one of its first bishops. Hastings founded a minister's college (now a part of Cambridge University) and encouraged the establishment of Princeton and Dartmouth Colleges. She also supported African American preachers and writers including John Marrant and Phillis Wheatley. However, Hastings endured a long and public dispute with John Wesley and Anthony Benezet over her continued investment in American slavery after she inherited Whitefield's orphanage in Georgia, built and maintained by enslaved Africans. For all of these reasons, the significant power of the Countess of Huntingdon was controversial for many Methodist leaders.

96. The British and Foreign Anti-Slavery Society (BFASS) and the Society for the Promotion of Permanent and Universal Peace are referenced in the notes to the introduction.

97. Here, Elaw compares their skepticism to that of the Jews in 1 Corinthians who expected a victorious Messiah rather than a crucified man.
98. This is most likely Elaw's bookseller, Mr. B. Taylor.
99. John Coulson and J. Crompton were prominent supporters of Elaw's preaching career in Northern England. Both are listed as ministers and district supervisors in the records of the Primitive Methodists during her time in England. Coulson, in fact, was sanctioned more than once for improper conduct regarding engaging (and possibly providing steady salary for) Elaw to preach.
100. "Enter ye in at the strait gate: for wide is the gate, and broad is the way, that leadeth to destruction, and many there be which go in thereat," Matthew 7:13.
101. "Seals to my ministry," or converted souls, is a common phrase used in spiritual narratives to indicate God's validation of a person's call to preach. When Paul needed to prove his apostleship, he referenced his Corinthian converts as seals to his ministry in 1 Corinthians 9:2. Also in 2 Corinthians 3:1–3, he declares that "*Forasmuch as ye are* manifestly declared to be the epistle of Christ ministered by us, written not with ink, but with the Spirit of the living God; not in tables of stone, but in fleshy tables of the heart."
102. Mary Bosanquet Fletcher (1739–1815) grew up in a wealthy Huguenot family and by the age of seventeen had renounced her wealth and converted to Methodism. After being disowned by her parents for rejecting a wealthy suitor, Bosanquet and Sarah Ryan, friend and mentor, started the Cedars, an orphanage school. They later moved to a farm, Cross Hall, and developed it into a Methodist Society. Cross Hall (1768–1782) housed and educated many prominent women, including Sarah Lawrence. Soon after Ryan's death, Bosanquet married John Fletcher in 1781, closed Cross Hall, and started a co-ministry with Fletcher, who died four years after they married. Fletcher continued her popular ministry. In fact, she is credited with convincing John Wesley not only to admit women exhorters but also to allow women to preach directly from text, which he had formerly opposed. By the time of her death, she had authored several Methodist pamphlets, published letters in the monthly *Methodist Magazine*, and transcribed and preserved a previously unpublished dream manuscript (anonymous author). Fletcher's diaries and letters are collected and edited in Henry Moore's *The Life of Mrs. Mary Fletcher* (1817).

Anne Carr (1783–1841) was converted to Wesleyan Methodism at eighteen but found Primitive Methodists more appealing and began preaching with them by 1820. Spending much of her time ministering to the poor, Carr helped to open the Methodist chapel in Hull and later in Leeds. In 1821, tired of the constant rebukes from male leaders, Carr left the Primitive Methodists and founded the Female Revivalist Society. Martha Williams, Carr's protégé, published *Memoirs of the Life and Character of Ann Carr* in 1841.

103. The superintendent minister of Bradford was sanctioned for employing a Black woman to preach.
104. William Dawson (1773–1841) was a Yorkshire farmer and famous preacher known for the dramatic power of his sermons. Elaw's reference to Garland was most likely Rev. Thomas A. Galland from Leeds.
105. Elaw references the story of Deborah, a biblical heroine. One of the very few women prophets, she was also the fourth (and only female) judge of Israel mentioned in the Old Testament. Judges 4 tells the story of Deborah's deliverance of the Israelites from twenty years of severe oppression under Jabin. However, it is also a story of cunning and agency in the face of dangerous men. Although Deborah devises the plan that fells Jabin's army, it is another woman who actually kills the army general, Sisera.

When Sisera runs to the tent of a family loyal to Jabin, Heber's wife, Jael, offers him drink and a hiding place. When Heber falls asleep, Jael drives a tent stake through Sisera's temple.

The prophet Huldah is mentioned only once, but her prophecy is renowned for saving a nation. When King Josiah needs verification that they have found the lost book of laws given to Moses, his highest priest seeks counsel from Huldah, trusting that only through her will they receive word directly from God. Huldah validates the discovery and delivers a prophecy that revived the covenant of God for Josiah and his kingdom (2 Kings 22:14–20; 2 Chronicles 34:22–33).

106. Elaw's allusion to Tekel references Daniel 5:27 and signifies deficiency: "Thou art weighted in the balances, and art found wanting." In the story of Daniel and King Belshazzar, a divine disembodied hand appears and writes on the wall during a great banquet. No one can read the writing, and the terrified king sends for Daniel to interpret. Daniel tells him that his lack of humility before God has resulted in the writing on the wall: that his days are numbered, he has been judged deficient, and his kingdom would be divided between two new rulers.

107. Manchester's first and only such school at the time was Henshaw's Blind Asylum, established in 1839. The education of blind and deaf children was not compulsory until the Elementary Education Act of 1893.

108. "Trust in the Lord with all thine heart; and lean not unto thine own understanding. In all thy ways acknowledge him, and he shall direct thy paths," Proverbs 3:5–6.

109. The year 1843 seems to be a misprint in both editions of the original memoir and should have been recorded as June 13, 1842. In August of this same summer, Elaw states that she went to "hear Bishop Soul[e] from America," and Soule toured England in 1842. In fact, his passport shows that he left England on August 7 (the same day Elaw reports he preached at Great Queen-street chapel) and was back in the United States later that month. Also, a few pages later Elaw reports that it's January 1843, so the chronology suggests that, at this point, she is still referring to events in 1842.

110. Sarah, a revered figure in the Old Testament, is best known as Abraham's beautiful wife and half-sister who gave birth to a miracle child at the age of ninety. Soon after they were married, Abraham, the patriarch of Judaism, Islam, and Christianity, asked Sarah to reveal herself only as his sister (and not his wife) to the Egyptians, who might kill him to get to her. She did so, and Abraham received their special favor, but soon the pharaoh took Sarah as his wife. He returned her to Abraham only after being punished by God for taking another man's wife. Sarah's sacrifice for her husband and late-life motherhood marked her as a long-suffering, dutiful wife and mother of nations.

111. Joshua Soule (1781–1867) served as deacon, elder and book agent for the Methodist Episcopal Church. He was elected bishop in 1820 but declined over a policy issue, then was elected again and accepted in 1824. Soule traveled to England and Ireland as an American delegate to the Wesleyan Methodist General Conferences from April to August 1842. Immediately upon his return to the United States, Soule was embroiled in the heated debates about the church's stance on slavery. When the MEC split in 1844 over the issue, Soule left the New England Conference and presided as bishop over the newly formed Methodist Episcopal Church, South. For a comprehensive analysis of early evangelicalism in the South, see Heyrman's *Southern Cross*.

112. In the book of Genesis, the populations of two cities on the Jordan River, Sodom and Gomorrah, are judged impenitent and beyond redemption. God destroys the cities with the exception of one penitent family, Lot and his daughters. The city names

became modern-day metaphors for behavior considered to be "unnatural," especially pertaining to sexuality.

113. Rainton Hall, a mansion in the center of West Rainton, was approximately four miles northeast of Durham, built in 1688 by Sir John Duke. The region was populated largely by tenements occupied by coal miners.

114. "Nor thieves, nor covetous, nor drunkards, nor revilers, nor extortioners, shall inherit the kingdom of God," 1 Corinthians 6:10.

115. Thomas Dudley, a bookbinder on Charterhouse-lane, was listed under "Insolvent Debtors" in the 1848 *Jurist*. Dudley filed bankruptcy with a court date for May 11, 1848.

116. See figure 14 in appendix B for a rendering of London's Jewin Street Wesleyan Chapel.

117. Elaw references the Parable of the Virgins (Matthew 25) in which five of the ten virgins missed the bridegroom (Christ) and midnight wedding banquet because they were not prepared for his arrival at any hour.

118. Matthew 24 lists signs of the physical return of Jesus Christ, indicating the end of earthly existence for all Christians.

Appendix A

1. Thomas most likely died at sea. The 1847 crew list for the whaling vessel, Junior, includes Thomas Pierce. The whalers were often at sea for three to four years.

2. An 1855 crew listing of the *Emily* notes a Thomas Pierce, eighteen years old, Black with "wooly" hair. Rebecca's son, like his father, may have been a mariner. His 1858 death records note that he died in Massachusetts and is buried in the Crawford family plot.

3. Ann Crawford's sister, Julia, was married to the famous minister Henry Highland Garnet. Garnet's family escaped Maryland enslavement and settled in New York when he was a child. Garnet became a well-educated minister and radical abolitionist who delivered "An Address to the Slaves of the United States of America" at the 1843 National Convention of Colored Citizens in Buffalo, New York. His speech called for armed resistance to enslavement citing moral suasion as a failed tactic. The Garnets were in England when Diana was kidnapped and sold.

WORKS CITED

1790 U.S. Federal Census. Bucks, Pennsylvania, series M637, roll 8, p. 52.

1800 U.S. Federal Census. Middletown, Bucks, Pennsylvania, series M32; roll 36, p. 306.

1810 U.S. Federal Census. Middletown, Bucks, Pennsylvania, roll 46, p. 933.

1830 U.S. Federal Census. Utica, Oneida, New York, series M19, roll 99, p. 6.

1840 U.S. Federal Census. Nantucket, Massachusetts, roll 193, p. 417.

"1841 Census of England, Middlesex, St. Clement Danes, Ralph Shum." *Census Returns of England and Wales, 1841*. National Archives of the UK, Public Record Office, folio 30, line 11.

"1841 Census of England, Yorkshire, Addingham, Zilpha Elaw." *Census Returns of England and Wales, 1841*. National Archives of the UK, Public Record Office, p. 14, folio 32, line 20.

1850 U.S. Census, Population Schedule. National Archives and Records Administration, record 328.

"1851 Census of England, Middlesex, Mile End Old Town, Thomas Shum Household." *Census Returns of England and Wales, 1851*. National Archives of the UK, Public Record Office, p. 33, folio 563.

1860 U.S. Census, Population Schedule. National Archives and Records Administration, series M653, roll 1,438.

"1861 Census of England, Middlesex, Mile End Old Town, Tipha Thurn Household." *Census Returns of England and Wales, 1861*. National Archives of the UK, Public Record Office, p. 7, folio 115, lines 19–20.

"1871 Census of Kew, Surrey, and England." *Census Returns of England and Wales, 1871*. National Archives of the UK, Public Record Office, class RG10, piece 554, p. 5, folio 140, roll 823397.

"Advertisement." *Salem Gazette*, vol. 5, no. 49, 22 June 1827, p. 3. *Readex: America's Historical Newspapers*.

"A Novel Preacher." *Bicester Herald*, 1 November 1856. *British Newspaper Archive*.

Andrews, William L. *Sisters of the Spirit: Three Black Women's Autobiographies of the Nineteenth Century*. Indiana University Press, 1986.

"Anniversary of the Wesleyan Centenary Chapel, Kirkby Stephen." *Kendal Mercury*, 5 June 1847. *British Newspaper Archive*.

Blanton, Wyndham B. *Medicine in Virginia in the Nineteenth Century*. Garrett & Massie, 1931.

Blockett, Kimberly. "Disrupting Print: Emigration, the Press, and Narrative Subjectivity in the British Preaching and Writing of Zilpha Elaw, 1840–1860s." *MELUS: Multi-Ethnic Literature of the U.S.*, vol. 40, no. 3, 2015, pp. 94–109.

Boch, Susie, Joseph S. Wood, Maureen Elgersman Lee, Howard M. Solomon, and Abraham J. Peck. "Liberating Visions: Religion and the Challenge of Change in Maine, 1820 to the Present." *Publications (Annual Event Catalog)*, 2006, p. 3.

Boudinot, Elias. *The Age of Revelation: or, The Age of Reason Shewn to Be an Age of Infidelity*. Philadelphia: Asbury Dickins, 1801.

Bourque, Monique. "Women and Work in the Philadelphia Almshouse, 1790–1840." *Journal of the Early Republic*, vol. 32, no. 3, 2012, pp. 383–413. *JSTOR*, www.jstor.org /stable/23315160.

Brekus, Catherine A. *Strangers and Pilgrims: Female Preaching in America, 1740–1845*. University of North Carolina Press, 1998.

Brown, Candy Gunther. *The Word in the World: Evangelical Writing, Publishing, and Reading in America*. University of North Carolina Press, 2004.

Bucks County, Pennsylvania, Tax Records, 1782–1860. Bucks County Historical Society, Doylestown, Pennsylvania.

"Burial Record, Ralph Bressey Shum." *All Souls Cemetery, Kensal Green, Kensington, Transcript of Burials, Jan. 1854–Dec. 1854*, London Metropolitan Archives, 1854.

Byron, Gay L. *Symbolic Blackness and Ethnic Difference in Early Christian Literature*. Psychology Press, 2002, pp. 105–15.

Caballero, Chamion. "Interraciality in Early Twentieth Century Britain: Challenging Traditional Conceptualisations through Accounts of 'Ordinariness.'" *Genealogy* vol. 3, no. 2, 2019. https://doi.org/10.3390/genealogy3020021

Carey, William. *An Enquiry into the Obligations of Christians, to Use Means for the Conversion of the Heathen*. Leicester: Ann Ireland, 1792.

Carroll, Robert P., and Stephen Prickett, editors. *The Bible: Authorized King James Version*. Oxford University Press, 2008.

Carwardine, Richard. *Trans-Atlantic Revivalism: Popular Evangelicalism in Britain and America, 1790–1865*. Westport: Greenwood, 1978.

Cater, Philip. *Punch in the Pulpit*. 3rd ed., London: William Freeman, 1863.

Connolly, Michael C. "Black Fades to Green: Irish Labor Replaces African-American Labor Along a Major New England Waterfront, Portland, Maine, in the Mid-Nineteenth Century." *Colby Quarterly*, vol. 37, 2001, p. 18.

Conroy-Krutz, Emily. *Christian Imperialism: Converting the World in the Early American Republic*. Cornell University Press, 2015, p. 75.

Cooley, Steven D. "Manna and the Manual: Sacramental and Instrumental Constructions of the Victorian Methodist Camp Meeting during the Mid-Nineteenth Century." *Religion and American Culture: A Journal of Interpretation*, vol. 6, no. 2, 1996, pp. 131–59.

"County Petty Sessions, July 22: Brutal Assault." *The Bury and Norwich Post, and Suffolk Herald*, 28 July 1857. *19th Century British Library Newspapers*.

"Death Certificate [Ann Shum]." *England and Wales Civil Registration Indexes*, vol. 1, 1850, p. 304.

"Death Certificate [Zilpha Shum]. 20 August 1873." *England and Wales Civil Registration Indexes*, vol. 1, 1873, p. 370.

Douglass, Frederick, and William Lloyd Garrison. *Narrative of the Life of Frederick Douglass, An American Slave*. Boston: Anti-Slavery Office, 1849.

Dudley, Myron S. *Churches and Pastors of Nantucket, Mass. from the First Settlement to the Present Time: 1659–1902*. Press of D. Clapp & Son, 1902.

Dudley, Myron S. "Two Centuries of Churches and Pastors in Nantucket, Mass." *New England Historical and Genealogical Register*, January 1902.

Dunbar, Erica Armstrong. *A Fragile Freedom: African American Women and Emancipation in the Antebellum City*. Yale University Press, 2008.

"Early History of Bristol." *Bucks County Historical Society, Vol. 1*, Published by B. F. Fackenthal, Jr., Pennsylvania State University Libraries, pp. 515–36.

Elaw, Zilpha. *Memoirs of the Life, Religious Experience, Ministerial Travels and Labours of Mrs. Zilpha Elaw, An American Female of Colour; Together with Some Account of the Great Religious Revivals in America*. Published by Zilpha Elaw, sold by T. Dudley, 1846.

Elizabeth. *Memoir of Old Elizabeth, a Coloured Woman*. Philadelphia: Collins, 1863.

———. *Elizabeth, a Colored Minister of the Gospel Born in Slavery*. Philadelphia: Tract Association of Friends, 1889.

Finke, Roger, and Rodney Stark. *The Churching of America, 1776–2005: Winners and Losers in Our Religious Economy*. Rutgers University Press, 2005.

Foreman, P. Gabrielle, Jim Casey, and Sarah Lynn Patterson. *The Colored Conventions Movement: Black Organizing in the Nineteenth Century*. University of North Carolina Press, 2021.

Foote, Julia. *A Brand Plucked from the Fire: An Autobiographical Sketch*. Cleveland: Lauer & Yost, 1879.

Gewehr, W. M. "Some Factors in the Expansion of Frontier Methodism, 1800–1811." *Journal of Religion*, vol. 8, no. 1, 1928, pp. 98–120.

Goode, Gloria Davis. *From Bucks County, Pennsylvania to Nantucket, Massachusetts: Zilpha Panco Elaw, African-American Spiritual Autobiographer*. Nantucket Historical Association Research Library and Archives, 1996.

Hanley, Ryan. *Beyond Slavery and Abolition: Black British Writing, c. 1770–1830*. Cambridge University Press, 2018.

Hempton, David. *Methodism: Empire of the Spirit*. Yale University Press, 2005.

Herndon, Ruth Wallis, and John E. Murray, editors. *Children Bound to Labor: The Pauper Apprentice System in Early America*. Cornell University Press, 2009.

Hindmarsh, D. Bruce. *The Evangelical Conversion Narrative: Spiritual Autobiography in Early Modern England*. Oxford University Press, 2007.

———. *The Spirit of Early Evangelicalism: True Religion in a Modern World*. New York: Oxford University Press, 2018.

Heyrman, Christine Leigh. *Southern Cross: The Beginnings of the Bible Belt*. Chapel Hill: University of North Carolina Press, 1997.

Jackson, Rebecca. *Gifts of Power the Writings of Rebecca Jackson, Black Visionary, Shaker Eldress*, edited by Jean M. Humez, University of Massachusetts Press, 1987.

Jacobs, Harriet. *Incidents in the Life of a Slave Girl: Written by Herself*, edited by L. Maria Child. London: Hodson and Son, 1862.

Jay, Elisabeth. *The Evangelical and Oxford Movements*. Cambridge University Press, 1983.

Jones, Margaret. "From 'The State of My Soul' to 'Exalted Piety': Women's Voices in the Arminian Magazine/Methodist Magazine, 1778–1821." *Gender and Christian Religion*, edited by R. N. Swanson. Suffolk: Boydell and Brewer, 1998, pp. 273–86.

Lane, Laura. "Documents Confirm Large Presence of African-Americans in Colonial Oyster Bay." *Long Island Herald*, 9 February 2018. www.liherald.com/stories/docu ments-confirm-large-presence-ofafrican-americans-in-colonial-oyster-bay,99946. Accessed December 8, 2019.

Leask, Nigel. *Curiosity and the Aesthetics of Travel Writing, 1770–1840: "From an Antique Land."* New York: Oxford University Press, 2002.

Lee, Jarena. *Religious Experience and Journal of Mrs. Jarena Lee: Giving an Account of Her Call to Preach the Gospel*. Revised and corrected from the original manuscript written by herself, Philadelphia: printed and published for the author, 1849.

Letter from Zilpha Elaw. John Harfield Tredgold. Secretary of the British Foreign Anti-Slavery Society. Mar 13 1839–May 30 1842. C 6/1–151 Chap-Fen. Correspondence from the Secretaries and Other Officials of the Society. Oxford, Bodleian Libraries, MSS. Brit. Emp. s. 18 / C6.

Lyght, Ernest. *Path of Freedom: The Black Presence in New Jersey's Burlington County, 1659–1900*. E. & E. Publishing House, 1978.

"Marriage Certificate [Ralph Shum and Ann Hayden], 1824." *Pallot's Marriage Index for England: 1780–1837*, The Generations Network, Inc., 2001.

"Marriage Certificate [Zilpha Elaw]. 9 Dec. 1850." *England and Wales Civil Registration Indexes*, vol. 2, General Register Office, 1850, p. 381.

McNeill, John J. *The Church and the Homosexual*. 4th ed., Beacon Press, 1993, pp. 63–65.

———. *Freedom, Glorious Freedom: The Spiritual Journey to the Fullness of Life for Gays, Lesbians, and Everybody Else*. Lethe, 2010, p. 211.

Methodist Episcopal Church. *Minutes of the Annual Conferences of the Methodist Episcopal Church for the Years 1773–1839, Volume 1*. T. Mason and G. Lane, 1840.

Mitchie, Helena. "Looking at Victorian Honeymoons." *Common Knowledge*, vol. 6, no. 1, 1997, pp. 125–36.

Moody, Joycelyn. *Sentimental Confessions: Spiritual Narratives of Nineteenth-Century African American Women*. University of Georgia Press, 2001.

Moon, James. *An Account of Negroes Set Free, Kept by James Moon of Woodburn, Son of Roger Moon Who Came from England, 1776–1782*. Manuscript journal from Haverford Quaker Collection.

Moore, Henry. *The Life of Mrs. Mary Fletcher*. London: J. Kershaw, 1824.

"Mrs. Elaw Again! To the Editor of the Kendal Mercury." *Kendal Mercury*, 21 August 1847. *British Newspaper Archive*.

"Mrs. Elaw. To the Editor of the Kendal Mercury." *Kendal Mercury*, 14 August 1847. *British Newspaper Archive*.

M.S.W. "The Story of the Schumm Family by M.S.W.: *The Methodist Recorder* Winter Number. December 1893." *Schumm*. http://thurman.org.uk/roots/shum/methodist.html. Accessed 7 March 2016.

Noll, Mark. *American Evangelical Christianity: An Introduction*. Malden: Blackwell, 2001.

"Obituary [Rebecca (Elaw) Crawford]." *The Inquirer and Mirror*, 27 October 1883.

"Obituary [Zilpha Shum]." *The Methodist Recorder and General Christian Times*, 1 September 1873.

"Organ Opening." *Leeds Mercury*, 17 April 1841. *British Newspaper Archive*.

Osgood, Charles Stuart, and Henry Morrill Batchelder. *Historical Sketch of Salem, 1626–1879*. Salem: Essex Institute, 1879, p. 98.

Paine, Thomas. *Paine: The Collected Writings*. New York: Library of America, 1955.

Palin, William. "The Lost Squares of Stepney." *Spitalfields Life*, 30 December 2012, https://spitalfieldslife.com/2012/12/30/the-lost-squares-of-stepney/. Accessed 3 August 2020.

Park, Eunjin. *"White" Americans in "Black" Africa: Black and White American Methodist Missionaries in Liberia, 1820–1875*. Psychology Press, 2001, p. 4.

Perry, Seth. *Bible Culture and Authority in the Early United States*. Princeton: Princeton University Press, 2018.

"Petition of Edward Pompey and 104 Others of Nantucket for Amendment of the Common School Law." Massachusetts Anti-Slavery and Anti-Segregation Petitions; Passed Acts; St. 1845, c.214, SC1/series 229. Massachusetts Archives, Boston. 10 March 2015.

Philip, Robert Kemp. *The Shopkeeper's Guide*. London: Houlston and Stoneman, 1853.

Primitive Methodist General Committee Minute Book of 1842. Itinerant Preachers' Friendly Society, (PM) Minutes, Membership Registers and Ephemera. Methodist Archives and Research Centre, Manchester, UK. Reference MA 1977/121 (GB 135). 8 July 2005.

Primitive Methodist Itinerant Preachers' Friendly Society Minutes, 1841–58. Itinerant Preachers' Friendly Society, (PM) Minutes, Membership Registers and Ephemera. Methodist Archives and Research Centre, Manchester, UK. Reference MA 1977/121 (GB 135). 8 July 2005.

"Primitive Methodists." *Cambridge Chronicle and Journal*, 25 October 1856. *British Newspaper Archive*.

"Primitive Wesleyanism." *Nottinghamshire Guardian*, 5 March 1857. *British Newspaper Archive*.

Prince, Nancy. *A Narrative of the Life and Travels of Mrs. Nancy Prince*. Boston: Published by Nancy Prince, 1853.

Railway, Locomotives and Cars. vol. 3, July–December 1834, Bristol, Conn., etc., Simmons-Boardman Pub. Corp.

"Ralph Bressey Shum." *Electoral Registers*, London Metropolitan Archives, 1856.

Religious Society of Friends. "Philadelphia Yearly Meeting of the Religious Society of Friends." *The Ancient Testimony of the Religious Society of Friends, Commonly Called Quakers, Respecting Some of Their Christian Doctrines and Practices*. Philadelphia: Joseph Rakestraw, 1843.

Richey, Russell. *Early American Methodism*. Indiana University Press, 1991.

Rogers, Jack. *Jesus, the Bible, and Homosexuality*. Westminster John Knox, 2009.

Rule, John. "Methodism, Popular Beliefs and Village Culture in Cornwall, 1800–50." *Popular Culture and Custom in Nineteenth-Century England*, edited by Robert Storch, Routledge, 2016.

Sernett, Milton C. *Black Religion and American Evangelicalism: White Protestants, Plantation Missions, and the Flowering of Negro Christianity, 1787–1865*. Scarecrow Press, 1975.

Sharpless, Isaac. *Quakerism and Politics: Essays*. Ferris and Leach, 1905.

Smith, Amanda. *An Autobiography: The Story of the Lord's Dealings with Mrs. Amanda Smith, the Colored Evangelist: Containing an Account of Her Life Work of Faith, and Her Travels in America, England, Ireland, Scotland, India, and Africa as an Independent Missionary*. Chicago: Meyer & Brother Publishers, 1893.

Snowden, Frank M. *Blacks in Antiquity: Ethiopians in the Greco-Roman Experience*. 3rd ed., Harvard University Press, 1970.

Stanley, Susie C. *Holy Boldness: Women Preachers' Autobiographies and the Sanctified Self*. University of Tennessee Press, 2002.

Stowe, William. *Going Abroad: European Travel in Nineteenth-Century American Culture*. Princeton: Princeton University Press, 1994.

Stuart, James. *Three Years in North America*. Edinburgh: Printed for Robert Cadell, 1833.

"The Confessions of a Rambler." *The Repository*, vol. 3, no. 8, 1824, p. 278.

The Small Edition of the Post Office London Directory. London: W. Kelly & Co., 1843.

The Nature, Design and General Rules of the Methodist Societies: To Which Is Added an Extract from the Rev. John Wesley's Advice to the People Called Methodists with Regard to Dress: An Address to Class-Leaders: And a Word of Advice. The Works of John Wesley, Volume 8: Addresses, Essays, Letters. Books for the Ages Software. Albany: Version 1.0, 1997.

The Primitive Methodist Magazine, for the Year of our Lord 1873. Vol. 11 of the new series, London: George Lamb, 1873.

The Wesleyan-Methodist Connexional Record and Year Book, 1876-7. London: Wesleyan Conference Office, 1876.

Thomas, Robert. *A Century of Methodism in Germantown*. Press of the Germantown Independent, 1895, p. 98.

Thompson, Carl. *Travel Writing*. New York: Routledge, 2011.

"To the Editor of the Kendal Mercury." *Kendal Mercury*, 24 July 1847. *British Newspaper Archive*.

Watchman and Wesleyan Advertiser, 15 January 1851.

Watring, Anna Miller and F. Edward Wright. *Bucks County, Pennsylvania Church Records of the 17th & 18th Centuries. Volume 2 Quaker Records: Falls and Middletown Monthly Meetings*. Family Line Publications, 1994.

"Wesleyan Methodists, Appleby." *Kendal Mercury*, 13 February 1847. *British Newspaper Archive*.

Wesley, John. *A Plain Account of the People Called Methodists*. 9th ed. London: G. Paramore, 1795.

Westerkamp, Marilyn J. *Women and Religion in Early America, 1600–1850: The Puritan and Evangelical Traditions*. Routledge, 1999.

"Whaling Crew List Database." *New Bedford Whaling Museum*, www.whalingmuseum.org /online_exhibits/crewlist/about.php. Accessed March 2016.

Will [Ralph Shum]. Prerogative Court of Canterbury and Related Probate Jurisdictions, Will Registers. Class PROB 11. Piece 219. National Archives, Kew, England.

"William Wood Letter Concerning Zilpha Elaw." Syracuse University Libraries, Special Collections Research Center.

Williams, Martha. *Memoirs of the Life and Character of Ann Carr*. Leeds: H.W. Walker, 1841.

Wilson, Harriet. *Our Nig, Or Sketches from the Life of a Free Black*, edited by P. Gabrielle Foreman and Reginald H. Pitts.

Witherington, Ben. *The Acts of the Apostles: A Socio-Rhetorical Commentary*. Eerdmans, 1998, p. 295.

Select Bibliography

Primary/Archival Sources

Books

Crowell, Seth. *The Journal of Seth Crowell: Containing an Account of His Travels as a Methodist Preacher for Twelve Years / Written by Himself*. New York: Printed by J.C. Totten, 1813.

Towle, Nancy. *Vicissitudes Illustrated, in the Experience of Nancy Towle, in Europe and America*. Portsmouth: Printed for the authoress, by James L. Burges, 1832.

Walker, David. *Walker's Appeal, in Four Articles; Together with a Preamble, to the Coloured Citizens of the World, but in Particular, and Very Expressly, to Those of the United States of America*. 3rd and last ed., Boston: D. Walker, 1974.

Ware, Thomas. *Sketches of the Life and Travels of Rev. Thomas Ware: Who Has Been an Itinerant Methodist Preacher for More than Fifty Years / Written by Himself; Revised by the Editors*. New York: Published by G. Lane and P.P. Sandford, for the Methodist Episcopal Church, 1839.

Newspaper Articles

"A Black Female Orator!" *Cambridge Independent Press*, 18 October 1856. *British Newspaper Archive*.

"A Dark Lady Evangelist at Turnbridge Wells." *Sussex Advertiser: Surrey Gazette and West Kent Courier*, 19 August 1862. *British Newspaper Archive*.

"A Lady of Colour on Board a Cunard Steamer." *Derbyshire Courier*, 21 July 1860. *British Newspaper Archive*.

"A London Paper Advertises that 'Zilpha Elaw,' a Lady of Colour,' Was to Preach." *Devizes and Wiltshire Gazette*, 24 October 1844. *British Newspaper Archive*.

"A Negro Female Preacher." *Caledonian Mercury*, 6 July 1855. *British Newspaper Archive*.

"A Slave Once, A Bishop Now." *Durham County Advertiser*, 16 October 1891. *British Newspaper Archive*.

"A Useful Lady in the Camp." *The Ulsterman*, 22 August 1855. *British Newspaper Archive*.

"Adam Black (Not the M.P.)." *Falkirk Herald*, 18 October 1860. *British Newspaper Archive*.

"American Persons of Colour." *Morning Chronicle*, 9 January 1860. *British Newspaper Archive*.

"American Railway Carriages." *Sheffield Independent*, 26 December 1857. *British Newspaper Archive*.

"American Slavery." *Hampshire Telegraph and Sussex Chronicle* [Portsmouth, England], 6 April 1840. *19th Century British Library Newspapers*.

"American Slavery." *The Bristol Mercury*, 6 April 1850. *19th Century British Library Newspapers*.

"American Slavery." *The Derby Mercury* [London, England], 3 June 1840. *19th Century British Library Newspapers*.

"American Slavery." *Worcester Journal*, 13 September 1856. *British Newspaper Archive*.
"Any Lady (of Colour) Requiring." *Shipping and Mercantile Gazette*, 7 July 1860. *British Newspaper Archive*.
"City of London Working Men's Teetotal Alliance." *Clerkenwell News*, 19 November 1859. *British Newspaper Archive*.
"Coloured Justice." *Cumberland and Westmorland Advertiser, and Penrith Literary Chronicle*, 24 June 1856. *British Newspaper Archive*.
"Concert." *Bury and Norwich Post*, 25 March 1862. *British Newspaper Archive*.
"Disgraceful Case." *Nottinghamshire Guardian*, 19 March 1857. *British Newspaper Archive*.
"Dr Guthrie on Lady Lecturers." *Dundee, Perth, and Cupar Advertiser*, 1 April 1862. *British Newspaper Archive*.
"Epitome of News. British and Foreign." *Roscommon Journal, and Western Impartial Reporter*, 14 January 1860. *British Newspaper Archive*.
"Female Preacher." *Stamford Mercury*, 17 December 1841. *British Newspaper Archive*.
"London, December 16." *Limerick Chronicle*, 18 December 1841. *British Newspaper Archive*.
"Miss Grace Egerton." *Glossop-Dale Chronicle and North Derbyshire Reporter*, 26 May 1860. *British Newspaper Archive*.
"Miss Grace Egerton's Highly Successful Entertainment 'The Christmas Party.' " *Leigh Chronicle and Weekly District Advertiser*, 14 April 1860. *British Newspaper Archive*.
"Mrs M. E. Webb's Readings." *Leicester Chronicle*, 6 December 1856. *British Newspaper Archive*.
"Negro Slavery in America." *York Herald*, 8 October 1859. *British Newspaper Archive*.
"Once Coloured, Always Coloured." *Walsall Free Press and General Advertiser*, 8 November 1856. *British Newspaper Archive*.
"Opening Services." Norfolk Chronicle, 4 December 1858. *British Newspaper Archive*.
"Persons of Colour." *Carlow Post*, 14 July 1860. *British Newspaper Archive*.
"Shameful Treatment of a Lady of Colour." *Salisbury and Winchester Journal*, 14 January 1860. *British Newspaper Archive*.
"The Dark Lady of Plumpton Woods." *Westmorland Gazette*, 1 November 1856. *British Newspaper Archive*.
"The Prejudice of Colour." *Cheltenham Chronicle*, 10 July 1860. *British Newspaper Archive*.
"United Methodist Free Church." *Kentish Mercury*, 20 August 1864. *British Newspaper Archive*.

Secondary Sources

Books and Book Sections

Andrews, William L., and David A. Davis. *North Carolina Slave Narratives: The Lives of Moses Roper, Lunsford Lane, Moses Grandy & Thomas H. Jones*. University of North Carolina Press, 2003.
Armistead, Wilson. *A Tribute for the Negro: Being a Vindication of the Moral, Intellectual, and Religious Capabilities of the Coloured Portion of Mankind: With Particular Reference to the African Race*. London: W. Irwin, 1848.
———. *Five Hundred Thousand Strokes for Freedom; A Series of Anti-Slavery Tracts, of Which Half a Million Are Now First Issued by the Friends of the Negro*. London: W. & F. Cash, 1853.

Balfour, Clara Lucas. *The Women of Scripture*. London: Houlston and Stoneman, 1847.

Bassard, Katherine Clay. *Spiritual Interrogations: Culture, Gender, and Community in Early African American Women's Writing*. Princeton University Press, 1999.

Beetham, Margaret. *A Magazine of Her Own?: Domesticity and Desire in the Woman's Magazine, 1800–1914*. Routledge, 1996.

Blight, David W. *Frederick Douglass' Civil War: Keeping Faith in Jubilee*. Louisiana State University Press, 1989.

Blockett, Kimberly. "Writing Freedom: Race, Religion, and Revolution, 1820–1840." *The Cambridge History of African American Literature*, edited by Maryemma Graham and Jerry M. Ward, Cambridge University Press, 2011.

Brekus, Catherine A. "Female Evangelism in the Early Methodist Movement, 1784–1845." *Methodism and the Shaping of American Culture*, edited by Nathan O. Hatch and John H. Wigger, Abingdon Press, 2001, pp. 135–74.

British and Foreign Anti-Slavery Society. *Proceedings of the General Anti-Slavery Convention Volume 1*. London, 1841.

Brooks, Joanna. "The Unfortunates: What the Life Spans of Early Black Books Tell Us about Book History." *Early African American Print Culture*, edited by Lara Langer Cohen and Jordan Alexander Stein, University of Pennsylvania Press, 2012.

Burchfield, R. W. *Murray, Sir James Augustus Henry (1837–1915), Lexicographer*. Oxford University Press, 2017.

Carter, Tomeiko Ashford. *Powers Divine: Spiritual Autobiography and Black Women's Writing*. University Press of America, 2009.

Chesson, Frederick William, and Wilson Armistead. *God's Image in Ebony: Being a Series of Biographical Sketches, Facts, Anecdotes, Etc., Demonstrative of the Mental Powers and Intellectual Capacities of the Negro Race*. Partridge and Oakey, 1854.

Church, Thomas. *Sketches of Primitive Methodism*. T. Ward and Co., 1847.

Cima, Gay Gibson. *Early American Women Critics: Performance, Religion, Race*. Cambridge University Press, 2006.

Clinton, Catherine. *The Other Civil War: American Women in the Nineteenth Century*. Hill and Wang, 1999.

Collier-Thomas, Bettye. *Daughters of Thunder: Black Women Preachers and Their Sermons, 1850–1979*. Jossey-Bass, 1998.

Cullen, Margaret. "Holy Fire: Biblical Radicalism in the Narratives of Jarena Lee and Zilpha Elaw." *The Force of Tradition: Response and Resistance in Literature, Religion, and Cultural Studies*, edited by Donald G. Marshall, Rowman & Littlefield, 2005.

Davis, William Watts Hart. *History of Bucks County, Pennsylvania: From the Discovery of the Delaware to the Present Time*. 2nd ed., Lewis Publishing Co., 1905.

Dodson, Jualynne. "Nineteenth-Century A.M.E. Preaching Women: Cutting Edge of Women's Inclusion in Church Polity." *Women in New Worlds: Historical Perspectives on the Wesleyan Tradition*, edited by Hilah F. Thomas, Louise L. Queen, Rosemary Skinner Keller. Abingdon, 1981.

Douglass-Chin, Richard J. *Preacher Woman Sings the Blues: The Autobiographies of Nineteenth-Century African American Evangelists*. University of Missouri Press, 2001.

Eslinger, Ellen. *Citizens of Zion: The Social Origins of Camp Meeting Revivalism*. University of Tennessee Press, 1999.

Evans, Curtis. *The Burden of Black Religion*. Oxford University Press, 2008.

Fisch, Audrey A. *American Slaves in Victorian England: Abolitionist Politics in Popular Literature and Culture*. Cambridge University Press, 2000.

Fish, Cheryl J. *Black and White Women's Travel Narratives: Antebellum Explorations*. University Press of Florida, 2004.

Foster, Frances Smith. *Written by Herself: Literary Production by African American Women, 1746–1892*. Indiana University Press, 1993.

Fulop, Timothy Earl, and Albert J. Raboteau. *African-American Religion: Interpretive Essays in History and Culture*. Routledge, 1997.

Gardner, Eric. *Unexpected Places: Relocating Nineteenth-Century African American Literature*. University Press of Mississippi, 2009.

George, Carol V. R. *Segregated Sabbaths: Richard Allen and the Emergence of Independent Black Churches, 1760–1840*. Oxford University Press, 1973.

Glaude, Jr., Eddie S. *Exodus!: Religion, Race, and Nation in Early Nineteenth-Century Black America*. University of Chicago Press, 2000.

Graham, E. Dorothy. *Chosen by God: A List of the Female Travelling Preachers of Early Primitive Methodism*. Wesley Historical Society, 1989.

Grammer, Elizabeth Elkin. *Some Wild Visions: Autobiographies by Female Itinerant Evangelists in Nineteenth-Century America*. Oxford University Press, 2003.

Hatch, Nathan O. "The Puzzle of American Methodism." *Methodism and the Shaping of American Culture*, edited by Nathan O. Hatch and John H. Wigger, Abingdon Press, 2001, pp. 3–40.

Haynes, Rosetta R. *Radical Spiritual Motherhood: Autobiography and Empowerment in Nineteenth-Century African American Women*. Louisiana State University Press, 2011.

———. "Zilpha Elaw's Serial Domesticity: An Unsentimental Journey." *Gender, Genre, and Identity in Women's Travel Writing*, edited by Kristi Siegel, Peter Lang, 2004, pp. 181–91.

Haywood, Chanta M. *Prophesying Daughters: Black Women Preachers and the Word, 1823–1913*. University of Missouri Press, 2003.

Heyrman, Christine Leigh. *Southern Cross: The Beginnings of the Bible Belt*. University of North Carolina Press, 1998.

Horton, James Oliver, and Lois E. Horton. *In Hope of Liberty: Culture, Community, and Protest Among Northern Free Blacks, 1700–1860*. Oxford University Press, 1997.

Humez, Jean M. " 'My Spirit Eye': Some Functions of Spiritual and Visionary Experience in the Lives of Five Black Women Preachers, 1810–1880." *Women and the Structure of Society: Selected Research from the Fifth Berkshire Conference on the History of Women*, edited by Barbara J. Harris and JoAnn K. McNamara, Duke University Press, 1984, pp. 129–43.

King, Wilma. *The Essence of Liberty: Free Black Women During the Slave Era*. University of Missouri Press, 2006.

Lloyd, Jennifer M., and Jennifer M. Lloyd. *Women and the Shaping of British Methodism: Persistent Preachers, 1807–1907*. Manchester University Press, 2010.

Mack, Phyllis. *Heart Religion in the British Enlightenment: Gender and Emotion in Early Methodism*. Cambridge University Press, 2008.

May, Cedric. *Evangelism and Resistance in the Black Atlantic, 1760–1835*. University of Georgia Press, 2008.

McKay, Nellie. "Nineteenth-Century Black Women's Spiritual Autobiographies: Religious Faith and Self-Empowerment." *Interpreting Women's Lives: Feminist Theory and Personal Narratives*, edited by Joy Webster Barbre, Indiana University Press, 1989.

McLoughlin, William G., editor. *The American Evangelicals, 1800–1890: An Anthology*. Harper Torchbooks, 1968.

Nash, Gary B. *Race and Revolution*. Madison House, 1990.

Nowatzki, Robert. *Representing African Americans in Transatlantic Abolitionism and Blackface Minstrelsy*. Louisiana State University Press, 2010.

Peterson, Carla L. *Doers of the Word: African-American Women Speakers and Writers in the North (1830–1880).* Oxford University Press, 1995.

———. "Subject to Speculation: Assessing the Lives of African-American Women in the Nineteenth Century." *Women's Studies in Transition: The Pursuit of Interdisciplinarity,* edited by Kate Conway-Turner, Suzanne Cherrin, Jessica Schiffman, and Kathleen Doherty Turkel. University of Delaware Press, 1998.

Pierce, Yolanda. *Hell without Fires: Slavery, Christianity, and the Antebellum Spiritual Narrative.* University Press of Florida, 2005.

Procter, Margaret, Michael Cook, and Caroline Williams, editors. *Political Pressure and the Archival Record.* Society of American Archivists, 2005.

Quarles, Benjamin. *Black Abolitionists.* Oxford University Press, 1969.

Raboteau, Albert J. *Slave Religion: The "Invisible Institution" in the Antebellum South.* Oxford University Press, 2004.

Rezek, Joseph. "The Print Atlantic: Phillis Wheatley, Ignatius Sancho, and the Cultural Significance of the Book." *Early African American Print Culture,* edited by Lara Langer Cohen and Jordan Alexander Stein, University of Pennsylvania Press, 2012.

Scotland, Nigel. *Apostles of the Spirit and Fire: American Revivalists and Victorian Britain.* Wipf & Stock, 2009.

Taft, Zachariah, and John Wesley. *Biographical Sketches of the Lives and Public Ministry of Various Holy Women Whose Eminent Usefulness and Successful Labours in the Church of Christ Have Entitled Them to Be Enrolled Among the Great Benefactors of Mankind: In Which Are Included Several Letters from the Rev. J. Wesley Never Before Published.* Printed for the author and sold by Mr. Kershaw, 1825.

Taves, Ann. *Fits, Trances, and Visions: Experiencing Religion and Explaining Experience from Wesley to James.* Princeton University Press, 2000.

Valenze, Deborah M. *Prophetic Sons and Daughters: Female Preaching and Popular Religion in Industrial England.* Princeton University Press, 1985.

Welter, Barbara. *Dimity Convictions: The American Woman in the Nineteenth Century.* Ohio University Press, 1976.

White Gray, Deborah. *Ar'n't I a Woman?: Female Slaves in the Plantation South.* W.W. Norton and Co., 1985, p. 165.

Wigger, John H. *Taking Heaven by Storm: Methodism and the Rise of Popular Christianity in America.* Oxford University Press, 1998.

Wilson, Carol. *Freedom at Rise: The Kidnapping of Free Blacks in America, 1780–1865.* University Press of Kentucky, 1994.

Wood, Marcus. *Blind Memory: Visual Representations of Slavery in England and America, 1780–1865.* Manchester University Press, 2000.

Zackodnik, Teresa. *Press, Platform, Pulpit: Black Feminist Publics in the Era of Reform.* University of Tennessee Press, 2011.

Magazine and Journal Articles

Alexander, Ben. "Excluding Archival Silences: Oral History and Historical Absence." *Archival Science,* vol. 6, 2006, pp. 1–11.

Avilez, GerShun. "Housing the Black Body: Value, Domestic Space, and Segregation Narratives." *African American Review,* vol. 42, no. 1, 2008, pp. 135–47.

Billington, Louis. " 'Female Laborers in the Church': Women Preachers in the Northeastern United States, 1790–1840." *Journal of American Studies,* vol. 19, no. 3 (1985), pp. 369–94.

Bloch, Ruth H. "American Feminine Ideals in Transition: The Rise of the Moral Mother, 1785–1815." *Feminist Studies*, vol. 4, June 1978, pp. 101–26.

Buell, Lawrence. "Religion on the American Mind." *American Literary History*, vol. 19, no. 1, Spring 2007, pp. 32–55.

Conway, Stephen. "The Politicization of the Nineteenth-Century Peace Society." *Historical Research: The Bulletin of the Institute of Historical Research*, vol. 66, no. 161, October 1993, pp. 267–83.

Cuffee, Sallie M. "Reconstructing Subversive Moral Discourses in the Spiritual Autobiographies of Nineteenth-Century African American Preaching Women." *Journal of Feminist Studies in Religion*, vol. 32, no. 2, Fall 2016, pp. 45–62.

Fetterley, Judith, and Susan K. Harris. "Introduction." *Legacy*, vol. 15, no. 1, 1998, pp. 1–9.

Foote, Kenneth. "To Remember and Forget: Archives, Memory, and Culture." *American Archivist*, vol. 53, no. 3, July 1990, pp. 378–92. doi:10.17723/aarc.53.3.d87u013444j3g6r2.

Foster, Frances Smith. "Genealogies of Our Concerns, Early (African) American Print Culture, and Transcending Tough Times." *American Literary History*, vol. 22, no. 2, June 2010, pp. 368–80. doi:10.1093/alh/ajq004.

———. "A Narrative of the Interesting Origins and (Somewhat) Surprising Developments of African-American Print Culture." *American Literary History*, vol. 17, no. 4, 2005, pp. 714–40.

Hammond, W. L. "The Old Black Mammy." *Confederate Veteran*, 26 January 1918, p. 6.

Harwood, Thomas F. "British Evangelical Abolitionism and American Churches in the 1830's." *The Journal of Southern History*, vol. 28, no. 3, August 1962, pp. 287–306. *JSTOR*, doi:10.2307/2205310.

Hunter, William R. "Do Not Be Conformed unto This World: An Analysis of Religious Experience in the Nineteenth-Century African American Spiritual Narrative." *Nineteenth Century Studies*, no. 8, 1994, pp. 75–88.

Jimerson, Randall. "Archivists and Social Responsibility: A Response to Mark Greene." *American Archivist*, vol. 76, no. 2, 2013, p. 11.

———. "Embracing the Power of Archives." *American Archivist*, vol. 69, no. 1, January 2006, pp. 19–32. doi:10.17723/aarc.69.1.r0p75n2084055418.

Kaplan, Elisabeth. " 'Many Paths to Partial Truths': Archives, Anthropology, and the Power of Representation." *Archival Science*, vol. 2, 2002, pp. 209–20.

———. "We Are What We Collect, We Collect What We Are: Archives and the Construction of Identity." *American Archivist*, vol. 63, no. 1, January 2000, pp. 126–51. doi:10.17723/aarc.63.1.h554377531233l05.

Lambert, David R. "Blind Memory: Visual Representations of Slavery in England and America, 1780–1865 (Book Review)." *Journal of Historical Geography*, vol. 28, no. 3, July 2002, p. 456.

Lapsansky, Emma Jones. " 'Since They Got Those Separate Churches': Afro-Americans and Racism in Jacksonian Philadelphia." *American Quarterly*, vol. 32, no. 1, Spring 1980, pp. 54–78. *JSTOR*, doi:10.2307/2712496.

Lockley, Tim. "David Margrett: A Black Missionary in the Revolutionary Atlantic." *Journal of American Studies*, vol. 46, no. 3, August 2012, pp. 729–45. doi:10.1017/S0021875811001277.

Maclear, J. F. "The Evangelical Alliance and the Antislavery Crusade." *Huntington Library Quarterly*, vol. 42, no. 2, Spring 1979, pp. 141–64. *JSTOR*, doi:10.2307/3817500.

McFarlane-Harris, Jennifer. "Pauline 'Adoption' Theology as Experiential Performance in the 'Memoirs' of African American Itinerant Preacher Zilpha Elaw." *Performance, Religion, and Spirituality*, vol. 2, no. 1, 23 Mar. 2019. press.utoledo.edu.

Nord, David. "The Evangelical Origins Of Mass Media In America, 1815–1835." *Journalism Monographs*, vol. 88, 1984.

Ritchie, Daniel. "Abolitionism and Evangelism: Isaac Newton, The Evangelical Alliance, and the Transatlantic Debate over Christian Fellowship with Slaveholders." *The Historical Journal*, vol. 57, no. 2, June 2014, pp. 421–46.

Robinson, Amy. "Authority and the Public Display of Identity: 'Wonderful Adventures of Mrs. Seacole in Many Lands.'" *Feminist Studies*, vol. 20, no. 3, 1994, p. 537. *WorldCat Discovery Service*, doi:10.2307/3178185.

Smith, Mitzi J. "'Unbossed and Unbought': Zilpha Elaw and Old Elizabeth and a Political Discourse of Origins." *Black Theology*, vol. 9, no. 3, 2011, pp. 287–311.

Smith, Ruth L., and Deborah M. Valenze. "Mutuality and Marginality: Liberal Moral Theory and Working-Class Women in Nineteenth-Century England." *Signs*, vol. 13, no. 2, Winter 1988, pp. 277–98.

Tusan, Michelle. "Gleaners in the Holy Land: Women and the Missionary Press in Victorian Britain." *Nineteenth-Century Gender Studies*, vol. 6, no. 2, Summer 2010, www.ncgsjournal.com/issue62/tusan.htm.

Welter, Barbara. "The Cult of True Womanhood: 1820–1860." *American Quarterly*, vol. 18, no. 2, Summer 1966, pp. 151–74. *JSTOR*, doi:10.2307/2711179.

Williams, Delores S. "Visions, Inner Voices, Apparitions, and Defiance in Nineteenth-Century Black Women's Narratives." *Women's Studies Quarterly*, vol. 21, no. 1–2, 1993, pp. 81–89.

Wolffe, John. "Transatlantic Visitors and Evangelical Networks, 1829–61." *Studies in Church History Subsidia*, vol. 14, 2012, pp. 183–93. *Cambridge Core*, doi:10.1017/S0143045900 003926.

Zackodnik, Teresa. "'Rich Thought and Polished Pen': Recirculation and Early African American Feminism." *Nineteenth-Century Gender Studies*, vol. 6, no. 2, Summer 2010.

WEB PAGES AND BLOG POSTS

"'Protestant Nonconformity,' A History of the County of York East Riding: Volume 1, the City of Kingston Upon Hull (1969), pp. 311–30." *British History Online*. Accessed 2 March 2016.

Woodward, Josiah. "An Account of the Rise and Progress of the Religious Societies in the City of London &c. and of the Endeavours for Reformation of Manners Which Have Been Made Therein / by Josiah Woodward." *Early English Books Online*, February 2016.